The Path of the
Shaman

Anna Franklin

LEAR

www.learbooks.co.uk

LEAR

This first edition published in 2007 by
Lear Books
Windrush, High Tor West,
Earl Shilton,
Leicestershire,
LE9 7DN
England
www.learbooks.co.uk

The Path of the Shaman © Anna Franklin 2007
Anna Franklin has asserted her rights under the Copyright, Designs and Patents Act, 1988 to be identified as the author of this work.

All rights reserved. No part of this book may be used or reproduced in any form without permission of the author, except in the case of quotations in articles or reviews.

Cover artwork © Anna Franklin.
Internal illustrations © Paul Mason

Cover design by Paul Mason

ISBN 978-0-9547534-4-3

Chapter 1
WHAT IS A SHAMAN?

The word 'shaman' is generally thought to derive from the Tunguso-Manchurian (Siberian) word *saman* from the verb *sa* which means 'to know', so a shaman is 'one who knows'. Strictly speaking, the term is properly applied only to the traditional religious systems of the native peoples of Central Asia, Siberia and the circumpolar region of the Northern Hemisphere, though it is more broadly used in anthropology to categorise similar religious practices and ideas found in other areas of the world:

- The shamanic crisis, during which the shaman undergoes death and rebirth
- A belief in a tiered Cosmos, consisting of the middle realm, upperworld(s) and underworld(s)
- A cosmic axis or World Tree that connects the realms
- Trance journeys to those realms
- The use of various methods to achieve trance
- Conversing with, and being helped by, spirits, including those of animals and plants
- Shapeshifting and travelling in animal form
- Animism- a belief that everything has spirit, whether human, animal, plant or inanimate object
- Working with spirit helpers to heal, divine and perform various forms of magic
- A common, though not universal, belief in the Great Shaman, the Lord of the Animals

Anthropologists classify a shamanism as a magical/religious practice during which the shaman enters a trance state in order to enter a realm of non-ordinary reality beyond everyday consciousness in order to encounter spirits. Sometimes non-shamans get glimpses of this sphere and its possibilities through visions, miracles, clairvoyant experiences and so on, but through the shaman's intimate knowledge of the Otherworld, its geography and denizens, he can step into it at will.

The encounter is an entirely personal one and not shared by others as a group of people might share a religious ceremony or ritual. Indeed, everything important the shaman learns comes through personal experience and not through received teaching, though elder shamans may oversee the process of his initiation.

THE PATH OF THE SHAMAN

The shaman's ability is won through personal hardships. In all parts of the world the dawning of the shaman's enlightenment begins with a 'shamanic crisis', often in adolescence, but sometimes much later.[1] This is a severe illness or breakdown which actually threatens his life, and he lingers for a time between on the threshold of life and death. The shaman is reduced, by the trauma of this incident, to a primal way of thinking and being, and only then can he enter the archetypal primordial state where humans can converse with gods, animals and plants. He experiences the sensation of dissolution and the separation of body from spirit, something that only usually occurs in physical death, and which cannot be compared to astral travel or out of body experiences, or even an initiation in other magical traditions.

Returning from his crisis, the shaman knows, from his own encounters, that the world is alive, that everything has spirit and that we are surrounded by spirits, a viewpoint called animism by anthropologists. When he interacts with the world of spirit, he is practising shamanism, and only then. He may work with a variety of supernatural beings and from these learn how to cure specific illnesses, divination, the mastery of fire, weather magic, hunting magic, the retrieval of lost souls or the accompanying of the souls of dead to the Otherworld, and the removal of curses. He can travel great expanses in spirit flight, hear what is going on at a remote place, send messages over a distance and even 'shapeshift'. Furthermore, he may take on the role of the priest of a community, becoming the bridge between the world of spirits and humankind. Shamanism is not a doctrinal religion, but it *is* a religious practice.

Shamanism was probably the first religious approach of humankind. Our earliest evidence of shamanic practice dates from 30,000 years ago at the end of the last Ice Age. Our ancestors explored deep limestone caves – probably believing the down-sloping vanes led to the underworld – and there seeking spirit animals in visions. People did not live in these particular caves; they were reserved solely for religious use. Human bodies were not buried in the caves either- they were the realm of spirit animals- human dead were buried at the entrances to the caves or in large rock shelters, i.e. on the threshold of the underworld. [2]

Cave paintings of animals, human figures in animal costume and statuettes of female figures began to appear, and this form of artistic expression continued for a further 20,000 years amongst the hunter-gatherer tribes. We know that these ancient artists did not portray all of the animals they saw and hunted, while certain animals appeared more frequently than others, especially horses, bison, deer, oxen, mammoths,

4

THE PATH OF THE SHAMAN

ibexes, bears and lions. By their arrangement, the pictures seem to have been thought effective only in certain caves, and only in specific places within the caves. Usually only one representative of any species was depicted within a single cave, and the animals pictured were not necessarily the ones that people most relied on for food or were in greatest danger from. Too often for coincidence, certain animals appear in proximity to others: oxen by horses, bison next to mammoths and so on, making systematic and significant pairings shown in symbolic relationships.[3]

Animals are often shown with darts and javelins piercing them, and are depicted one on top of another, suggesting that the effect was not for art, but magic.[4] The paintings do not seem to represent animals in their natural state, but they are rather spirit animals, floating within the natural features of the rock, reflecting not a realist depiction of the mundane plane, but the inner reality that the artist *saw*. Blood and fat were mixed with the painting pigments as a ritual act of restitution, the paintings thus uniting the spiritual and material planes. Furthermore, they were not painted and left, but continually renewed. With the painting and the blood, the animal spirit was returned to the earth (cave) womb, with the animals sometimes shown entering or leaving the rock itself through natural fissures, suggesting that the rock itself is the membrane between the human world and the world of spirits. People passed pieces of animals back into the rock and therefore back into the spirit realm, making ritual restoration for the lives they had taken in the hunt.

The paintings demonstrate a sophisticated and highly evolved religious framework - these were not simple, ignorant people. As with other religious symbolism, one needs to understand the concepts to understand the imagery; the culture we are brought up in defines and shapes our perceptions. In the modern world, we are accustomed to accepting what we see with our eyes and define with our logic as being 'reality'. We know that other cultures have a much less definite perception of what reality actually is.

The paintings were situated deep within the caves, often only reached through dark labyrinthine corridors and after risking potholes and drops *en route*. It is likely that these journeys were designed to be spiritual experiences, walking through the darkness was probably ritually identified with travel through the spirit realms, with the revelation of the mystery at the end. Imagine approaching the deep cave through a passage of shadowy tunnels lit only by flickering torch light, sometimes walking, sometimes crawling through the silence, constantly aware that you are approaching the magical womb of the earth. This itself would work on the imagination and raise the level of consciousness. It may have been an initiatory journey

THE PATH OF THE SHAMAN

designed to bring about insight, to illuminate experience and ensure a permanent transformation of perceptions. The candidate was thus forever separated from his previously accepted ordinary-consciousness of the world, to become a 'man of knowledge'.

The revelation of the inner cave showed animals in new relationships, demonstrating that life is both interconnected and interdependent. In the heart of the cavern male animals and symbols were painted, while at the back of the cave, in a tunnel perhaps, were the same images but this time along with horned men. In the cave of Lascaux are animals, leaping bulls, stags, ponies, bison and what is sometimes taken to be a shaman, a prostrate man wearing a bird mask, with an erect phallus, while beside him is a staff with the image of a bird upon it.

At Trois Frères, the caves contain hundreds of images and were used for at least 20,000 years. Its most famous painting is the so-called 'Sorcerer of Trois Frères,' a dancing humanoid figure, two and a half feet tall, with antlers, stag ears and owl eyes, a bushy tail and a phallus. The figure may be a god, the Lord of the Animals, or a shaman who has donned the costume of the god who controls the game that surrounds him. Certainly, the cave depicts some form of hunting magic; the people of the Old Stone Age did not grow food, but hunted it.

The Lord of the Animals would stare down at the initiate, showing the mutual dependence of man and animal. Such symbiosis is part of the lore of all hunting tribes to this day. The candidate was being prepared to hunt and kill animals in a sacred manner, and shown that the interior world of the spirit is more important than the external world of matter. Real animals were a mere reflection of their spirits. Hunting and killing was a mystical as well as a practical experience and the hunter identified with his prey. Life, of necessity, preys on life, and this is a mystery in itself and was celebrated in a sacred manner; life would be reverenced as it was taken. The cave paintings depict all the essential elements of the shaman – the ritual dance, the animal costumes, trance, the possession of animal familiars and identification with an animal or bird.

Though in the early Palaeolithic Age the entrance to the spirit realms was through the caves, by the Neolithic it was through structures built above ground to reflect the make-up of the Cosmos, mirroring its structure in the ordinary realm, with heaven above and the underworld below. It may have been thought that in this way people could gain greater control of the Cosmos (an idea reflected in the sacred architecture of much later periods). Selected dead were buried under the floors of living areas, and were sometimes exhumed, the bones dealt with in certain ways before being re-buried with the object of gaining greater control over the dead – who were obviously part of the spirit realm – and keeping them active longer so the shaman could commune with them.

Joseph Campbell (*Primitive Mythology*) suggested that the shamans of a hunting society and the shamans of an agricultural society had different practices and approaches, and this is true even in modern tribal societies.[5] Stephen and Christine Hugh-Jones in their *Study of South American Peoples* codified this as Horizontal Shamanism and Vertical Shamanism. Horizontal Shamanism refers to individual shamans, associated with the forest, who contact spirits using hallucinogens, and in trance make contact with the jaguar. The shaman works to provide game and animal fertility. Vertical Shamanism, on the other hand, is concerned with esoteric knowledge passed within a small elite group. These shamans are more associated with the house rather than the wild forest, and with crops and vegetable fertility, rather than animals. They use the hallucinogenic vine *yajé* and perform regular ceremonies for the community.

There is a growing body of evidence for shamanic practices among both the Celtic. Anglo-Saxon and later peoples of Britain. Both the ancient Celts and Saxons had gifted individuals who were able to journey at will into the world of the spirits. Furthermore, shamanism in Britain did not die out with the suppression of the Pagan religions by the Christian Church. The Witch Trial records of Britain and the rest of Europe show clear evidence of shamanic practice and the attempts of the Church and State to repress it.

Stories with shamanic themes certainly occur in pan-Celtic myths. The famous Gundestrup Cauldron gives us an image of the Lord of the Animals, or perhaps a shaman similar to those of the Palaeolithic cave paintings. He is depicted in the classic pose of the shaman, upright, cross-legged, "*staring forth at a world only he can see*".[6] He wears antlers and is surrounded by beasts who are possibly the spirit animals under his control, and in his left hand he holds the head of a serpent. A similar character appears in Celtic several stories. One of the most notable concerns a man called Cynon who entered the Otherworld, following a path through the woods to clearing in which there was a mound supporting the Lord of the Animals, who had one eye and one foot, surrounded by various animals. He instructed Cynon to go to a certain large tree where he would find a fountain and a silver vessel containing water which he should throw onto a slab. This would cause a great storm that would almost destroy him. The tree would be stripped of its leaves, but would soon be covered by sweet-singing birds.[7] This story seems to describe a shamanic initiation, with the

THE PATH OF THE SHAMAN

common elements of meeting the Master of the Animals, the World Tree and undergoing a shamanic crisis (the storm) before encountering the inspirational spirits of the birds.

John Matthews has explored at length the shamanic themes contained in the poetry of the bard Taliesin.[8] The poet described being three times in the Castle of Arianrhod, and had been 'born' (initiated) three times. He knew all the secrets of the world and could predict the future, he had been *"in the galaxy at the throne of the Distributor"* and refined in the Court of Ceridwen, where he drank from her cauldron to obtain the muse and the three inspirations of the goddess. He experienced shapechanging into various animals:

"...Since then I have fled in the shape of a crow,
Since then I have fled as a speedy frog
Since then I have fled with rage in my chains,
- a roebuck in a dense thicket.
I have fled in the shape of a red deer,
In the shape of iron in a fierce fire,
In the shape of a sword sowing death and disaster,
In the shape of a bull, relentlessly struggling..." [9]

A Scottish tale that describes an Otherworld initiation is that of Thomas the Rhymer. He had been playing his lute beneath a hawthorn in the woods when a beautiful fairy, riding a white horse, emerged from the trees to listen. Eventually she dismounted and he couldn't resist trying to kiss her. She warned him that such an act would bind him to her for seven years, but he did not hesitate. They journeyed together through the night to a bright meadow in which there were two paths, one to perdition and one to righteousness, but the Fairy Queen explained that for lovers and poets there was another path, a twisting third way that led to Fairyland. While in the fairy world Thomas was shown a mysterious tree which bore magical apples. The Queen of Elphame warned him that it bore all the plagues of hell, but it also conveyed the gift of prophecy.

After seven years Thomas returned home, but his songs were sweeter and more poignant than ever before. He was also able to foretell the future, as in Fairyland he had eaten an apple whose flesh had the power of truth, a parting gift from the Fairy Queen. On his seventy-eighth birthday, he was holding a party when he was told that two white deer, a male and a female, were heading through the village to his house. He knew this to be a summons to Fairyland and followed them back there, where he still sings and plays.

THE PATH OF THE SHAMAN

The apple is the fruit of Otherworld knowledge. The plagues of hell that accompany it are the suffering and pain the shaman must go through to win the sight. Once this is won, and the apple eaten, he or she will never be the same again and is forever changed. The third way described by the Fairy Queen is the way of the Walker between the Worlds, the shaman.

In Norse myth, Odin's experience of hanging on the World Tree to gain insight into the runes is a typical tale of shamanic initiation, and moreover, Odin was described as being able to shapeshift into a wolf, a man, a giant and an eagle amongst other forms, while the god Loki appeared as a horse, a raven, a man, and so on. Various humans had the ability to shapeshift like Ottar who could become an otter, and Fafnir who became a dragon.

Various forms of magic were practised among the Norse, including *seiðr* ('witchcraft') which employed a number of shamanic practices including spirit flights, soul recovery, removing elf-shot from sick patients, prophecy and weather magic. Norse literature relates that seiðr was learned from 'Finnish Wizards' i.e. Saami shamans who were reported to shapeshift into a variety of animals and take spirit journeys to far places to gain knowledge.

The seiðr-witch would undergo spirit possession and cast spells while in a trance, covered by her cloak or hood. She would begin by allowing her soul (*hamingja*) to leave her mouth during a great yawn. Skalds (bards) would also practice trance 'under the cloak', sometimes on top of a burial mound so that the practitioner could commune with the dead within, a practice known as *sitja á haugi* ('sit on a barrow'), though this was dangerous as he or she might be attacked *haugbui* or ghost and found insane in the morning.

In one legend, the seið-witch Gullveig was riddled with spears, burned three times and was called the thrice-born, recalling the story of Taliesin. Her name means 'gold intoxication' and her story is thought by some to refer to a chemical process to extract gold, though it has all the hallmarks of a shamanic initiation. She is often identified with the goddess Freyja, mistress of seiðr. [10] Seiðr was women's magic, said to be an art of the Vanir, the elder gods, and taught to Odin by Freyja.

A possible derivation of the word seiðr is from a root word meaning 'seat' or 'sitting', since seiðr magic often took place with the witch seated on the *seið-hjallr*, a high seat or scaffolding which she climbed to practice her art. [11] This bears a striking resemblance to shamanism in other parts of the world, where the shaman will ascend a stepped pole and chant

9

THE PATH OF THE SHAMAN

to call upon the spirits. Altaic shamans climb a nine stepped birch pole, and in the *Völuspá 2*, the prophetess also climbs a tree of nine steps. [12]

In *Eiríks Saga*, a woman named Þórbjörg sat upon a high seat, on a cushion stuffed with hen's feathers to help her attain spirit flight. Like shamans in other parts of the world, her costume comprised of animal skins and ornaments. She wore a blue mantle, a colour sacred to Hel, goddess of death and the underworld. On her head was a black lambskin hood lined with white catskin, while on her hands were catskin gloves. Cats were sacred to Freyja. Around her waist she wore a belt of touch-wood and a large skin pouch where she kept various talismans. She held a brass staff with a knob on it, set with stones, which she used to keep the rhythm for her chants by banging it on the floor. She asked those women present who knew the *Varðlokur* or Warlock-Song necessary to call the spirits to sing it for her.

In Britain, during the Ninth and Tenth centuries, there were many instances of Churchmen fulminating over Pagan magical practices, such as the brewing of love philtres and the practice of *wicce* to gain love, or *galdor*-craft of any kind. Ælfric denounced 'Wiccans' who taught the worship of trees, stones and wells, who brewed potions and interpreted dreams.

During the witch trials of the Middle Ages and later, we can see evidence of shamanic practice, such as conversing with spirits, animal and fairy familiars, the magical curing of disease, the removal or infliction of elf-shot, spirit flight and so on. This does not mean that there was a thriving shamanic culture among the underclasses, rather that shamanic consciousness is a potentially pan-human experience which does not rely on a culturally supportive setting, though it does require an underpinning of sympathetic mythology.

As well as trying to extinguish the shamanic practices of their own homelands, when Europeans travelled to the Americas they encountered people who claimed to speak with spirits by using trance-inducing techniques such as fasting, taking sacred plants or the infliction of pain. The disgusted explorers dismissed them as agents of the Devil. When the Russians began to colonise Siberia in the seventeen century, they found people who communicated with spirits, claiming to heal people, to influence the weather, game and the crops, as well as being able to divine the future. The Christian Russians dismissed them as dealers with demons.

It was not until the twentieth century that anthropologists made detailed studies of shamanic practices in places as widely distributed as the Amazon, Australia and the Arctic, and though they had local names, applied the encompassing term 'shamanism' since they all had practices akin

THE PATH OF THE SHAMAN

to those of the Siberian shamans. In 1951, the Romanian historian of religions Mircea Eliade finished his seminal book *Shamanism: Archaic Techniques of Ecstasy*, which documented the striking correspondences in shamanic practices, worldviews and symbolic behaviours in hundreds of societies around the world. Shamanism is *"the religious experience par excellence,"* he wrote, *"The shaman, and he alone, is the great master of ecstasy."*[13] Eliade's work demonstrated that shamanic practices and conceptions were ancient. He concluded that shamanic features could be found in any ethnic or cultural group, citing, for example, the Scandinavian story of Odin's initiation on the World Tree and the Orphic Mysteries of Greece, concerning as they do Orpheus's descent into the underworld to retrieve the lost soul of his wife Eurydice.

Such works caused a stir of public interest in shamanism, including amongst those westerners who were keen to try it for themselves. In the 1960s, with its emphasis on the drug culture, many were especially drawn to the use of the hallucinogenic plants employed by shamans in their sacred ceremonies, finding they could experience similar visions to those described by shamans. This was fertile ground for the works of Carlos Castaneda, an anthropology student who claimed to have studied with a Yaqui Indian sorcerer in Arizona and Mexico, publishing a firsthand account of his apprenticeship in 1968, *The Teachings of Don Juan: A Yaqui Way of Knowledge*. The book and its sequels became worldwide bestsellers. The veracity of these books has since been questioned, and at least one critic claimed that Casteneda spent his time in the library, not out and about with a shaman. It is certainly true that Casteneda made up parts of his books, but they seem to draw on real experiences and real knowledge of shamanism.

On the basis of these books, the spark of public interest became an explosion, and thousands of neo-shamans appeared in first America, then round the world. Many were interested only in the experiences of drugs; others barely studied classical shamanism at all. Sadly, the modern neo-shaman has a tendency to loot other nation's religions, cherry-picking odds and ends of disconnected knowledge from a variety of traditional cultures. The more distant and exotic the places they are stolen from the better, because he seems to think that they must be purer and truer, closer to some imagined primordial shamanism unchanged since the dawn of time.

While the experience of the shaman is universal, timeless and constant, its interpretation and practice relies on a complex net of mythology, symbolism, taboo, tradition and a setting in place and time. The shaman is intimately connected with the land around him, and accesses the greater

11

Cosmos through it. The myths and stories of his people contain the knowledge of how to shamanize expressed in local terms. Those of foreign places, on the other hand, are unhelpful, except in the most general sense. The path every real shaman forges is his own. He must undergo his own trials, face his own crisis and make his own contact with local spirit allies. His knowledge must be rooted in an understanding of his place in the land around him, and its place in the Cosmos, or he cannot properly orientate himself and operate in the Otherworld.

Chapter 2
THE SHAMANIC CRISIS

The Bluffer's Guide to the Occult [14] defines a shaman as a 'hippy with a drum' and this encapsulates for me the difference between a real shaman and a wannabe. 'Shamanism' has been a buzz word in the Pagan community since the early 1970s, and many people claim to be shamans without having much idea of what it actually means, attaching to it instead a wide variety of bowdlerized New Age practices such as waving smudge sticks and feathers and bashing the hell out of *bodhrans*, or simply wearing fancy-dress costumes and amulets, exploiting genuine native cultures to procure skins, eagle feathers, crystals and so on. Some simply think that the recreational use of psychotropic substances whilst raving the night away gives them the right to be called shamans.

Others suppose that they can adopt odds and sods of shamanic techniques, isolated from the cultures they were practiced in, as a way to spiritual illumination without having to undergo the very real hardships traditionally associated with gaining shamanic knowledge. This in no way reflects the experience of the tribal shaman whose central experience is the shamanic crisis, triggered by mental trial or severe physical illness. You can drum and wave feathers to your heart's content, but what makes a real shaman is undergoing – and surviving – the shamanic crisis, remembering, and afterwards acting as a shaman.

A person cannot just decide to become a shaman: only the spirits can choose and make a shaman. Though anyone can offer themselves to the spirits, there is no guarantee that the spirits will accept. The candidate is *always* subjected to trial and testing before his initiation in the Otherworld can take place, encapsulating a very real dissolution, death and rebirth in the core of his being, a process entirely out of the shaman's control, and often sudden and violent in its onset.

"... the initiation consists in an ecstatic experience, during which the candidate undergoes certain operations performed by mythical Beings, and undertakes ascents to Heaven or descents to the subterranean World. [15]

In folk tradition, a person sometimes marked from birth as a future shaman by being born under certain stars or marked with particular omens. In Slovenia, for example, the *kresnik* is known by a white caul at birth and can shapeshift into various animal forms. The kresnik may be the seventh child or one who has won the love of a fairy (*vila*). [16] Though the position of shaman is hereditary in some cultures, steps will be taken to ensure that the spirits accept the legacy, and the crisis will be provoked by

13

THE PATH OF THE SHAMAN

inflicting brutal pain, cold, starvation, sleep deprivation, or induced by drugs. The genuine shaman's work is accomplished with the aid of local spirits. These spirits have to be honoured and revered, and a lasting relationship has to be built up with them in order to gain their acceptance.

The curious thing about the shamanic crisis is that it is experienced in a similar way all over the world, which suggests it is potentially a fundamental and universal part of the human experience, whether or not it ever manifests within an individual.

Though dealings with spirits may be an everyday occurrence in a tribal shaman's society, and their stories and attributes part of his people's lore, his experiences are nonetheless personal and very frightening. Even though his society may systemise and oversee an initiation, for the individual who undergoes it, it is still a horrific experience, and the shaman is inevitably forced to confront his own fears, his death and mortality, and the power of the Otherworld.

The shamanic crisis brings the potential shaman to the brink of annihilation, forcing him to walk the boundaries between life and death. During the process, he is stripped of everything that makes him an individual and must totally relinquish his ego; all that restrains him in this is experienced as monsters that devour him - manifestations of fears, doctrinal beliefs, hang-ups and so on. Usually this is only possible when the candidate becomes ill to the point of death, or suffers what feels like endless pain and suffering, sometimes with visions of torture and spirit battles.

In Celtic myths, madness (the shamanic crisis) is often associated with poetic inspiration. In one tale Suibhne was a warrior-king who insulted a cleric. The cleric cursed Suibhne with insanity so that he leapt into the air, like a bird. He lived alone in the wilderness and became a poet. There are many accounts of people going to live in the woods as wild men and women, and this seems to be another metaphor for shamanic initiation. Merlin spent time as *Merlin Wyllt*- the Wild Merlin. He fled into the forest after losing a battle, insane with grief, to live like a beast. It was there that he learned the deep truths of the shaman, living between madness and ecstasy. In this account we have the universal experience of the shaman paralleled: the crisis event that leads to a period of illness, madness or withdrawal from the world, communing with the spirits of nature, including animal guides, before integrating the experience and returning to the world with enhanced magical powers.

Saxo, in his *History of the Danes* (written in 1182-1210 CE), said that one had to be a gifted person to see spirits, and went on to explain that

14

THE PATH OF THE SHAMAN

such people had probably experienced prophetic dreams in childhood, or had later undergone a sickness that opened the world of spirits to them.[17]

Similar evidence is found in records of the witch trials. In 1588, Alison Pearson was introduced to the world of fairies, as she lay sick in bed, by her dead cousin William Sympson who appeared to her in fairy form. He came to her as a 'green man' and told her he would help her if she would be faithful to him. Then he vanished and reappeared with a group of fairies who persuaded Pearson to take part in their merrymaking. Sympson also taught her how to use herbal remedies. Whenever Pearson spoke about the fairies to others, she was tormented with blows that left insensitive spots on her skin. She was convicted of witchcraft and burned at the stake.

The shamanic crisis is a terrible and harrowing journey that you wouldn't wish on your worst enemy, and would never seek willingly. I recently read a book recently that chirpily suggested 'think back and see if you might have had an illness that could have been a shamanic crisis'. Believe me, if you had had one, it would be imprinted indelibly on your soul forever, and you wouldn't have to think back - mild hallucinations during a bout of flu don't count. Every illness is not a call to shamanism, though every illness can be a learning process and an opportunity for spiritual growth. A person who has spent their life fit and well understands nothing of the deeper mysteries of life and death. However, it usually takes another shaman to recognise when the crisis is a real one, part of a process, and not a dangerous symptom of psychosis or self-aggrandising/wish-fulfilling fantasy.

Having been brought low, the potential shaman exists for a time in the Otherworld, losing all that he believes to be 'self', undergoing utter destruction and dismemberment before recreation and rebirth, and returning to the everyday world with knowledge far beyond the ordinary. The experience opens a level of consciousness that leaves pathworking and meditation, theory and theology far behind.

This process culminates in the vivid experience of dying, often encountered as a vision of dismemberment. The ultimate disintegration of the shaman may take several forms: dissection of the shaman's body; dissolving in a cauldron; or the smithing and hardening of his skeleton and muscles. Among the Tungus, future shamans fall ill and are pulled apart and eaten by demons (actually ancestor shamans); their heads are melted with bits of metal, which then become part of the shamanic costume. Elsewhere future shamans are shot with arrows by the souls of dead shamans, dismembered, and told whether or not any of their bones are

15

THE PATH OF THE SHAMAN

missing and if any are, they cannot become shamans. The Buryat, Altaians and Kazak Kirgiz are similarly cut up by their ancestors while sick. Eskimo shamans get torn up by an animal and then new flesh grows on their bones. In Central Australia:

> *"The Binbinga hold that medicine men are consecrated by the spirits Mundaji and Munkaningi* (father and son). *The magician Kurkutji told how, entering a cave one day, he came upon the old Mutidaji, who caught him by the neck and killed him. Mundadji cut him open, right down the middle line, took out all of his insides and exchanged them for those of himself, which he placed in the body of Kurkutji".* [18]

One of the oldest extant tales of a shamanic dismemberment is the Sumero-Akkadian story of Inanna's descent into the underworld, first written down in 1750 BCE, but almost certainly much older. According to the story, the goddess Inanna prepared for her descent to the underworld by donning seven articles of clothing, each symbolic of her royal power, which the gatekeepers then forced her to remove as she passed through the seven gates of Hell, where her sister Ereshkigal, goddess of death and the netherworld, waited. Finally, stripped naked, Inanna was killed and hung up on a peg on the wall to rot for three days and nights until she was brought back to life by the food of the *kurgarra* and the water of *galatur* (two little sexless creatures formed of the god Enki's fingernail dirt). This story is often told as *The Descent of the Goddess* in modern Wiccan first or second degree initiations. These initiations are not shamanic, though if properly nurtured and performed they are far more than purely symbolic death and rebirth experiences.

The story of Lleu in Welsh mythology has clear shamanic themes including shapechanging and dismemberment. He transformed into an eagle when he was wounded by his wife's lover, and was discovered by his uncle Gwydion with his flesh rotting and dropping off.

In Hungary, the folk sorcerer the Taltos was marked at birth by a caul or an extra finger, and was instructed in dreams by an older Taltos in the form of a bull or horse. The initiation was heralded by the 'long sleep' lasting three days when, in dreams, the candidate was dismembered, among other ordeals.

There is always a point where the potential shaman remains for a time on the threshold, experiencing the primal void - a state of un-being - and its greatest mysteries. Only when he has surrendered himself utterly can he be reborn.

Classically this rebirth is experienced as a light or crystal being placed inside the skeleton by another shaman, god or ancestor, and the new flesh reformed about it:

16

THE PATH OF THE SHAMAN

"At the same time he put a number of sacred stones in his body. After it was all over the younger spirit, Munkaninji, came up and restored him to life, told him that he was now a medicine man, and showed him how to extract bones and other forms of evil magic out of men. Then he took him away up into the sky and brought him down to earth close to his own camp, where he heard the natives mourning for him, thinking that he was dead".[19]

In South East Australia, one shaman said:

"When I was a small boy he (his father) *took me into the bush to train me to be a Wulla-mullung. He placed two large quartz crystals against my breast, and they vanished into me. I do not know how they went, but I felt them going through me like warmth. This was to make me clever and able to bring things up. He also gave me some things like quartz crystals in water. They looked like ice and the water tasted sweet. After that I used to see things that my mother could not see. When out with her I would say, 'What is out there like men walking?' She used to say, 'Child, there is nothing.' These were the air* (ghosts) *which I began to see.'*[20]

In Central Australia, such stones are called *atnongara*, small crystalline structures which every medicine man is supposed to be able to produce at will from his body, and it is the possession of these crystals which gives the shaman his powers.

A central Australian shaman said that when he was made into a medicine man, a very old witch doctor came one day and threw some of his atnongara stones at him with a spearthrower. Some hit him on the chest; others went right through his head, from ear to ear, killing him. Then the old man then cut out all his organs and left him lying on the ground all night. In the morning the old man came and looked at him and placed some atnongara stones inside his body and in his arms and legs, and covered his face with leaves. Then he sang over him until his body was all swollen up. Afterwards, the witch doctor provided him with a complete set of new internal organs, placed a lot more atnongara stones in him and patted him on the head, which caused him to jump up alive. The old medicine man made him drink water and eat meat containing atnongara stones. When the new shaman awoke he had no idea as to where he was, and said, "I think I am lost," but the old man replied "No, you are not lost; I killed you a long time ago." [21]

Among the Kwakiutl Indians, a quartz crystal was installed:

"Then Lebid spoke and said, 'Indeed, friends, you fellow-shamans, thus you must do to a new shaman. Now I will tell you, friends. I was very sick, and a man came into the place where I was lying in another house and invited me to follow him. Immediately I arose and followed him. Then I saw that my body

17

THE PATH OF THE SHAMAN

was still lying here groaning. We had not gone far into the woods before we arrived at a house and we entered the house. I was asked by the other man to go and sit down in the rear of the house. When I had seated myself, then spoke the man who was sitting on the right hand side of the doorway of the house. He said, "Go on, speak, Naualakume, he who is the great shaman, of what we shall do to him who has come and is sitting among us," said he. Then a man came who had tied around his head a thick ring of red cedar bark and a thin neck ring of cedar bark. He spoke and said, "Our friend will not stay away, for I wish him to go back to his tribe so that he may become a great shaman and that he may cure the sick in his tribe. And he shall have my name for his name. Now he shall have the name Naualakume. And I shall take out the breath from his body so that I may keep it," said he as he went out of the door of the house. It was not long before he came back. He spoke and said, "Now his body is dead on the ground, for I am holding his breath, which is the owner of the soul of our friend. Now I shall give him my shamanistic power," said he and he vomited a quartz crystal. Then all the men beat fast time on the boards. He sang his sacred song as he threw the quartz crystal into the lower part of my sternum, and now I had become a shaman after this as it was getting daylight." [22]

Other traditions involve "singing" a piece of crystal into the initiate's forehead or pouring "liquefied quartz" over the candidate's body. During an Eskimo shaman's initiation, his master will help him to obtain *angakok*, the 'lightning' or enlightenment, a mysterious luminosity which the shaman suddenly feels in his body that enables him to see in the dark and perceive things and coming events that are hidden from others:

> *"The candidate obtains this mystical light after long hours of waiting, sitting on a bench in his hut and invoking the spirits. When he experiences it for the first time 'it is as if the house in which he is suddenly rises; he sees far ahead of him, through mountains, exactly as if the earth were one great plain, and his eyes could reach to the end of the earth. Nothing is hidden from him any longer; not only can he see things far, far away, but he can also discover souls, stolen souls, which are either kept concealed in far, strange lands or have been taken up or down to the Land of the Dead".* [23]

During the initiation period, the shaman visits the worlds of above and below. One Somoyed man, unconscious for three days with smallpox, felt himself carried into the middle of a sea. The Lords of Water gave him the shamanic name 'Diver', implying one who could travel underwater (i.e., in the underworld). He then journeyed to a mountain where he met a naked woman who suckled him. Her husband, the Lord of the underworld, gave him two animal guides and led him to the

THE PATH OF THE SHAMAN

netherworld where he met the Spirits of the Great Sickness (syphilis), the Lord of Madness and the Spirit of Nervous Illness, and thus he learned which sicknesses he would be able to cure. Then he went to the land of the Shamanesses, who strengthened his voice and throat, so that he could chant and invoke the spirits. Afterwards he was taken to an island in the middle of the Nine Seas, where a young birch tree rose to the sky. It was the Tree of the Lord (the World Tree) and the Lord told him to make three drums from one of its branches, one for each of the major rituals he would later conduct for helping women in labour, men lost in the snow and curing the sick. He then went to a mountain cave where there were two reindeer women; one gave him a reindeer hair with which he could shamanize, while the other gave birth to two reindeer which would be his helpers. Then he travelled to another mountain cave where a naked man seized him, chopped off his head, cut his body into pieces and threw them all into a cauldron where they boiled for three years. Then the man put the shaman back together, but giving him new eyes so that he could see more than ordinary people, and piecing his ears so that he could understand the language of plants. The man woke after three days to find himself in his own yurt, but whenever he wanted to shamanize, he mentally took himself back to the cave of the reindeer women. [24]

As can be seen from the above tale, during his initiation, the shaman meets and learns from spirits, gains his own spirit allies and animal familiars. The first spirit the candidate meets is extremely important, and he must be able to recognise this being, as well as the importance and significance of all the places and objects he is shown. For example he might meet spirits of certain sicknesses, such as fever or headache, and once he knows them and can name them, he can cure people so affected. It is the spirits who instruct the shaman, not a human teacher, and shamanic experience cannot be purchased at a weekend residential course or over the internet.

Remembering the experience is crucial, and the shaman must be able to describe it in words to others, or make a song of it. The shaman's songs are descriptions of his spirit journeys and helping spirits, and are usually gained during the initiation period.

REFUSING THE GIFT

Becoming a shaman is a dangerous procedure, and not all survive it. Once the spirits have called the potential shaman, the progression is inevitable, and it must be seen to its conclusion. If the process is not completed, the candidate may wander forever in the hinterland populated by his internal monsters - the powers he refuses to acknowledge torment him in distorted forms until they drive him insane. Eliade called this *"a total disintegration of the personality"*. The interruption of the process, or resistance to it, is a particular danger in a culture like ours which is more likely to medicate the candidate than provide a mentor to see him through and teach him the techniques he needs. The lessons go unlearned, and the candidate will face another catastrophe and another until the process can be completed or until the candidate is utterly destroyed.

The shamanic gift is not offered to many, and to decline it also leads to dire consequences. Refusing to practice as a shaman after the initiation will lead to crisis after crisis until the gift is finally accepted or the candidate is annihilated.

THE SHAMANIC CRISIS IN MODERN BRITAIN

It seems to be a national characteristic that we can admire other cultures, and can accept remnants of shamanic traditions in other lands, but deny them in our own. Historians and archaeologists have a tendency to esteem such practices in the history and anthropology of other cultures, but ridicule and treat with contempt those striving to practice shamanism in the West. Many writers today claim that it is not possible for modern, western man to experience the same mystical relationship with the Otherworld experienced by tribal shamans, or that if they do, this is somehow not valid.

We are not born as blank slates to be written on by the culture that surrounds us. The human body and brain, and the way our consciousness functions, has changed little since the time of the cave shamans and this, more than environment, shapes our lives. Our fundamental concerns are the same- What can I get to eat? Where will I live? Can I attract a mate? Is my family safe? Do I have enough possessions to gain status in the tribe? Am I respected? Can I get well if I am sick? What happens when I die? From that time to this, there are also commonalities of human religious experience; stories of visions of the other realms, moments of epiphany, of and encountering supernatural beings. These can be found in all the world's religions up to, and including, Christianity. It is only the way a society interprets and codifies these experiences that differs.

We are all capable of encountering the realm of spirit and surviving the transition. I know people in Britain who have done so, me included:

Anna

I had already been a witch for twenty years, working with spirits on a daily basis, when the gods decided I needed to go deeper into the mysteries. My own shamanic crisis was spread over several years. It began when I had a parathyroid tumour, and after the operation to remove it I was catapulted into full body tetany when each muscle in my body contracted, one by one, until I could not breathe. I knew then that my heart muscle would be the next one to cease functioning – I was dying. Despite this, I realised that while my body was panicking around me, experiencing its own fears and the desire to survive, my conscious self was separated from these sensations, and was utterly calm. Above me I could see a doorway, the exit from life, and was silently begging for it to be opened so that I might pass through, but this was not to be. It had taken the medics nearly thirty minutes to respond to my panic button, but eventually I was given emergency treatment and brought back.

Later that night, shocked and now very frightened, the world became nothing but crimson light, out of which shadowy figures emerged, the only clear parts of them threatening teeth and pincers. They haunted me nightly while I was in hospital, and I was plunged into a state of such severe trauma that I began to experience my surroundings in a completely different way. Every sound around me, from the rumbling of hospital trolleys to the calls of the other patients, resonated in a different chakra: low tones were experienced in my root and spleen chakras, while high notes reverberate in my throat and third eye chakras.

A few months later I was slowly recovering when I had a vision: I found myself in our circle in the woods. In the northern quarter was a door opening onto a staircase that went downwards into the earth. I went down the steps which gave way to a labyrinth of natural rough stone tunnels, each going further down into the netherworld than the last. I came to a narrow spar of rock that stretched over a deep abyss; below me was molten lava and I was afraid to cross - it didn't seem possible without missing my step and plunging to oblivion. I edged away from the precipice and took another route.

Eventually, the passageway I was following opened out into a cavern. A leather curtain covered an archway at the other end and I sensed a presence behind it. I waited quietly and the curtain moved. An old man wearing stag horns came into the room; I knew he was neither Cernunnos nor Herne, since I was well acquainted with both of them. He looked at me for some time before speaking, "I am the Ancient One," he said "as old as time," and I felt that I was seeing some greater mystery than any other I had yet witnessed. "This is for you, but you must not wear it yet," he warned, handing me a silver chaplet, set on its brow with a moonstone cradled by two silver swans.

THE PATH OF THE SHAMAN

Clasping it in my hands I began to go back down the shafts. After some time, I heard the sound of hammering and came on a dwarf-like man with a pickaxe, chipping shiny black stone from the cave walls. He looked at me angrily "What have you got there?" he asked. I showed him the chaplet and he seemed annoyed to see it. Impulsively I placed the circlet on my head and felt a white swan feather cloak around me or rather growing from me. The Smith began to hammer furiously at the walls and a black powder, like coal dust, began to fly from it. My white cloak turned darker until all the feathers were ebony.

Confused I ran away down the corridors until, before I knew it, I stumbled on the rock spar that crossed the precipice and I was falling, screaming, down towards the boiling lava. Then I stretched out my arms and I was soaring, gliding round in expanding circles upwards. I burst into the night sky moving ever upwards towards the full moon. As its hoary light struck my wings they transfigured and became snow-white once more. Heartened, I pressed onwards into the northern skies, drawn by the bright ember of the Pole Star, into a swirling spiral of brilliance.

I came to a bridge of light and folded my wings to land on it. Beyond it was a world of energy and light without material substance. Beings of pure energy emerged from a pearly mist and looked at me silently. I wanted to ask them questions but they gently turned away and were reabsorbed by the haze. I tried to follow them but an infinitely sweet voice said "This is not yet for you. It is time to return," and I felt soft arms around me, guiding me back to the Earth.

I found myself back in the grove and took the circlet from my head, and the vision ended.

The experience marked the end of a cycle when the group I was working with decided to split up for a while, but it heralded the beginning of greater difficulties to come. I developed a constant sore throat to the point where it became painful to speak, and eventually impossible; I had developed another growth, this time on one of my salivary glands. Even after this was removed, I began to grow more ill and the medication I was given caused a stroke. Trying to push through this and continue working as well as I could, I felt worse and worse, and eventually developed severe ME – my body and my psyche just could not cope with any more strain. From going about the world I became confined to the house, then to a room, and eventually to a bed. I was in constant pain so severe I wept. I was unable to feed myself and had to be spoon fed. I was unable to take myself to the toilet, to wash and clothe myself. I couldn't hold a book to read it, and then I lost my eyesight for a time.

22

THE PATH OF THE SHAMAN

Everything I was had been stripped away from me. For the greater part of two years I lay in bed, feeling myself to be an empty shell, completely separated from the world and no longer part of it- it went on around me but I was caught in some hinterland between life and death. Each night I prayed that I wouldn't wake up in the morning; that the gods would take me, but every day I woke up just the same. Each night I was plagued by dreams and visions of dark tunnels and monsters were teeth and claws that wished to devour me, that *were* devouring me. I was nothing, and I must either change or die. I surrendered myself to death.

Then one night I lay beneath an open window. The wind was fierce, and gusts played about my bed. "Come with us," they said, and I left my body to travel the night with the storm, across the paddock and away over the fields. The next morning a phrase from a dream lingered in the air 'the earth soul and the fire soul'. I understood that the earth soul stayed anchored in one place, while the fire soul was free to roam. From then on, each night I travelled the world with the breeze.

Gradually, little by little, by sheer effort of will, I would crawl from my bed, and Chalky would take me out in the car. Each tree I passed was an immense presence, vibrating with life. I was taken to lie in the garden, and found I could understand the language of plants. Human speech was mostly just a buzz and a blur, but I, who had worked with herbs for many years, finally understood the spirits of plants directly. As I later described to my friend Sue, it seemed to me that I had slowed down so much that I had sunk deeper and deeper into a new level of consciousness, like a person falling into the mud at the bottom of the pond, while on the bright surface other people skittered, moving too fast with their everyday concerns to see what was really going on at the root of things.

I dreamt that I went to visit a witch. She was young and dressed in black, and lived in a cottage. The place was hung with drying plants and charms. She gave me some herbs, and as I left I thought "This is how I am meant to be living. She doesn't allow any intellectual discourse to come between her and what she simply believes." I had felt patronising towards her, since I knew far more than she did, but there she was, living her beliefs, and so sure of them that I envied her.

Later the same evening I dreamed I stood before a large window which looked out over a landscape towards the sea. The night was deep cobalt blue and the full moon very bright. I saw myself reflected in the window, long hair and a blue dress floating in the breeze.

In my hand was a goblet of red wine, and as I willed it, it levitated to the ceiling where it touched a beam, then back down as I willed it. I did this several times and the power surprised me pleasantly, and the feeling pleased me.

23

THE PATH OF THE SHAMAN

I began an invocation. After a while a weak, thin-looking creature with white skin and yellow eyes came to the outside of the window. "You are not the one," I said, "you are not human," and I sent him easily away.

I went outside where numerous streams mingled and parted again, running down to the sea. An old woman crouched beside them, and dropped a poppet with an orange rag tied around it into the water. "When it reaches the sea," she said, "he will come". I sensed he had been a long time gone, and he was the one I have been trying to invoke, and though I wondered how he could be human when he had been in the sea for so long, it seemed not to matter.

This began a series of intense dreams and visions, and in one of the last of the sequence, in the way of dreams, I was myself, and also an elderly highlander on the moors of Scotland. The man was ill, but he was able to enter into and capture animal souls, mainly birds, and fly with them. There was one bird that he could not capture, however, a large gull, but it allowed him to touch its soul, which appeared pale, opaque and granular, like a piece of glass washed in the sea. "At least," he thought, "I have touched it". He also came across a bear and thought to himself "Why should I not have the soul of a bear, since I am the chief of my people?" but the bear was unwilling and reared up so that he was unable to take it.

He kept the souls in a plain wooden box. They looked like glass bird shapes, and on top of the other souls was one in the shape of a gull with its wings spread in flight. One day, he determined to get his daughter 'a bit of a soul for herself,' since she needed some cunning and wisdom, so he took up his gun and set off after a fox. I knew she was me too, and the gift was mine.

Then, one autumn equinox, Sue suggested that we go out for a drive. We decided to go where fate drew us, feeling for the pull of the web at the end of each road to decide which way we should turn. Fate took us to Croft Hill. Though it is only a few miles from my present house, I had never been there before.

Two women with severe ME climbing a steep hill doesn't seem sensible, but we both knew this is what we were meant to do, struggling with trembling and weak muscles, panting with unfit lungs. Half way up, we stopped and looked back at the landscape laid out before us in the bright September sunshine. For the first time since falling ill, I felt a rush of joy and a sense of being part of the world. Nevertheless, as I struggled to the summit, I felt that the effort was too much and that I would literally die on reaching it. I laid myself on the cleft rock that tops the pinnacle, having the

THE PATH OF THE SHAMAN

impression it was like a sacrificial altar, and I was willing to die there, in a beautiful place on a beautiful day, and be happy to do so; let the gods take me.

Instead I was aware of being drawn through the rock to deep within the hill. There the spirit of the hill appeared to me, the presence we were later to call Old Man Croft. He showed me many things, including how the hill mediated the power around the local landscape, how energy flowed in and flowed out, and how the rocky crest was the backbone of the hill, his backbone.

After what seemed like aeons I surfaced again and was led to a grove of hawthorns, which I realised made a perfect circle on the hillside. I sat beneath one, and the dryad of the tree emerged and told me to eat one of her fruits. I did. The hill had become part of the tree, and the tree became part of me, and thus we were all connected. I witnessed the souls of the other hawthorns come out and dance on the hillside, weaving a web with the land, the wind, the birds and the sunshine; I knew that the dance would change as the seasons changed. They drew me into the dance; I swayed as a tree, flew with the birds among the branches and blew with the wind about the summit, vibrantly aware of the energy flowing into and out of the hill.

As I looked into the blue distance I felt myself travel back in time, witnessing a procession sailing towards me along a river (though there was no river nearby as far as I knew then), coming to make offerings on the holy hill.

Though I should, by rights, have been exhausted by the trip, when we returned I felt more vigorous than I had for several years, as though my soul was returning to my body. I was brimming with an inexpressible joy- the magic was back. Though I was not cured, my recovery began on that day. I may never be fully recovered, but I left off the harrowing of hell, and returned to life.

Croft Hill became a place of pilgrimage for us. On the Summer Solstice of 1999 I poured a libation of water into the summit cleft, and laid a bunch of camomile flowers at its foot. The hawthorns were beginning to form fruits and I reflected on how this was the time of fertilisation, the impregnation of the Earth Mother. However, it was not the day to linger at the hawthorns, so I set off to visit the oak in the hollow. As I sat beneath it, I watched a pillar of light travel upwards from the trunk into the sky, then down again through it into the earth: a cosmic axis. The oak explained that in each place, one tree takes on this role, though not necessarily the oldest one. I thought about the role of the World Tree with its branches in the heavens and thought 'Well, trees are not *that* tall, not like mountains' and

25

the tree replied that its leaves were in more than one realm and that each leaf was a realm in itself.

The next day I was visiting my friend Angie, and when we returned to her house in Rugby we noticed a colossal flock of gulls circling the cornfield. What were so many sea birds doing inland at that time of year? More were flying in to join them all the time. I went across the road to see what was attracting them and they followed me. I went back to the house and again they followed me. Angie and I went inside to get them some bread and water, but when we went out again, they had completely vanished. I knew this must be an omen of something coming along the Web towards me.

That night I entered a trance and began to dance slowly. As I moved, I felt the energies fluctuate around me. I saw the strands of the Web and how things were connected. I understood how to change things by weaving the threads of the web, feeling and seeing which threads I needed- maybe this energy from an oak tree thread, this energy from the grass and the energy from this location and so on. I only needed to pull the energies along the web without involving physical objects at all. I discovered how to draw and weave the energies of stars, moonlight, place and people in ritual. Manipulating and moving energies became an important focus of my work.

Kathy:

Kathy had been diagnosed with a rare and life-threatening illness in the summer of 1987, with any treatment for the condition carrying a high risk of stroke. A growth was taking up 60% of her cardiac output and the alternative to treatment was heart failure. She lost a great deal of weight and her hair started falling out. She writes:

"I was thirty years old, my mortality staring me in the face, a dread of possible stroke and an uncertain future. I was at my most frightened and at my lowest ebb. Life over a three year period had taken on a very different perspective; I felt weak, alone and very isolated. Anna, a life-long friend, had been very supportive and suggested I might like to join her Outer Circle to explore alternative methods of healing and inner energies, which I did. Very slowly I began to feel as though I had taken back some control.

It was during these monthly meetings while meditating that my shamanic journey began. What was about to evolve was a life-changing experience of which I had no previous knowledge; it just happened to me, and though the journey was not an easy one, it was powerful and brought knowledge of healing. A total metamorphosis took place- a journey of life, death and rebirth.

THE PATH OF THE SHAMAN

After a time, I realised that one journey was connecting to the next. I knew that there had been a beginning and that I had to continue to see what the end would bring, but was reluctant and fearful of what it would be, so each month I entered into another meditation into the unknown.

In one journey, at the very beginning, I stood on an island, just a small mound of earth surrounded by water. Flocks of ducks with emerald green and midnight blue necks passed overhead, bringing a sense of joy and splendour to my eyes and soul. Sharks circled the island, only their fins visible.

The ducks landed, making them seem more ordinary and everyday than when they were in flight. They seemed unafraid to swim with the sharks and splashed happily in the water as the sharks continued to circle- each going about their business. There was total acceptance of the other's right to be in the water, even though one would have expected the sharks to be predators. The ducks began to feel hungry and looked towards the land for food, their faces now looking distressed and mouths opening like chicks waiting to be fed, their eyes squeezed tight and beaks clapping together frantically. They were blinded and desperate.

Only one solitary being remained on the land- another bird, scraggy in appearance and arrogant in manner as he watched the hunger and pain before him. He could have helped: he had wings to fly and he wasn't stranded and desperate like the others. Instead, he pecked and teased the ducks, sometimes almost forcing his beak into their mouths, tempting them as if to give them food but leaving them almost choking with starvation, he could have helped but didn't

I took off then, on the back of a beautiful white horse, on an almost fairyland journey over the land then down into a valley where the horse came to a gentle halt as I took in the beauty around me. Below, a river bent and wove into a serpent. Surrounding me were giant rock formations soaring above to the sky. Being in this grandeur I felt minute, but not insignificant. Then, in the near distance between some rocks, a giant spider appeared; he was bigger than the mountains. I was not frightened, but my sense of purpose altered- I was not only minute when surrounded by the grandeur of the landscape, but also minute compared to the spider. I was tiny in the grand scheme of things, and this was an important lesson - we should never forget how small we are: it is the very thing that makes us grand.

I left this place and for a brief moment was in two places at once. First there was a procession of soldiers in a castle, like the changing of the guard, but with a threatening war-like feel to the occasion. The soldiers walked around a turret, their spears pointing upwards and becoming the only thing visible above their heads. The scene changed and I looked down from the castle wall, and the image of the spears remained, only now they were not spears but oars held by slaves, still pointing to the sky, regimentally arranged along the side of a Viking boat that was leaving the river below. This was a vision first of authority and then helplessness.

THE PATH OF THE SHAMAN

I noticed the scraggy bird from the island was looking on. It had been around forever, not belonging, but just going from place to place causing havoc, which seemed to give it a feeling of self-satisfaction and importance, yet it knew the consequences and felt them, making it alone and cast out. But how could he put right the rot of many lifetimes? As he watched the two situations he felt lonely and unloved; for many lifetimes he had travelled from place to place, looking for a new start, only to find that he carried himself with him, like a noose around his neck.

Then, from nowhere, came a bigger, blacker, bird, like a giant deformed raven with piercing red eyes like rubies. It swooped upon the smaller bird, its grasping claws outstretched, wings arched to envelope and mouth open to devour. It seized and flew off with the scraggy bird but dropped it in the water accidentally, leaving the bird weak, injured and dying.

I followed and found the bird in the shallows, waiting to die, the gentle tide lifting his wings as the water rolled over him. Then a shark came out of the sea and pushed the bird to safety with his long nose. The bird revived slowly, remembering that he had been saved by the shark - the shark that could have eaten him. It could have devoured him as the monster bird had tried to devour him. It could have eaten the ducks, yet it allowed them the right to live. As he recovered his strength he thought on all of this and realised this he had been given his chance. He had been given the gift of life, an opportunity to halt the destructive force within him which had pushed others away and caused his own isolation- something it had taken him many lifetimes to see. He could help.

He took flight with the other birds feeling welcome, that he belonged. Looking down at the water he paused for a moment and then dived into it, transforming into a shark. He had decided against the freedom of flight and glory, and chose instead circling the island, allowing others to be, just as the other sharks had done earlier

Later I realised the bird was Self, vulnerable; during my illness I felt that isolation from the rest of the world. This story came as a lesson. The large bird came to devour me, but it didn't, though it tried, which was a near death experience in the vision. The shark, which might have appeared threatening, was the one that helped. It was a story about your right to be, that you don't have to be flying in the heights to help, but you can just give a littlie nudge which saves a life. You can watch people suffer or try to help, which I think is what this story was trying to say to me. You could be devoured but were given a chance to live and should do something with it: what doesn't devour us makes us stronger. This was an experience quite early on, and seemed to be a moral or life lesson.

Another series of journeys took place which were almost like a slow death, one consisting of wading through a murky place - swampy, dull, green and sludgy - which was hard work to pull myself through. In another vision creatures were tearing my flesh, flashing here and there before me. I was inside myself somehow and could see my

THE PATH OF THE SHAMAN

blood, as though I was actually travelling through my body. On another occasion I was in a complete void like a black hole, nothingness, though I was travelling through it, and I think this was a death.

The culminating experience of dismemberment and remaking came sometime later. I was feeling very low and Anna was away and I couldn't talk to her. I had been reading and I came across a passage to do with willpower and I realised its importance to me. For the first time I decided to do a meditation without Anna. I went into it feeling very positive. As I entered the dream state it seemed that the sequence carried on from previous visions.

I was lying on the ground and I was just a skeleton. I'd had meditations before that led to this state, this seemed to be the next stage. Basically, it was a feeling of being fragile; there was nothing left of me but the skeleton. There were shaman figures around me and animals in the background. I can't say what those animals were but they kept coming nearer and retreating. The shamans were trying to blow life back into me.

A snake came up from where I felt my feet were, though I couldn't see them. At this point I was very frightened of it; it was wrapping around my skeleton. I had seen it before in my previous meditations, a lot of which were frightening; it had always been threatening. It was crushing me and I was so fragile, brittle, with no strength left, and that was the way I was feeling in my everyday life. I was trying to resist being crushed by the snake. Somehow, through willpower, I unwound the snake and it went. This was an incredibly powerful realisation. I found my Will and that was the most profound thing.

A crystal ball was placed in my solar plexus. I don't remember my body all coming back to one piece, but the crystal was placed and left me with a really warm feeling of pure love. It was a whole turning point as though something had gone 'click'. In my everyday life for weeks after I had a sense of a really warm feeling where the crystal was. It filled me with a sense that I could handle everyday life in a calm manner with warmth and love. When I came out of the meditation I felt a bit disturbed but there was that really warm feeling.

After that, the snake would come and wrap itself round me but now it was comforting. I had made friends with my fear; it became an ally. It would come and go, at times winding through me, sometimes as though it was cuddling me, coiled round me, protective. I have had meditative experiences since when I have left my body to see things. Sometimes the snake went to look at other people and told me what was wrong with them.

Twenty years on, when I look back I realise that after the peak experience I had felt confusion and had a sense of inadequacy; this experience doesn't happen to everyone and I should be using it. I knew that I wasn't going to start dressing up and banging a drum, it wasn't me. I was not going to be a traditional shaman, but 'one who knows', helping people in both simple and more involved ways. The shark taught me

29

THE PATH OF THE SHAMAN

this way back in one of my early experiences. Now I understand that it is about healing and knowledge. Healing comes in many forms - it can be about compassion, love, empathy, understanding and setting seeds, but the knowledge of how to change energies is the most important thing of all. It took many more life experiences to realise what had come to me in 1986 and its value to me and others. The brain has the power to heal itself and tells us many things, and this should be trusted even when that trust is hard to summon.

The healing journey is a long one and it is first and foremost a process. I have had two more near death experience since 1986 with a fractured skull and car accident, and have since suffered post traumatic distress disorder. During this period I learned that we have a primitive brain (amygdale) and a thinking brain which developed through evolution. During times of crisis we directly experience the primitive brain and primitive emotions such as fear and the flight or fight response. At this point, the two brains are not connecting and we are locked into the primitive emotions without being able to rationalise them. I underwent a therapy that used REM work to connect the primitive and rational brain while concentrating on those deep fears and was able to release many of them by bringing them into the thinking brain. This was often accompanied by strange sensations such as things leaving me or things bubbling over. Some would say that crisis changes the chemical structure of the brain permanently, but I believe you can recover and relearn, and that is healing. Illness and crisis takes you back to the responses of the primitive brain, and the shamanic crisis comes with surrender to it.

If a person does not learn to heal themselves, then they are stuck forever in the primitive trauma state. I know that when I began the process of shamanic journeys I was driven by two things - I was intrigued by it, though frightened, and that there was an outcome, whatever it might be; if I didn't see it through see it through to the end I would be left suspended or worse.

The toxicity of negative emotions can kill you, and helping people to handle such emotions is healing. As a healer you can understand where people are, and use many methods to help them, including the use of animal powers to take people out of themselves and identify with and take on the characteristics and powers of a given animal to facilitate a change in energy. I feel what a person needs and call up the right animal for the work, sending out the right energy. I would only do this with the other person's permission.

Sometimes healing can just be the sowing of a seed in someone, which grows. For example I went to Canada to visit some friends and had a strong desire to find out about local shamanism and healing. My friends took me to a Native American site which had been discovered in the 1950s, surrounded by a wood where only the indigenous people were allowed because they understood where they could go and what they could touch. One of my friends thus became interested in shamanism, and now uses it to help

30

people. I set a seed- thus it passes on. I don't always feel it necessary to reveal myself or my experiences when helping others. In fact, I am drawn to helping people with no knowledge in this area (like I was in the beginning) and who don't have the support of shamanic/Pagan communities.

The shamanic journey is different for each person but leads to the same goal, the ability to help others. Better helping people manage their negative emotions "is a form of disease prevention".[25]

Nigel:

Nigel Pennick is well-known for his many books on the Northern Tradition, the runes, East Anglian Magic, geomancy and the Spiritual Arts and Crafts. He writes:

"When I was ten years of age, I suffered massive infection that left me deaf and struggling for my life. During this time I had a cosmic axis experience that in retrospect seemed to have gone on for three earthly days, but that is subjective and there is no way of knowing. I was present in both the upperworld and the underworld. I was elevated in an out-of-the body state to the right-hand corner of the room, where I saw myself lying in the bed. Then I was taken through the roof, which I saw from above before going to the upperworld inside a column whose walls were translucent and patterned like dark scales. In the upperworld I beheld the awesome light behind the light, a blinding whiteness beyond brilliance. Then I was cast down the column, back through my body and into the bones of the Earth where I experienced the presence of the human and animal dead, embedded in and part of the rocks, where, I, too, was buried in a kind of basalt sarcophagus, seemingly for thousands of years, before again I returned to my body and waking consciousness. A terrifying experience that I could not talk to anyone about for decades."

Shamanism is a life-long process of expanding consciousness. Further illumination began for Nigel with a vivid epiphany at the Pantheon in Rome, a place that was designed to represent the Cosmos, a physical manifestation of primal potential, encapsulating all time and space. Some months later, he experienced shamanic death and dismemberment.

Lying in hospital following a sixteen-hour heart attack, he felt triangular glass shards tearing through his body. These grew and multiplied, cutting through his flesh, shredding it in all directions, blood flowing out in streams. He felt that he was dying and accepted it, aware that his physical nature was spreading out in all directions, dissipating like liquid splattering on the ground, becoming boundless. He describes this as a timeless moment, like being on the rim. During this he felt he was identified with the giant Ymir:

"...Ymir, the primal giant, is dismembered by the gods as the primal act in the formation of the world. The various parts of Ymir compose the basic structures of

the world. Ymir's bones become the rock, Ymir's hair the plants growing upon the earth. Ymir's blood becomes the sea – the ebb and flow of the tides recalls the ebb and flow of blood in the body, the old way of viewing the pulse. The sea's tides are related to the waxing and waning of the Moon, paralleling the heart as the origin of the bodily blood-tides. The penetrated body bleeds, just as springs of water emerge from within the body of the Earth. The spiritual principle of "as above, so below" links the bodily blood to the tides, and also links the bodily breath to the winds. All is a symbolic way that humans can relate to the materials of the world, from which our bodies are formed, through the physical exchange that links our individual being in interbeing, in continuity, and in separation." [26]

Suddenly he was snapped back; the body rejoining like two powerful magnets slamming back together, or like the gravitational creation of the Cosmos itself (a potential existence that creates itself). He compares this to the massive, inexorable forces of Ice and Fire, which cannot be resisted:

"In the Northern Tradition coming-into-being story, the Primal Void - Ginnungagap - is a state of non-being that 'contains' all potential matter and possibilities, yet is nothingness. It is the potential of the division of unbeing, a state that all further being emanates from. Once initiated, a process of separation and accumulation proceeds, building up the two polarities of Is and Cen (ice and fire). These are the principles of static being and energetic change respectively.

Is (ice) is the immobile principle, a static form that is brought about through the örlog of ice's formation. Thus water frozen in a bucket takes on the form of the internal volume of the bucket. This is the form that it must retain until conditions change, and the ice becomes flowing water once more. In transvolution, these frozen forms are the fixed patterns in life that have come into being, the 'baggage' that causes blockages in progress. The Ice Giants personify these blockages. They come into being in a certain particular form through the processes of örlog, then have a long-lasting effect upon continuance. They may bring a useful stability for certain purposes, but they are inordinately difficult to change. The forms of orlog, manifested as Is (the frozen form) unavoidably turn the course of events in a particular way. They may limit possibilities, forcing events in a direction that, in time, brings the individual's destruction and dissolution, one's 'doom'. The individual is hemmed in by these giant forms and pushed forwards in a particular direction until the conditions can no longer sustain existence. Though static, they nevertheless interact with dynamic processes to produce a 'catastrophe'. [27]

When a friend came to visit, Nigel asked him to bring a copy of the *Eddas*. When he opened the book, there was Ymir…

Nigel felt that he had been recreated. Some time later, he was taken outside in a wheelchair to await transportation to Papworth Hospital, the first time he had been in the fresh air since his heart attack. Looking up he saw a birch and a pine tree and wept, because this was *beorc* and *cen*, new beginnings and knowledge through pain. He thought "It doesn't matter what happens to me now," and a line came to him from Beowulf: "Wyrd often spares a man who is not doomed, so long as his courage holds":

"The symbolic separation of Ymir's body to make the world gives us a sequence of forms that allows us to relate to the world, part to part. These are manifested in different ways in the thirteen types of the world that appear in the Old Norse spiritual text, Alvissmal, and the twenty-nine runes of the Old English Rune Poem. By isolating the perceptible parts of this interconnected continuum, we can gain insights and some understanding of them, and better relate our own part in this with the whole...The legend of Woden's discovery of the runes tells how he hung himself upon a tree for nine days and nine nights without food and drink in a rite of destruction of the self. Perilous and painful ordeals, whether self-inflicted or as the result of outside agency, are life-threatening events from which the individual cannot avoid being forever altered. They undergo a permanent alteration in conscious awareness...Woden's legendarium tells that he received from the eldritch the gift of knowledge of the runes. The story is quite clear that he did not devise the runes, they were revealed to him from the realm of Otherworldly existence, the eldritch wildwood. Like the tree-sprung Oghams, the runes are linked with natural things, appearing in the branches of trees, the veins of leaves and cracks in the earth. The runemaster is a liminal being who moves between the wildwood and the built environment, reconnecting civilization with the primal, pre-cultural world. The synthonal nature of the runes, where the open meanings of Nature are linked to the closed meanings of the alphabet, makes them a link between the intuitive and the rational or analytical. The runemaster thereby reinstates the eldritch wildwood in the realm of human preoccupations. [28]

Nigel says that the shaman is literally 're-membered' after his disintegration and that it is important he *remembers* the trauma. He is blessed, but must practice his art or suffer the consequences of rejecting it. Afterwards, Nigel dedicated his work to the Spiritual Arts and Crafts, the importance of which he realised so lucidly at the Pantheon. After his near death experience, he felt he was given a second chance in life so that he could fulfil this pledge, as he says: "life is short; you have to get on with it". As part of this quest, he began working in stained glass, created a window of Sophia with a cosmic egg. She is the exemplar of wisdom and illumination, brought about by the shamanic initiation. The cosmic egg represents the primal potential.

Chapter 3
THE SHAMANIC COSMOS

"The principle of universal order is that in one is all, and this naturally includes the spiritual innateness of the material world. Body, mind, spirit, fetch and soul are one with the Cosmos. No part of it is unworthy, for there is no part of us that is not of the divine and no part of the divine that is not within material existence."[29]

The shaman has a particular world-view in which knowledge is organised and interpreted in a specific way. In the shamanic Cosmos, there are unseen other worlds overlapping our own. As Nigel Jackson puts it (after Carlos Castaneda):

"The Otherworlds of the unknown press about the island of the known and from this no- time and all times the spirits cross into the boundary of our world."[30]

The shaman recognises his own place in the Cosmos, and his position relating to it, not a stranger in the universe, not a separate being apart from it, but a vital part of the whole, with no real difference between spirit and matter. For the shaman, gods, spirits, humans, animals, plants and even inanimate objects are part of each other, indivisibly connected.

We normally go through life blinkered by our five senses and restricted by our experiences. Each of us creates his own view of reality in the mirror of our memories; what exists outside our world-view, we cannot perceive or process. For example, natives in the West Indies were not able to see Columbus's ships approaching because they had no knowledge of such items - their brains could not process the information, because it had no context. The island shaman, on the other hand, with his expanded consciousness, was aware that something was happening. He could see ripples and waves on the water (because these were familiar things to him) but not the ships themselves. Eventually, after concentrating really hard, he saw the ships, and it was only after he explained and pointed them out to the others that they could see them too. [31]

From the moment we are born, we learn to assemble the perceptual structure of the everyday consensual reality, according to the cultural values that surround us.[32] It is true that we only take in a fraction of what goes on around us. Our eyes see far more than we process, but we only integrate the bits we need, or which seem to fit in with what we *expect* to see. If we see things we don't recognise, we may not process them at all, but when we recognise the new things that happen to us, they become part of our reality.

34

THE PATH OF THE SHAMAN

While some may dismiss the shaman's visions as mere fantasy, the shaman understands that the world we see is only part of reality. We think that science has given us a view of the world that establishes a concrete actuality, but much of science is theory designed to fit observed events, and these theories are continually revised. We don't *know* that black holes exist; they are a mathematical theory to explain certain observed phenomena. Newtonian physics gave us a mechanical view of the universe, solid objects reacting according to gravity; matter was thought of as static and predictable. Scientists now believe that the universe is not a concrete 'reality', but better explained in terms of energies. Atoms (once thought to be the smallest unit of matter) are not solid. An atom is a particle of dense matter surrounded by a cloud of electrons. Matter takes up a tiny part of an atom, and the rest is a vacuum - the universe, therefore, is not filled with solid objects- it is mostly empty. Moreover, the electrons pop in and out of existence, as does the nucleus itself. Where they go in between time is a big question, and some even speculate that they go into an alternative universe. There have been laboratory experiments where a single particle exists in two places simultaneously. Some have said that an atom is more like a thought than a solid speck of matter- it is made up of information.

The Otherworld is around us, eternal, timeless, where nature and human consciousness know no separation. It does not exist in some distant place, and space is only a metaphor for expressing our separation from it. We have an innate need to understand our place in the Cosmos, and cannot conceive of existence without the concept of space. It is here, not *there*. [33] The shaman's journey reunites the worlds.

THE LAYERED COSMOS

There are similarities in shamanic beliefs (and of those in post-shamanic societies) across the world, even though many of these societies never had any contact: all believe in a tiered Cosmos, usually of three realms —upper world, middle world and lower world. The ancient Babylonians spoke of the heavenly realm of Shamash (the sun god), the middle world of humans and the underworld of the dead. Even the Christian world-view sees man in the centre, with heaven above and hell below.

Middle Earth

Middle Earth or the Middle Realm is the everyday world where we live, the place of mundane life and ordinary consciousness, the place of revealed creation. It is situated between the realms of above and below. Spirits from the other realms may break through into the everyday world, sometimes in

35

the form of omens, signs and so on. Moreover, there are also other realms in the middle world, of which we are normally unconscious.

The Underworld
The underworld exists 'below' us. It is the primeval darkness, the realm of the dead and the unborn, a sometimes frightening and wild where dreams and nightmares take on substance.   The underworld is reached (in vision) through caves, wells, by sinking or diving under the sea or rivers, by climbing down a hollow tree into its roots, or through the tomb.

The Upperworld
Traditionally, the Upperworld ranges from the sky to the heavens, and contains the higher planes of existence, the realm of the sky gods. It is usually reached by climbing the World Tree or pole, or perhaps by flying on the back of a bird, in the form of a bird, or by crossing the rainbow bridge.

Subdivisions

Siberian shamans believe that the Cosmos is divided into three layers with the human world in the middle, though the upper world could be reached by a small hole. The upper world is further divided into several strata. The Somoyedic peoples spoke of a heaven composed of six tiers, while the Altai tribes thought of three, seven or nine provinces, with a separate realm in the north for evil spirits. [34] The Chukchee of northeast Asia believe in a tiered Cosmos, with one realm situated above another, so that the ground of one formed the sky of the world below. The number of worlds is variously given as seven, five or nine. All the worlds are joined by holes situated under the Pole Star. In pre-Columbian Mesoamerica the watery upperworld was divided into nine or thirteen layers arched over the Earth's surface, while below was the underworld of decay and death.

In Navaho legend, there are four layers above and four layers below the earth. [35] The first men lived in a dark first world, where there were insects, mountains and plants. After a while, the first beings climbed a reed into the second world. Conflicts caused them to climb the reed into a third world which had abundant life, light and rivers. Further troubles arose and they once again climbed the reed into this world.

In the Norse and Teutonic tradition there are nine worlds in creation. The names of these vary according to different sagas, but are generally thought of as Hel and Niflheimr at the bottom level (sometimes these are conflated into one world). At the middle are: Jotunheimr, the land of the giants; Midgardr, the land of mankind; Nidvallr, the land of the dwarves and Svartalfheimr, the land of the dark elves. In the upper world are: Alfheimr, the land of the light elves; Vanaheimr, the home of the Vanir and Asgardr, the home of the Aesir. [36]

THE PLACE AT THE CENTRE OF THE WORLD

The idea of things having a centre is one that is psychologically important to us and which allows us to orientate ourselves in relationship to it. English villages were once built around a central green and towns around the market cross, while sprawling conurbations still have a 'town centre'. We recognise other centres in our everyday lives: the navel is the centre of our bodies; our homes are the centre of our lives. According to Nigel Pennick, Pat Collins, the King of the Showmen, used to stamp his heel into the ground to mark out the geomantic centre of the fairground where the main ride, usually a carousel, would be situated with the rest of the amusements laid out around it. This sense of finding the centre was so important that when he died and was to be buried in a newly consecrated

THE PATH OF THE SHAMAN

extension to the graveyard, his son walked the area, stamping his heel into its geomantic centre, and declared that his father should be buried on that spot.[37]

The concept that the manifest world has a sacred centre, a foundation point where it connects to the upper and lower world, goes back to at least Neolithic times, and is virtually pan-global: *"As the individual's spirit is centralised in the body, and the body has a physical location, so the world's spirit was thought of as centralised at a fixed point."* [38]

Every nation has believed, at some point in its history, that it occupied that centre of the world, that its people were the original people or 'chosen race'. The centre of the world was understood to be a place of particular spiritual energies where the commonplace world was closest to the upper and lower realms. A rock or pillar marked the spot, and through this the world was connected to those domains; in other words, this was where the cosmic axis penetrated the earth. At noon, on the summer solstice, the sun stood directly above the pillar and cast no shadow, thus 'proving' it was the centre of the world. [39]

For the Greeks, the sacred centre was the Omphalos at Delphi. For the Babylonians it was Eridu where the sky god Anu first created humans from clay. The Islamic text *Midrash Tanhuma* stated that just as a human being had a central naval, so Israel lay at the middle of the world, with Jerusalem at the centre of Israel, with the Temple at its heart, and the Ark at the centre of the Temple, while the foundation stone in front of the Ark was the foundation stone of all the world. The latter was the Dome of the Rock from which the Prophet Mohammed ascended to heaven. In Christian lore the centre is Golgotha, founded on Adam's skull and the place where Jesus was crucified. The Church of the Holy Sepulchre is now built there and its summit is kissed by pilgrims. The centre of the Jewish world is nearby, the Rock of Foundation on the Temple Mount, which is meant to be the naval of creation, the first solid point God made.[40] In the mediaeval period, Jerusalem was also thought to be the sacred centre of the world and early maps, such as the *Mappa Mundi* in Hereford Cathedral, show Jerusalem as the hub, with the other known countries laid out around it.

Every Celtic country had its own sacred centre. For the Hebrideans, it was Iona. The Manx centre was at Keeill Abban, situated in the middle of the island where the north-south axis crosses the east-west axis. [41]. The earliest monument there is the Tynwald Mound alongside the Royal Road. Originally there may have been a Pagan temple on the site now occupied by St Luke's Church

In Ireland it was Tara, situated in the region of Midhe ('Middle'), the royal heart incorporating the *Lia Fail*, the Stone of Density, used for the coronation of the High Kings of Ireland. The kings met there every Beltane at a natural outcrop now known as *Aill na Mireann*, but probably earlier as *Carraig Choithrigi* ('the Stone of Divisions'), which is situated near earthworks on the Hill of Uisnech, the actual geographical mid-point of Ireland.

No such clear evidence exists for the use of a sacred centre in England, though one tale does imply that it was once extremely important. In the Celtic tale of Llud and Llevelys, King Llud was instructed to overcome the difficulties facing his kingdom by measuring the land to find the exact mid-point, where he would find two dragons fighting. When he did this and found the dragons, the problems were solved.

In 1941 Sir Charles Arden-Close, director general of the Ordnance Survey, located it on the Watling Street four miles ESE of Atherstone, between the villages of Higham-on-the-Hill and Caldecote. However, a stone cross in Meriden claims to mark the exact centre of England, though the monument was moved two hundred years ago by a few yards. At the Bulls Head pub there is a brass plaque on the floor inscribed with an eye, a target and crossed arrows (the village was a legendary haunt of Robin Hood) which is also said to mark the middle of England. It was made by Italian prisoners of war in the 1940s.[42]

For the Romans, the centre of England was a few miles away at Venonae, the modern High Cross where the old Roman roads of the Fosse Way and the Watling Street cross, five miles south of Hinckley. There is a monument there, in very poor condition, in the garden of a house set back from the road. It was erected in 1712 but was struck by lightening in 1791. Before that, there was a monument with four arms erected in 1640 by Anthony Flaunt of Claybrooke. The site lies on the boundary of Leicestershire and Warwickshire, and wrestling matches between youths of the rival counties took place there until the middle of the eighteenth century.

With a revival of interest in sacred centres amongst Pagans and earth-mystery enthusiasts in the 1980s, many efforts were made to identify the geomantic sacred centre of England. As well as the above, another suggestion includes Dunstable, which lies at the crossing of the Roman roads the Watling Street and Icknield Way. The four streets of the town were named after the four cardinal directions.[43]

The Omphalos- the Navel Stone

The Greek word *omphalos* means 'navel'. The navel is obviously the centre of the body, but it is also the place by which we are attached to the nourishment of the mother while in the womb. The Omphalos Stone stood at Delphi. *Delphys* means 'vagina' [44] suggesting this is the place where the Goddess gave birth to the world. Omphalos stones marked the hub of the world in various cultures, giving us an image of the sacred centre attaching us to the primal source of the Goddess as the creatrix at the core of creation. Omphaloi are usually near a well, cave or natural cleft in the earth, giving access to the underworld womb of the Goddess and its oracular powers. From the omphalos the four rivers of paradise are said to flow out, the source of all goodness, perhaps identified with local springs or streams.

Several other naval stones are known, and some of them were said to be meteoric black stones, fallen from the sky and thus creating a link between the earth and heaven. [45] Numerous standing stones in the British Isles are reputed to have fallen from the stars. The now-lost Star Stone marked the meeting of Leicestershire, Nottinghamshire and Lincolnshire. An also-vanished stone at Grimston, Leicestershire, was also said to have such an origin. [46]

Meteoric stones were used as representative of the Goddess in the ancient world. One such is the Ka'bah at Mecca which stands in the centre court of the Great Mosque. It was originally a shrine of Al'Lat ('Goddess') where she was served by seven priestesses, representing the seven known planets (pilgrims still circle the stone seven times). Nearby is an ever-flowing well, an image of the Goddess as giver of life. [47] The setting crescent moon, an ancient symbol of the Goddess, still appears in the national flags of many Islamic nations.

Goddesses of other cultures were also associated with stones. The earliest form of Cybele's name may have been Kubaba meaning either 'cube', 'a hollow vessel' or 'cave'. The ideograms for Kubaba in the Hittite alphabet are a lozenge or cube, a double-headed axe, a dove, a vase and a door or gate - all images of the Goddess in Neolithic Europe. [48] Aphrodite was said to have come ashore on Cyprus after her birth in the foam. She was represented by a black stone which can still be seen at the museum close by her temple. Astarte was represented by a stone at Byblos and Artemis of Ephesus by a sculpture carved from a black meteorite.

Chiefs and kings were installed at the world rock, giving them the power to speak from the gods. This was certainly true of the *Lia Fail* ('Stone of Destiny') at Tara and the various 'king stones' (such as Kingston upon Thames) where medieval English kings were crowned. British monarchs are still crowned on the Stone of Scone. In Celtic lore, a footprint was carved into the upper surface of a rock at the place of

THE PATH OF THE SHAMAN

installation, and it only fitted the foot of each rightful king. Such an indentation, known as 'the giant's footprint', can be seen near Boscawen-un circle in Cornwall, a place of *gorsedd* or law giving mentioned in the Welsh triads. The power of the king was drawn from the sacred centre, which was also regarded as the birthplace of the tribe. If he was a good king, and 'straight', the land prospered, if he was 'crooked', it failed, and battles were lost.

The centre of the city of London was once believed to have been the London Stone, an insignificant rock now housed behind a grating in Cannon Street, but once the old Roman *Terminus*, sacred to Jupiter, the stone that stood at the centre of every Roman city where the main axis of the north-south road crossed the east-west road.

Bob Trubshaw wrote about Croft Hill as a possible English omphalos, an idea first mooted in the nineteenth century by T.L. Walker, who suggested it as the British Druidic centre equivalent to the omphalos of the ancient Gauls on the River Loire.[49] The River Soar flows through the village of Croft, corresponding to the stream said to flow beside the navel, while the hill itself has an ancient and interesting history. Croft Hill is mentioned in a land grant by King Wiglaf of the Mercians in 836 CE, while the Mercian Court met at Croft Hill, giving it credibility as a central law-giving place. In the *Domesday Book* it is recorded as Crebre, or Crec, one of the few Celtic names in the area, from *bre* meaning hill and *cre* from *cræft* meaning a rotating machine, i.e. a mill. It is recorded as being held by Ralph,

> "...with 4 ½ carucates of land and one bovate. In the demesne is one plough and two slaves, eight villains with one sokeman, four bordars have two ploughs. There is a mill rendering 4s and twelve acres of meadow."

The hill itself is quartz-rich granite and much of it has been quarried away, with extraction beginning in Roman times. It is steeped in local legends with various UFO sightings and earth-lights witnessed. The low hills nearby are called 'Shepherd's Tables', where it is said herders gathered on Old May Day to sing and celebrate the turning out of their animals into the summer pastures. Trubshaw speculated that as Shepherd's Race was a name sometimes given to turf labyrinths, this perhaps indicated a ritual pathway up this hill, like the spiral path up Glastonbury Tor. It is one of the places where I work; indeed, it was instrumental in my own shamanic initiation. It is a brooding presence in the otherwise low landscape, a place of many moods, changing dramatically with the seasons. Sometimes it is welcoming, at others inhospitable when it would not be wise to stay; people the *genius locus* doesn't like are quickly discouraged and feel obliged to leave. There is definitely a correct

41

way to approach the hill and to climb it, with pockets of different energies which sometimes must be visited in turn.

The Mountain at the Centre of the World

Certain mountains are regarded as abodes of the gods, places where the human can approach the high realm of spirit. Moreover, the mountain considered to be the centre of the world held a special place in myth and shamanic practice. This 'cosmic mountain' was given different names in different cultures. The Egyptians knew it as the Primordial Mound, the Israelites as Sinai or Zion, and the Greeks as Olympus or Parnassus. The Hindus called the divine peak Meru or Sumeru, the Chinese Kun-lun, Sung-shan, or Bu-zhou, the Icelanders Himinbjörg, the Aztec Colhuacan, and the Choctaw Nunne Chaha.

In *Black Elk Speaks*, Black Elk described becoming sick before a shaman came and adapted him to the gods, and also the powers he encountered. He had prophetic visions of the future of his tribe and saw himself on the central mountain 'which is everywhere', the cosmic axis, the point where stillness and movement, time and eternity are together. He commented *"God's centre is everywhere and circumference nowhere"*.[50]

The idea of the world arising from a central mound occurs in several cultures which reproduced it in man-made structures and temples. The Egyptian pyramids may be reproductions of the primordial mound, and during the Ptolemaic Period, every temple was considered to be a replica of the original temple which had been built upon the prehistoric mound after it had emerged from Nun, the primeval waters. In ancient Sumer, the innermost sanctuary of the temple was sometimes referred to as the 'holy mound', and was again seen as the mound which first arose out of the abyss.

THE COSMIC AXIS

In the shamanic world-view, the cosmic axis bisects the realms at the centre of the world, connecting to the worlds of above and below. For some, the cosmic axis was located at a geographical place, such as the omphalos or sacred mountain, for others, it was constructed when needed. This was the means by which humans could travel the other realms, or speak with the gods. The cosmic axis and sacred centre is the still point around which creation turns.

The Central Pole or Cosmic Pillar

The central pole, the cosmic axis, was considered the legitimate source of human law, and was represented by the measuring rod, the king-post and the sceptre.[51] Every Celtic chief had a measuring rod which he received at his installation. By virtue of this rod he was able to mete out justice, as well as measure the kingdom to find its centre. The MacDuffies, hereditary lords of the small Hebridean island Colonsay, had such an axis, a staff thrust into a hole in a stone base. Their power and wealth depended upon it. When it was stolen in 1539 the last of the MacDuffies died and the lineage was broken.[52]

The great Irish hero Cuchulainn, when his last and greatest battle was going badly, strapped himself to a stone monolith which represented the central backbone of creation, and drew strength and support from it.

Irminsul, the sacred pillar at Eresburg in old Saxony, was said to connect heaven and earth. It was cut down by Charlemagne in 772 CE, though Grimm cites the twelfth-century *Kaiserchronik* as mentioning several Irmin pillars. Remains of an Irmin pillar apparently dating to Roman times are found in Hildesheim Cathedral, where it has been adapted as a candelabrum. The nearby village of Irminseul points to an older connection of the area with the concept.

The Maypole is often considered a phallic symbol, associated with the worship of fertility gods, but it may include symbolism relating to the cosmic pillar thrust into the earth.

Baltic people made representations of the cosmic axis as wooden-roofed poles topped with symbols of sky deities, sun, moon and stars, and guarded by stallions and snakes. Even in the twentieth century these poles were found in front of homes, beside sacred springs and in the forests. People erected them for marriages, to ward off illness and to ensure good crops.

The Omahas of North America had a sacred pole known as the Mystery Tree. It was the centre of the four winds and the home of the Thunder Bird.

The World Tree

Another representation of the cosmic axis is the World Tree, with its roots in the netherworld, trunk in middle earth, and branches in the heavens. The most famous example is the Norse Yggdrasil, an evergreen ash tended by the Norns, three goddesses of fate who live at its roots, moistening them with water from the Well of Urdur. Yggdrasil has three roots and a spring rises from beneath each. The first root reaches into Niflheimr, the land of

43

THE PATH OF THE SHAMAN

the dead, and the spring beneath it is Hvergelmir, the source of all the earth's rivers. The second root goes into Jotunheimr, the land of the Frost Giants and the place of the spring of Mimir, which gives great wisdom to all who drink from it. The third root goes into Asgardr, the home of the gods, and the Well of Urdr rises beneath it. At the base of the tree is a giant serpent called Nidhogger, along with smaller snakes that gnaw at the roots of the great tree. On the topmost branches is an eagle with a hawk called Vedfolnir between its eyes. The eagle and the snake are deadly enemies, and the squirrel Ratatoskr runs between them, carrying insults. Also living in the tree are the goat Heidrun and four stags called Dain, Duneyr, Durathor and Dvalin.[53]

It is likely that the reverence for sacred trees amongst the Germanic tribes was related to the concept of the World Tree. Many of the smaller forests of Germany are considered to have been holy groves, such as Odinswald, the grove hallowed to Odin, where sacrifices were made under certain trees and in which the bards were inspired to prophesy. Thor's Oak was an ancient tree sacred to the Germanic tribe of the Chatti. It stood near the village of Geismar, and was the main focus of the veneration of the god. In 723 CE, the Anglo-Saxon missionary Winfrid (St. Boniface) had the oak felled to demonstrate the superiority of the Christian god over the native Pagan religion. He used the wood of the oak to build a chapel in Fritzlar.

The Celts also worshipped in groves. The word 'Druid' is thought to derive from the Greek *drus*, meaning 'oak' and the Indo-European *wid* meaning 'know' suggesting that a Druid is a man of oak knowledge- in other words, he possessed the skill of travelling the realms via the World Tree. It has been suggested that 'bard' may be formed from the word *barr* meaning 'branch'. A silver branch with little bells was held over the heads of Celtic master poets as part of their insignia, possibly representing a branch from the World Tree and the inspiration the bard gains from the Otherworld.

The oak attracts lightening more than any other tree, a vivid representation of the channelling of energy from the heavens, via the lightening strike of the god, through the trunk and into the earth. Oak trees frequently occur in Celtic myths in conjunction with shamanic themes, like that of Arianrhod (the initiator whose Spiral Castle is at the centre of the heavens) and Llew, who undergoes death and dismemberment.

Arianrhod had two sons, Dylan and Llew, whom she refused to recognise. Dylan threw himself in the sea, but Llew was brought up by his uncle Gwydion ap Don. Arianrhod cursed him that he would never marry a woman born of the race of men, so Gwydion and the magician Math ap Mathonwy ("Bear son of Bearlike") gathered the flowers of oak, broom and meadowsweet to fashion him a wife called Blodeuwedd ("Flower Face"). All was well until Blodeuwedd met the handsome Gronw Pebyr and fell in love him, and the adulterous pair plotted to rid themselves of Llew. He was tricked into telling Blodeuwedd that he could only be killed when on the bank of a river with one foot on the back of a he-goat and the other on the rim of a bath. The weapon needed to kill him would take a year to make, working only on Sundays. Gronw set about making these preparations and when all was complete Blodeuwedd playfully asked Llew to show her how he could possibly balance on a goat and bath at the same time. Indulgently he demonstrated, but as soon as he was in position Gronw threw the fateful javelin. It wounded Llew in the thigh and he turned into a bird and flew away. Gwydion searched far and wide for his missing nephew until one day he discovered a sow behaving strangely. It was eating worms and gobbets of flesh which fell from an oak tree in which a rotting eagle was perched. Recognising Llew, he changed him back to human form and nursed carefully him back to health.

Other trees are important in Celtic lore. The yew was one of the five magical trees of Ireland descried as "the renown of Banbha" (a crone or death goddess), "the spell of knowledge" and "the king's wheel". Every ancient Irish king wore a yew brooch in the shape of a wheel to remind him of the turning of the life's circle and the inevitability of death. In ogham the yew is *Idho*. A mistake in the translation of a 5th century manuscript meant that the name of a sacred island off the western coast of Scotland was changed from Ioha to Iona. The traditional associations of Iona are linked to rebirth and reincarnation. The ancient bardic groves there were taken over by St. Columba, fleeing from Ireland to seek fresh lands in which to spread the Christian faith.

In Baltic lore, the World Tree or iron post stands beyond the Hill of the Sky, next to a grey stone. It usually described as an oak or a birch with silver leaves, copper branches and iron roots. The sun goddess Saule rests in it, hanging her belt up and sleeping in the crown. Two horses stand by the post.

In the mythology of Mexico a great cosmic tree forms the centre of the universe, its branches rising to the clouds from which flows the fertilising rain, while its roots stand in the primeval waters from which all things originate.

45

THE PATH OF THE SHAMAN

The Akawiros of Bolivia had a World Tree which bore all kinds of fruit and organic beings.

In the Persian *Avesta*, in the branches of the sacred tree growing on the Mountain of Paradise there are two birds roosting - Amru and Chamru, the two eagles of the sky.

In Britain, the inhabitants of Leamington Spa claimed that the centre of England was marked by the ancient Lillington Oak. This tree during World War II and was replaced in 1982 by a new sapling.

Siberian legend says that at the beginning of the world a tree was born without branches. God caused nine branches to spring at the foot, of which were born nine men, the ancestors of the nine human races. God allowed men and animals to nourish themselves with the fruits of the five branches turned towards the east, but forbade them to taste the fruit of the western branches. He appointed a dog and a serpent to guard these branches against men and the demon Erlik. While the serpent slept, Erlik climbed the tree and seduced Edji who ate part of the protected fruit and gave part to her husband, Törongoi. They were instantly covered with hair, became ashamed of their nakedness and hid themselves among the trees.

In Judaic and Christian myth, the tree of knowledge grew in Paradise ('orchard'), but the first man and woman, Adam and Eve, were forbidden to pluck its fruits. Tempted by the serpent at its roots, Eve plucked the fruit of knowledge and gave it to Adam. God grew angry at this trespass, and flung them from Paradise. The biblical Tree of Knowledge may not have been an apple tree at all, but a fig or date palm. It was only identified as an apple tree in the 2nd century AD., in a translation by Aquila of Pontus. Eve's original Hebrew name was Hawwah from the Akkadian word *Hayah* meaning "to live". She is thus called Hawwah because she was 'Mother of All Living' according to Genesis. This was a title of the Sumerian goddess Ninhursag, from whom the myth was appropriated by the Hebrews. In the Sumerian version the god Enki (possibly cognate with Yahweh or Jehovah) was cursed by Ninhursag because he stole forbidden plants from paradise. His health began to fail and the other gods prevailed on the Mother Goddess to help him. She created a goddess called Ninti (literally *nin*= lady, *ti*= rib i.e. 'lady of the rib', a play on words since the phrase also means "to make live"). Enki claimed his rib hurt him and she healed him. Eve is in fact the Great Goddess, who initiates Adam into her mysteries via the World Tree.

In Chinese legend the *Fu-sang* tree was where the ten suns resided, while a dragon curled round its base. It was located in the east in the Valley of the Morning as the sun rose from it, in Paradise.

The World Tree of Hindustan is the symbol of universal life and immortality. It is considered to be the god Brahma, who is known as 'The Tree of Skambha'. All the other gods of the Hindu religious system were considered to be branches from this divine tree which overshadowed the universe. Hymn 81 of the tenth book of *The Rig Veda* asks the question "What was the forest; what was the tree from which the sky and the earth issued?" the answer being that the forest, the Cosmic Tree was the god Brahma himself. It was visited by two heavenly birds, one symbolising day and the sun who visits the tree without eating; the other symbolising night and the moon, which comes to feed on the fruit. It is said the serpent fears this tree and avoids its shadow. If the shadow goes towards the east, the serpent flies towards the west. If the shadow of the tree falls to the west, the serpent flies east. By virtue of the tree the serpent cannot hurt the birds but if they leave the tree the serpent can devour them. The tree produced the first fruit which nourished the first men.

The idea that the World Tree has a serpent or dragon at its roots is widespread. In Greek myth the tree of the Hesperides, sheltered in the garden of paradise, was protected by the serpent Ladon. Its golden apples of the immortality were placed under the guardianship of the Hesperides, Nymphs of the Evening and Daughters of the Night. Their garden was in the far west, or in other words, where the sun sets in the evening. They were the nymphs of the setting sun Aegle (Brightness), Erythia (Scarlet) and Hesperarethusa (Sunset Glow). Herakles slew the serpent and stole the apples on a quest for shamanic knowledge, but they were later returned by Athene, the goddess of wisdom. The apple symbolises the sun, as it ripens to yellow it is the passage of the sun across he sky, as it turns red it is the dying or setting sun which will rise anew each morning, reborn. It is for this reason the apple represents immortality. The Norse Gods ate the apples of Iduna in order to preserve their youth and beauty, while in Greek myth Zeus and Hera were presented with a tree of golden apples by the Earth Goddess Titaea, which bestowed youth and beauty on those who ate the fruit.

Legendary isles of apples are common, and always lie in the west, the place of the dying sun, from which it proceeds to enter the underworld, or Land of Youth, travelling through the realms of death in preparation for its rebirth. In the story of King Arthur, after he is mortally wounded, he is taken on a magic barge to the Isle of Avalon, which means 'Isle of Apples', from the Welsh *afal* meaning 'apple'. The Elysian Fields of the ancient Greeks, the place of the afterlife, also translates as 'apple orchards'.

THE PATH OF THE SHAMAN

From its association with the Otherworld, the apple is seen as a passport to it, or symbol of it. The Greeks believed that carrying an apple bough that bore flowers, buds and fruit at the same time would enable them to enter the underworld. Bran, in Celtic myth, was summoned by the Goddess to enter the Land of Youth with a 'silver white blossomed branch from Emain, in which the bloom and branch were one'.

In Algonkian legend, the World Tree was created when the Bear spirit pushed it through the layers of the Cosmos, so that the Midewiwin (a society of shamans) were provided with a passage to travel the universe. [54]

Amongst the Plains Indians the sun dance is performed around a central post, an uprooted tree which represents the World Tree, with its roots in the underworld, trunk in the everyday world, and top in the sky. The three levels are marked on the post; an eagle at the top represents the sky, a buffalo skull represents this world, and tobacco offerings at its food are offerings to the underworld. [55] The dancers circle the tree for many hours a day, until the last day when they are attached to the tree by skewers through their flesh, and must endure this through the twenty-four songs of the ritual. This is done to engender visions.

The Australian tribe of the Achilpa had a World Tree, a gum tree, made for them by their divine ancestor. They carried it with them and it showed them where they should travel. When it was broken, they lost their power and contact with the ancestral spirits, and giving up hope, they laid down and died.

The ancient Chaldeans and Assyrians' World Tree was called 'the Great First Source' which grew in the forest of Eridhu. A cedar shoot sprouted, its white crystal root stretching toward the netherworld. Its seat was the centre of the earth, while its foliage was the home of Zikum (the heavens) the great primeval mother. During the initiation of an augur, the candidate was made to descend into an artificial imitation of the underworld, where he beheld the altars amid the waters, and the treasures of the gods Anu, Bel and Ea.

The Spindle

The sense of the world spinning about the still cosmic axis is reflected in the image of spinning wool about a distaff. Our Anglo-Saxon and Scandinavian ancestors believed that the goddess Freyja span out the web of destiny. In Norse tradition, the three stars we know as the belt of Orion are called 'Freyja's Distaff', or perhaps they represent the three Norns spinning each person's *wryd* (fate). [56] There are many other ancient spinning and weaving goddesses who spin the thread of the Cosmos and weave the web of destiny, such as the Greek Fates.

Amongst the Kogi it is claimed that at a certain spot, the Mother stuck her spindle and spun it, turning the world on its axis, spinning out the thread which is time as well as space, and which heaps up in the cone of the Sierra, and which then develops, in an ever-widening spiral, into the whole of the world.

The Cosmic Mill

In Scandinavian and Finnish myth is the story of the World Mill, a cosmic axis. A mill generally consisted of a one still stone at the bottom with another rotating above by means of a fixed handle at the centre. The still, lower stone represented the earth, and the revolving one the heavens and turning stars around the still point of the Pole Star at the centre. [57]

The Pole Star

The revolution of the stars around the apparently still Pole Star near the centre of the heavens could readily be taken to mean that the polar region of the stars was the centre of the Cosmos. It was the point in the heavens where the central pole connected. It was called the *Nowl* in Norse lore, which means 'navel' or the 'nail' which holds it in position. In Celtic tradition, the Spiral Castle of Arianrhod (the Corona Borealis) surrounds the North Star, and this is the place that souls travel to at death or for initiation.

THE FOUR DIRECTIONS

Wherever we stand is the centre for us. We stand on the earth. Above us are the heavens, the stars turning clockwise about the 'still' Pole Star. Below our feet is the underworld. Beyond this, we generally conceive of directional space as fourfold, what is on our left side, our right side, behind us and before us. The compass reflects this fourfold division, with the cardinal points of the east where the sun rises, the west where it sets, the north where the sun is low in winter, and the south, the high point of the sun in summer.

Direction is also important in the Otherworld, but before we orientate ourselves in the Otherworld, we must first establish our relative place in this. When the tribal shaman goes into a trance, he often looks one way and another, the so-called 'quest for the right path' which takes place during rituals.[58]

RECREATING THE COSMOS IN MIDDLE EARTH

The belief that control of the Cosmos and entry to its various realms can be gained by recreating it in miniature in a chosen spot is an ancient one, exemplified by the old Hermetic maxim 'as above, so below'. The creation of stone circles, temples, etc was an attempt to allow the priest, magician or shaman to manipulate the forces of the macrocosm by recreating it in the microcosm. In the past, augurs and geomancers would be employed to determine the correct place. In China such people still work with *feng-shui*. Caesar stated that the Druids were trained in 'land measurement' as well as astrology and geodesy. Strabo wrote that Zeus released two gold eagles and where their flights crossed marked the centre of the world, Delphi.

According to Plato's *Laws*, the cosmic order is taken as the pattern for any temple or shrine. Often a centrally placed stone, representing the omphalos, receives the world pole. Below lies the underworld, a sacred well or cave. Around the stone stood shrines to the gods, and the four directions were marked, as well as the twelve winds. The four streams of paradise may be represented by the four roads extending from the central point and divide the country into four sections, perhaps further subdivided into eight or more and marked by boundary stones. For anyone who created sacred space, the first thing was to locate the central axis of the country, preferably on the north-south, east-west line passing through the centre, a ritual path reflecting the Milky Way, an image of the cosmic axis in the sky. Overlooking the omphalos was a central, conical mountain, the mountain at the centre of the world where the chief god lived. Plato stated that the capital city should be placed as near as possible to the centre of the country.

The sacred centre of any locality lay at the hub of local roads, usually at the nexus of a north-south and east-west crossing. In other words, in ideal circumstances, a road would run off to each of the cardinal points of north, south, east and west. The contenders for the Royal Roads of England are the Fosse and Watling Street, or the Icknield Way and Ermine Street. [59] They are ancient Roman roads, a byword for straightness; Royal Roads were always straight. In many European languages the words for 'kingship' link to 'correctness' and 'straightness'. The clearest example in English is 'ruler' which refers either to a monarch or to a straight edge. The origin of this seems to be buried in the earliest Proto-Indo-European languages, and a root word-element '*reg-*' is generally accepted as being the origin of this complex concept. A bad king was called 'crooked'

In Pre-Columbian Mesoamerica each town and village had their own version of the tiered Cosmos, incorporating local mountains, streams,

THE PATH OF THE SHAMAN

caves etc. the sun and moon delineated the outer boundaries of the Cosmos, with a central tree growing out of a mountain, linking the realms. On the vertical plain, the four quarters were pictured as a four-petalled flower. The central point of the Cosmos sometimes required sacrifice to be made upon it to keep the Cosmos living. Temples embodied the Cosmos, and were orientated to the turning of the heavens. The temple itself materialized the path of the king on his shamanic journey and enabling him to travel in the sacred world as a public performance.

The concept of the home being the centre of the every family's world or its navel is also common. The Kogi Indians, for example, see the world in the form of a quartered circle, with other disc-like worlds both above and below. The circular ceremonial house of the Kogi has four fires, which represent this quartered earth. The conical roof symbolises the top half of the universe and, within its construction, contains symbols of the worlds above. A series of underworlds lies below the house. The Kogi priests, the Mamas, sit in the ceremonial house as though it were a womb, and they are at the foot of an umbilical cord which reaches down from the centre of the roof. [60]

The Desana of South America drink hallucinogenic *yajé* and the house becomes a model of the universe, and the men's door the eastern entrance to the Earth we inhabit. Movement through the house becomes movement through the Cosmos. [61]

The Neolithic round-house with the fire at the centre, in the square hearth, the smoke escaping through the open roof, was also a representation of the Cosmos- the walls of the hut were the circumference of the universe, the hearthstone was the earth, its four sides the four directions and the four seasons. The presence of the gods was manifested in the living fire, with the smoke ascending through the smoke-hole to the gods.[62] The hearth has been the centre of human life for at least 400,000 years. The business of the home rotated around it, and it was the traditional place to house the shrine of the guardian spirit of the dwelling, and provided a place for worship within the household. The Latin word for it was *focus*, since it was the focus of the home.

In Greek myth the hearth goddess was Hestia. She refused a throne on Olympus to look after the hearth, and never took part in the wars and arguments of the gods. Instead she was the calm centre, the safe haven of the home, where people could seek refuge and shelter. She was worshipped as that centre, whether the centre of the city, the house, even the centre of the world, the omphalos. As the domestic hearth is the sacred centre of the home, the hearth of the gods is the centre of the Cosmos. According to Plato, the

51

twelve Olympian gods, who represent the twelve constellations of the zodiac, circle the House of Heaven, while Hestia remains still at the centre, tending the hearth, which is called 'the Everlasting Place'. Hestia was the first born of the Olympian deities and last released by her father Cronos (Father Time), who had swallowed all his offspring to prevent them usurping his throne. Thus it is said that she is both the beginning and the end- *alpha* and *omega*.

Her Roman equivalent was Vesta. As well as being worshipped daily in the home, at the hearth fire, she was also worshipped in an important state cult, maintained in a sacred building on the Forum Romanum with a circular chamber housing an eternal flame that was never allowed to die out. It is said that the cult was founded by king Numa Pompilius (715-673 BCE) and the sacred fire burned until 394 CE. The cult of Vesta probably originated in tribal society, when a fire was the central focus of the village.

When we cast a circle or create sacred space, its function is to orientate us in relationship to this world and the Otherworld, recreating the form of the Cosmos, and linking us to the Otherworld. We draw the cosmic axis from the Pole Star above, through the middle realm, into the underworld. We align the north of the circle with the true north, and the south, east and west likewise. The gateways to these realms are then opened in the quarters, and the four royal roads of power are opened to meet at the centre of the circle, above the hearth fire.

THE WEB

The shaman's view of the Cosmos is a holistic one, with everything in all the realms connected by an interwoven and interdependent fabric of energy and consciousness, beyond time and beyond space. We are an integral part of this whole, we do not stand outside it, and through it, we are indivisibly connected to everything else. The concept of the unitive field being a net or woven cloth is widespread: in India it is called *Tantra*, meaning 'web' or 'fabric' or it is called the 'jewelled net of Indra. In South America it was called 'the net of power'. Here in Britain it was called the Web of Wyrd. Through it, we can communicate with every other consciousness or 'spirit' in the Cosmos, whether human, plant, animal or mineral. The shaman practices various techniques of being able to attune to the threads of the web.

This web was often thought of as being woven by a goddess or trio of goddesses. In Greece, they were the three Fates or *Moerae* who control human destiny. The thread of life is spun on Clotho's spindle, measured by the rod of Lachesis and snipped by Atropos' shears. In stature, Atropos was the smallest of the three, but by far the most feared, as she is 'she who cannot be stayed'. Prayers and pleas would not move the Fates, and even the gods could not alter their decrees.

In Norse myth, their equivalents were the Norns, three goddesses who dwelt beneath the World Tree. They were Urdr ('Fate'), Verdandi ('Being') and Skuldr ('Necessity'/ 'Debt'). Urdr and Verdandi wove the complex golden threads of wyrd (fate), which Skuldr destroyed in time. They appear in Shakespeare's *Macbeth* as 'the Wyrde Systres'.

In Welsh legend, the weaver was Arianrhod, mistress of Caer Arianrhod, the Spiral Castle of death, initiation and rebirth. Out of her own body she span the thread of being, fate and destiny, weaving it to form matter of the Cosmos, the web that joins all life together. Her spinning wheel was the wheel of the stars, her threads the threads of life, death and rebirth. Her castle reflected the spiralling thread. The ancients saw it as the Corona Borealis around the Pole Star, where souls regenerated. The spiral shape, which is the basis of the spider's web, is an ancient and almost universal symbol of regeneration and rebirth.

It is possible that The Fates were the original Fairy Godmothers who were believed to assist at the birth of humans. Long after the coming of Christianity, mothers would make ready for them when a baby was due, spreading out food and gifts to ensure their favour for the child. Just as the fairies were called 'good people' in supplication, the Fates were respectfully titled *Parcae*, or 'merciful'. Belief in them survived in parts of Greece well into the twentieth century. The Latin word *fatum* or fate referred to a pronouncement of destiny, a spoken sentence of doom fixed by the gods at birth (the word 'fairy' is probably derived from it).

Chapter 4
TRAVELLING THE COSMOS

"If the doors of perception were cleansed, everything would appear as it is – infinite."
William Blake

Carlos Casteneda coined the terms 'ordinary reality' and 'non-ordinary reality'. Ordinary reality is the consensual reality we all experience everyday – we can all agree that there is a big house over there, rain is wet, a metre is thirty centimetres and so on. We experience this reality through our five senses. It is often called the physical or material plane, the time-space world. In ordinary life, we are focused on the business of living, yet while we are dreaming or meditating, we experience other kinds of realities. In dreams and visions, we might meet dead relatives, other beings, speak with animals and visit places thousands of miles away in an instant. Non-ordinary reality is only encountered during an altered state of consciousness. This form of reality is experienced by an individual; he sees things that are meant for him alone, and they are generally witnessed by no one else.

The word 'consciousness' is derived from the Latin *con-scire* meaning 'with-knowing'. Consciousness is a spectrum from wide-awake, left brain logical thinking to daydreaming, dreaming and deep trance. In the modern western world, only logical thought is considered important, while dreams and visions are dismissed, though in the past people firmly believed that god and spirits communicated with them in dreams and visions. This was true even in Christian countries where the clergy used meditation, fasting and flagellation to induce visions which gave the recipient both status and power. (However, any non-clergy having visions were subject to investigation and suspicion, especially of they were women.[63]) While in the west, only the state of being wide-awake is given credence as reality, in the shamanic world-view, other levels of consciousness are equally valid. The shaman deliberately alters his level of consciousness in order to be able to journey to the Otherworld.

Two hundred years ago you would have been laughed out of any scientific establishment for saying that time is flexible, but Einstein proved (by mathematical theory) that time is relative, and depends on the observer. Quantum physics goes further, and according to its principles, it is possible not only to go forward in time, but also backwards. According to quantum theory, reality only exists as potential until we observe it. We are used to thinking that things exist without our input, but they exist only as possible movements of consciousness. Things are not things, but tendencies. As we observe, we choose which possibility manifests; it has now been proved that the observer shapes the outcome of any experiment - in other words, reality in not concrete, but only one of multiple potentials. We create our own reality moment by moment.

In the world-view of tribal people everywhere, the realms we know from dreams and visions, the worlds inhabited by gods, spirits, animal powers and ancestors, are recognised as equally real. Moreover, these realms hold the key to solving problems, healing and knowledge.

METHODS OF CHANGING CONSCIOUSNESS

To travel to the Otherworld, it is necessary to change the level of consciousness from 'ordinary reality' to 'non-ordinary reality'. Human brains and physiology are the same all over the world- what the Siberian shaman experiences can equally be felt by a twenty-first century Englishman.

There are many methods of changing consciousness, some safe and some positively dangerous, proving the extent to which a shaman will go to seek his goal, and the seriousness with which he takes his art. Shamanism is not a game for dabblers, but a life and death matter. In any act of magic, whether it be shamanism or Wicce, it is necessary to fully commit to the enterprise, and to sink into it utterly and completely in order to reach the ecstasy. However, it should be remembered that the shaman usually carries out his shamanising in a state of light trance rather than a deep trance in which he is unconscious of the everyday world, which is usually reserved for his initiatory experiences and vision quests.

Hypnogogia

The hypnogogic state occurs between waking and sleep, when we experience vivid images, sounds and so on, while the hypnopompic state happens on awakening from sleep where dreams may linger. It is possible to extend both the hypnogogic state and hypnopompic state, and both Dali and Magritte encouraged this to in order to gain inspiration for their artwork.

Lucid Dreaming

Lucid dreaming involves the control of the dream state- to know that you are dreaming and act consciously within the dream realm, in real time as events unfold. This usually entails determining the intent of the dream experience beforehand, perhaps using post-hypnotic suggestion to do so.

Near-death Experience

Near-death experiences often include elements that with similarities to shamanic initiations, occasionally including dismemberment. Other commonly encountered themes include bright lights, music or a humming sound, a sense of leaving the body and floating, moving along a tunnel, approaching a door or portal, encountering spirits and communicating with them, a review of life and a return to the ordinary world with altered views and perceptions.

Dance

Through dance and physical contact, we can experience spirits far more powerfully than by meditation alone. Dance is widely used to take the shaman into the spirit world, or even to summon spirits to possess his body, particularly those of his animal allies. He might call upon a fox or other burrowing animal to take him to the underworld by imitating its movements, or a bird to take him to the upperworld by emulating its flight. This necessitates abandoning himself to the dance, to its movements and allowing possession by the animal, leaving behind the ego completely. As someone who has tried to lead shamanic workshops among the self-conscious British, I know that this is something many people struggle to do.

The shaman may have been taught the dances by the spirits themselves during his visions or initiation. He may ask the community to support his journeys by singing his songs as he dances to call his spirits. When they arrive and possess him, it can cause a certain amount of pain and discomfort before he comes into alignment and harmony with the spirit powers. Once he has their power, he can then use it to divine why people are sick, or use the energy directly to heal them.

Another way the dance might be used is to summon fertility spirits to bless a society, with the dance being the focus of the community's prayers, or a way of honouring the spirits and thanking them. The Pueblos of South West America use the power of *kachina* dancers to bring the benevolent power of the kachinas into the villages. Kachinas represent the powers of nature and include the Cloud Beings, Corn Maidens, Star Spirits, Dawn Spirits and Lightning Spirits. They visit from midwinter to midsummer, then return to the Otherworld for six months. The spirits keep themselves to themselves unless they are specifically summoned by humans, when they cannot refuse to attend. Their help is sought on various occasions such as seasonal celebrations, house building, harvesting, hunting, *kiva* building, road making, rain making, or soliciting better crops, more babies and healthier animals. Kachina dancers wear masks that

THE PATH OF THE SHAMAN

represent the spirits and imitate the kachina in order to become possessed by them becoming the spirit whose power resides in the mask.[64]

In the Craft, we use dance to raise power for ritual. In group rituals, even non-initiates have felt the power flowing about the ring and the presence of spirits summoned by the dance, blurring the boundaries between the human and spirit worlds.

Chanting

The chanting of repeated words and phrases has the power to alter consciousness and connect the singer with the divine, as well as to magically invoke the energies associated with the words. The chant is rhythmic, monotonous, often creating a dense vocal texture that might last for hours. The shaman might sing or chant different themes and songs from the different worlds he visits, with different rhythms and voices for the middle world, the lower world and the upper world. He might imitate the sounds of the birds or animals he wishes to invoke. Chanting is often accompanied by drums and clapping. Each shaman may have his own power song, often given to him at the time of his initiation.

In South America, chants may be sung all night for a shaman on the verge of initiation, and he will feel a chill creeping up his stomach into his chest. He may smell rotting corpses and during the following days he experiences dreams during which he travels to the Otherworld, meets guides and finally the spirit of someone recently deceased.[65]

Norse shamans had their own form of song magic called *galdr* with sung spells and incantations. Some of these would be passed on for many years, others invented on the spot as needed. These might be used to ease the pain of childbirth, for example, or for healing, as in the case of the giant witch Groa, who attempted to sing a whetstone out of the god Thor when he had been injured by it.

In shamanic societies, chanting is used to effect healing, exorcism and magic. Native Americans chant in preparation for ceremonies such as healing, hunting, battles, controlling weather, rites of initiations and funerals. [66] The Navajo healing chants are interwoven with myths telling how the spirits first performed the chants, which show how the chants should be performed. The chanters must chant the prescribed texts correctly, or they will themselves be struck by the disease they are trying to cure.

Witches and Pagans use chanting today as a way of invoking gods and spirits, and sometimes as a way of altering consciousness.

57

THE PATH OF THE SHAMAN

Drumming and Clapping

The most common method of altering consciousness employed by tribal shamans is the use of monotonous percussion sound, usually with a drum, but also with sticks, rattles and other instruments. This disengages the conscious mind, allowing a meditative state to occur, and the pattern of a repeated steady beat can induce trance. The drum is even called the shaman's horse or mount, as in this Siberian chant:

Oh! My many coloured drum
Ye who standeth in the forward corner!
Oh! My merry and painted drum,
Ye who standeth here!
Let thy neck and shoulders be strong.
Hark, oh hark my horse –ye female maral deer!
Hark, oh hark my horse – ye bear! [67]

There are many rhythms that can be used to invoke trance states, but most important is that the tempo should be kept steady and not speeded up. Native American ritual drumming, for example, is slow and simple, reflecting the pulses of the earth, sky and the elements. A drum beat contains many sound frequencies, which produce changes in electrical activity in many areas of the brain. The shaman may also use a rattle to distract the conscious mind from running off with stray thoughts. Some drummers paint their allies onto the drum, along with other symbols and totems.

In the west, the use of the drum, associated with the old Pagan religions, was suppressed, though it continued to be used in folk traditions, often largely remnants of Pagan seasonal ceremonies.

Electrical stimulation

Research suggests that people with high electrical activity in the brain's temporal lobes are more imaginative and artistic than others. The electrical stimulation of the hippocampus produces lucid dreams in a waking state (don't try this at home, folks).

Changes in consciousness are triggered by magnetic fields and places of geological stress, explaining why some places are more prone than others to generate Otherworldly experiences. Places rich in granite, like Croft Hill, are always associated with apparitions, magic, earth lights and fairies.

Sleep Deprivation

Sleep deprivation generates hallucinations and disconnection from the

THE PATH OF THE SHAMAN

everyday world. Some tribal shamans deliberately keep themselves awake for extended periods to bring about a change in consciousness.

Fasting

Fasting is a discipline practiced in many religions, not only to purify the body, but because it alters consciousness. Fasting Christian mystics saw visions of God and the saints, for example. In the Hearth, we always fast coming up to a ritual.

Sensory deprivation

We surmise that in the Paleolithic period of the cave shamans, a priest's or initiatory candidate's journey through the darkness and seclusion of the cave heightened his awareness, while he travelled to the realm of the spirit animals. Rituals in many cultures employ similar techniques of isolation, darkness and deprivation of the sensory input of the outside world.

In the 1950s, scientists began to experiment with isolation tanks as a method of altering consciousness. This is a lightproof, soundproof tank in which the subject floats in salt water. After forty minutes or so, the brain waves shift from alpha or beta to theta, i.e. deep trance or hypnogogia.

Pain

In some tribal societies, pain is one of the methods used to enter non-ordinary reality, and anyone who has experienced severe and prolonged pain will readily testify that a shift in consciousness eventually occurs. The Navaho Sun Dancer was pieced in the breast and tethered to a pole, making a sacrifice of his agony during the lengthy dance, with his suffering the price of his vision. The tribesman of Borneo undergoes a seven day ordeal of tattooing which covers his body from neck to knee. Australian Shamans sometimes embed quartz crystals in an open wound and sew it shut. In ancient Mexico, a Mayan Queen would bear ceremonial tongue piercing in order to seek a vision from the Serpent of The Smoking Mirror. Among Caribs, novice shamans have hot pepper rubbed into their eyes. Blinded and in great pain, they are given drugs to induce visions.

Meditation

Meditation and pathworking can help train the mind to access the Otherworld, while the shaman maintains one foot in the Otherworld while viewing the 'real world' with a heightened state of consciousness, in which the spirit realm is visible. This is described as shamanic ecstasy, from the Greek *ekstasis* meaning 'to stand aside' or 'stand beside'.

59

Drugs

In some shamanic societies, though by no means the majority, hallucinogenic drugs are the favoured means of altering consciousness. Plants played a part in most of the world's early religions, and still do so in those traditions which are closely bound to the natural world. Richard Evans Schultes, Director of Harvard's Botanical Museum, catalogued ninety four different hallucinogenic plants around the globe, most of which were used for healing or spiritual purposes in a shamanic manner.

MAINTAINING INTENT

Carlos Castaneda, in his writings on the principles of Yaqui shamanism, emphasised that intent is the master key to sorcery, and that neglecting to focus on the intent would mean that the shaman would be distracted from his purpose, only to wander aimlessly in the Otherworld, captured by whatever first took his attention.

The shaman never takes a journey just to see what it is like, for recreation or for fun, as this angers the spirits. Every journey is taken for a specific purpose. Before the shaman goes on a journey, he or she must be clear what the intention of that journey is. As with ritual, if there is no specific purpose it should not be done. In shamanism, as in other forms of magic, the great dictum is 'intention is everything'. You have to be very clear what the intention of a ritual or journey is, i.e. what it is meant to achieve, and express it unambiguously. You have to let the people and spirits invited to the ritual know what they are being invited to, what the event is for. Anything open to misinterpretation *will* be misinterpreted by mischievous or malevolent entities.

TRAVELLING IN THE OTHERWORLD

The way in which the shaman views his means of travel around the Cosmos often reflects ordinary life around him. South American Tapirapé shamans travel the Cosmos in a canoe, reflecting the river life of the Amazon. The spirit boat is also a technique used in aboriginal Australia, on the northwest coast of North America. The Siberian shamans of the Steppes visualise travelling the Cosmos on horses. In Celtic myth, this is echoed in the tales of those who have ridden fairy horses into the Otherworld, like the Irish hero Conan, who was carried there by the horse Aonbharr. Thomas the Rhymer was taken to the realm of the fairy by the milk white steed of the elf queen, and Tam Lin escaped from Fairyland on a stolen white horse.

If we read between the lines of these stories, to the heart of the spiritual truth they contain, the horse is a metaphor for the method that conveys the seer into Otherworld consciousness. A shaman's drum is often referred to as his 'horse', since the drumbeat is the method that helps him induce a trance that enables him to attain Otherworld consciousness. The horse spirit carries the shaman into other worlds. It is said that the shaman tethers his horse to the World Tree, the cosmic axis that links the three realms.

In Celtic myth, the horse goddess Epona ('Pony') carries a key which unlocked both the stable door and the gates of the Otherworld. She rides between the worlds at will, to carry souls to the afterlife on horseback, accompanied by blackbirds and larks. She is also a shamanic deity, who carries the seer or bard to the Otherworld. She is, in fact, the Fairy Queen who travels between the realms on her white horse. In Wales, she was called Rhiannon, whose seven blackbirds called dreamers into Fairyland.

In Greek myth, the horse of Otherworld journeying was Pegasos (Latin Pegasus) who was the horse of Apollo and the Muses, and the inspiration of poetry. On Mount Helicon there was a spring called Hippocrene ('the Horse Well') which was horse-shoe shaped and was said to have been made when Pegasos ('of the springs of water') stamped there; poets drank its waters for inspiration. If a poet said 'I am mounting my Pegasos' he meant that he was inspired to write poetry. Poetry and bardship was a serious business, not mere rhyme making, it meant being given divine inspiration from the Otherworld. Many famous poets and musicians are said to have learned their craft in the Otherworld.

Ascent of Soul
The upperworld is usually experienced as a realm of light and energy. The shaman travels to it by flying, soaring, riding his horse there, or by climbing the World Tree, a ladder or the cosmic axis.

South American shamans speak of changing into birds and flying through the realms. The Tupinamba of Brazil and Caribs of Guyana talk of flying as the soul leaves the body. The Inuit shamans transform into birds or piece the sky on drums. In South Africa, shamans fly through the Cosmos as birds.[68] The Taltos of Hungary can straddle a reed and fly up into the clouds. In front of his house stands a staff with a carved bird upon it, representing his bird soul, which is sent out on journeys. [69]

The Caribs envision climbing to heaven on the ladder of Grandfather Vulture. Sora The Siberian Tungus take a young larch, cut off its branches and fix two cross beams to make a ladder for the shaman to climb to the upper realm. In the Bible, Jacob dreamed of a ladder set upon the earth, its top in heaven, and he saw angels ascending it. The Egyptian Book of the Dead declares "*I set up a ladder to heaven among the gods*", and amulets of ladders have been found in Egyptian tombs. Dante described a ladder rising to the highest celestial sphere.[70]

A petroglyph near Toronto relates to an Algonquin myth of the creation of the Midewiwin, a society of shamans. The Great Spirit told Shell and Bear that they must bring the Midewiwin from its birthplace in beneath the bowels of the earth. They came up through successive layers and paused at the layer between earth and sky. In this myth there is a cosmic axis located at the centre of the world which is the pathway between the openings in the layers of the universe. These openings were made when Bear pushed the World Tree through the layers, prior to the creation of the Midewiwin, as he wanted to provide a passage for the shamans to travel the universe.

Middle World Journeys
In Middle World travels, the movement is straight across, but the Otherworld appears as strange and different, possibly fairytale landscapes, forests and so on.

Descent of Soul:
Descent into the underworld usually involves going down into the earth, through a tunnel, into a cave, or travelling under water. The Yakut shamans of Siberia wore symbols called 'Opening into the Earth' or 'Hole of the Spirits' to travel downwards. The Tungus of Central Asia went into trance, travelled down through a narrow hole and crossed three streams into the lower realm. The Maya saw all openings into the earth as entrances to the underworlds. [71] The Piro of South America go through a hole and cross a shallow river. In South America submersion in pools, whirlpools, springs and so on provide access to the netherworld. Lapp shamans speak of immersion when they are referring to altered states, and Inuit shamans say that the underworld is a sea. A Siberian shaman was taken by a sprit into the underworld where he found a river with two streams flowing in different directions and was told one flows to the centre in the North, the other to the south and the 'sunny side'. In South America, submersion in pools, springs etc, provides access to the Otherworld. Inuit shamans say the Otherworld is in the sea.

THE PATH OF THE SHAMAN

Following the Thread

In trance, people often see threads and lines, or nets. The Tukano people of South America see undulating parallel lines as representing the thoughts of the Sun Father. The San think that brilliant threads are lines of light that healers use to climb up to the Great God in the sky. In Australia, shamans climb threads to reach the upper world; shamans also speak of following a line into the underworld. Manchurian shamans create spirits roads from red thread as a path between the dimensions. In Britain, Europe and Asia, straight threads are said to make paths for the spirits. It is unlucky to spin by moonlight as they get to the moon that way. In India ghosts use magic thread to enter houses, while everywhere, tangled threads are said to trap spirits.

These ideas are intimately connected with those of magic all around the world, and the concept of the web of wyrd or destiny spun by the weaver goddesses. The circular action of the spinning wheel is associated with the turning of the zodiac through the heavens, the turning of day and night, the passage of the seasons and the cycle of life itself. Spirals are marked on many ancient tombs, coins, floors, and cave walls. It represents the journey through the labyrinth that the soul travels into death and the underworld and outward to rebirth. The spiral maze is the one created by the spinning and weaving goddess, which encompasses the Cosmos itself.

In the ancient world, the goddesses who created the Cosmos with their spinning were also deities of magic. Magic is often spoken of as knotting or weaving, and magicians as spirit weavers, web weavers or net weavers. In fact, the word 'religion' comes from the Latin *religare* meaning 'to tie'. Magic was performed by moving and weaving the threads of the Cosmic net, or by knotting them.

The Egyptian goddess Isis was the patroness of weaving but she also wove magic. The knot was one of her symbols, usually depicted as a knotted cloth between her breasts and represented in an amulet called a *tyet*. The Egyptians used knots for many magical purposes, symbolising the controlling and releasing of both creative and destructive forces. In particular, seven knots were tied in a cloth to invoke the seven Hathors, of goddesses of childbirth, but Isis, Sekhmet, Amun and Thoth were also invoked during rituals as knots were tied. The ancient Romans were so in fear of the power of the knot to bind and limit energies, that the high priest, the *Flamen Dialis,* was forbidden to wear any knot or closed ring on his person, in case it bound up his powers. Similarly, Roman women who tied knots of twisted threads when they were passing crops were suspected of trying to 'bind' the crop and cause its failure.

63

THE PATH OF THE SHAMAN

The Cosmic threads weave in and out of this world and the Otherworld, since we are all part of the same Cosmos. By following one of these threads it is possible to pass through into the Otherworld. The Egyptian goddess Meith was a magician and her symbol was a weaver's shuttle. She was titled 'The Opener of the Ways' and conducted souls to the Otherworld, following a linen thread. This idea of following yarn into or out of the Otherworld is also found in other cultures. Ariadne, daughter of King Minos of Crete, helped her lover, the hero Theseus, find his way into the labyrinth by giving him a clew - a ball of thread (this is where our modern word 'clue' comes from). Many young men and women had lost their way and their lives in the maze before him, but the magic clew unwound itself and lead him to the centre of the maze where he slew the monstrous Minotaur. He then wound the yarn up to find his way out of the labyrinth. In Greek myth, the witch goddess Hecate led the corn goddess Demeter into the underworld by means of a thread, to find her daughter Persephone (Spring).

Large numbers of fairies are associated with spinning, either spinning themselves or maliciously destroying the spinning of others. They can be seen through the holed stones that are used as spindle whorls. They are said to have taught the skill of spinning to humans. Some of these fairies are traceable to ancient spinning and weaving goddesses. Like goddesses of fate, Fairy God-mothers appear in a triad to bless or curse a child at birth: one who spins, one who weaves and one who cuts the thread of life.

Several fairies are said to destroy any spinning left on the wheel at Yule. This has its origin in the fact that many sun gods and goddesses spin the Cosmos or the sunbeams in the hours before dawn. At Yule ('Wheel'), the midwinter solstice, when the sun stands still, all forms of spinning and weaving were forbidden. The Lapps forbade the turning of any kind of wheel, including cartwheels and churns. In the Old Norse literature, the goddesses of spinning inspected the spindles and distaffs of women of the household at Midwinter, rewarding the families of industrious spinners with good luck, and lazy spinners with disaster for the coming year.

The German Berchta ('The Bright One' or 'White Lady') carries a distaff and will blind anyone who spies on her activities, or some say, anyone who gets in her way on Twelfth Night will fall into a trance. When he wakes, he will be able to foretell how next year's crops will turn out. She is busiest at between Christmas and New Year, destroying any spinning that is unfinished by the time the Old Year is over. The Epiphany was originally known as Perchtun Night, since she is also Perchta who takes the souls of dead children into her care.

Holda brings the snow by shaking out the feathers from her bed in the sky. Between Christmas Day and Twelfth Night, she rides around in a wagon. Her realm is reached through the bottom of a well and she is associated with water and lakes. Though she is generally benign, and particularly interested in spinning, she gets annoyed by ill kept houses. Holda was originally a goddess of the hearth and spinning, demoted to a fairy bogey woman in Christian times.

Lucia ('Light') leads the Wild Hunt in Swedish tales. She is an old Pagan goddess also transformed into the Christian saint St. Lucia, whose festival is celebrated on 13th December. The festival is called 'Little Yule' and it is the start of the Yule festivities which celebrate the reborn sun. The house must be cleaned in preparation, all the spinning and weaving finished, and candles lit.

Irodeada is a fairy goddess of the Slavs to whom the spindle is sacred. It is a traditional symbol of the witch. In Rumania nine spindles were thrust into graves to prevent vampires rising. Magic thread and ghost ways were used by spirits to travel.

Holed stones were symbols of the Goddess and the power of her womb, and were regarded as powerful talismans. Holed stones have been found in Stone Age dwellings. They were used as spindle whorls, a function that continued for millennia. In ancient times, spinning was a magical act, the province of women under the auspices of the spinning and weaving goddess.

Germanic women's grave sites on the Continent and Britain often contain large, rock crystal spindle whorls that would have flashed in the sunlight. Others of amber and of jet have been found in Scandinavian and Anglo-Saxon contexts. Jet was 'black amber' and sacred to Freyja, as was true amber. They were used in seiðr to weave spells. Eligius of Noyon preached that a woman should not *"name other unfortunate persons either at the loom, or in dyeing, or in any kind of work with textiles."*

In the coven, the role of the Weaver is taken by a woman who acts as an intermediary between the worlds, calling in the spirits of place and ward.

FETCHES AND CO-WALKERS

There is an old British belief that everyone has a double in the Otherworld which is sometimes called a co-walker, a fetch, a waff, or a reflex man. It is said that if you catch sight of this double, it is an omen of death; the Irish and the Scots would refuse to eat meat at funeral gatherings, in case this brought them into contact with their spirit double.

THE PATH OF THE SHAMAN

Such an indwelling spirit was called a *genius* by the Romans, a *daemon* by the Greeks, a *fylgia* in Old Norse, which was rendered into English as a fetch. This is the part of the human soul that can act independently of the body, which some say already dwells in the Otherworld. Shamans send out their fetches, often in animal forms, while they are in a trance or sleeping.

The kresnik (Croatian shaman) allows his soul-fetch to leave his mouth in the form of a fly or small insect (in Lancashire butterflies are still called 'souls'), or sometimes he takes the form of a flaming wheel. Lapland sorcerers lay in trance, while their spirits flew out in the form of sparks. African witches' souls travel as supernatural lights. In Slavonic teaching, the Strigele ('little witches') are the fetches of witches seen as seven or nine dancing lights. The mysterious lights seen in bogs and marshes, often called will o'the wisps are sometimes called corpse candles or fetch lights, and were seen as the luminous manifestation of a soul, and the appearance as an omen of death. The gypsies called them Dood Lights (ie dead lights) which betoken activities of ghosts or Mullos.

This idea of the fetch travelling in the Otherworld recalls the stories of people who have been said to be in fairyland, though their bodies remain in the mortal world - in other words, it is their fetches that visit the Otherworld. In Ireland, a person who has been kidnapped by the fairies is said to be 'away with the fairies' when their spirits may have been taken, leaving behind a passive body. In one story, this happened to Ethna who was kidnapped by the Fairy King, Finvarra. She lay with her eyes closed and never spoke a word, or smiled, or gave any sign that she knew where she was. Everyone grew sad and realised that she must have eaten fairy food. After this had gone on for a year, a voice was heard to say "Though her body is present, her spirit is still with the fairies," and another voice answered, "She will remain so forever unless her husband breaks the spell. The girdle about her waist is fastened with an enchanted pin. He should unloose it, burn the girdle and throw its ashes before the door, then bury the enchanted pin. Only then will her spirit return from the sidhe." The young man hastily carried out these mysterious instructions, burying the pin beneath a fairy thorn. Then Ethna's soul returned to her body and the couple was truly reunited. She remembered her time in the realm of the sidhe as no more than a dream.

In the coven, the role of the Fetch is taken by a man in order to converse with, and deal with, the spirits raised.

THE PATH OF THE SHAMAN

THRESHOLDS TO THE OTHERWORLD

Certain places are better than others for making contact with the Otherworld. Those magical doorways are usually (though not exclusively) in remote areas: the spirit worlds are linked to sacred Nature. The ancients marked places where the veils between the worlds of men and spirits were thinnest with standing stones, circles, temples and groves. Many have been forgotten, and some were never known by humankind. However, the sensitive person may recognise them as places of numinous power by the slight feeling of tension in the air, and by the fact that they are physically unusual in some way. They stand out from the landscape around them, perhaps having unusual rock formations, strangely twisted trees and so on. They are all thresholds of some kind. Boundaries are charged with power, they are magical places between places – or times between times- belonging to neither one thing nor the other, forming points where the Otherworld can intersect with this one. These boundaries might include such in-between things as crossroads, the shore between sea and land, thunderstorms, midnight (the time between one day and the next), dawn, sunset.

Doorways

The threshold of a house is an uncertain place, neither inside nor outside, but a boundary between the two. When a person crosses a threshold they move from one state to another and may be in danger from the spirits that dwell *between*, as many spirits do. In many cases, it was thought unlucky to tread on the threshold itself, and people were always careful to step over it. This is why brides, in a transitional stage of life, are carried across it. A number of fairies live beneath thresholds, including the French Follets (who are bad tempered but will act as house fairies if you win their respect) and the Russian house fairy the Deduška Domovoy. Because not all spirits are kind or welcome, the Irish scattered primroses on the doorsteps to keep them from crossing it, and in England thresholds were made of protective holly wood for the same reason. In parts of Britain, defensive designs called 'step patterns' were drawn on the doorstep in salt or chalk, or reproduced in mosaic. These took the form of knot work and 'tangled thread' patterns since spirits like to follow straight paths when travelling, and get caught up in trying to follow the twisting lines.[72]

Hearth

Hearth stones were similarly decorated, since the hearth is a threshold too. There are many spirits associated with human hearths, and they often gain entrance to homes via the chimney or smoke hole. One such is the Italian

67

THE PATH OF THE SHAMAN

house fairy the Attilio who, like his Welsh cousin the Bwciod, likes to warm himself by the fire. Both become angered if people try to keep them out by such methods as putting ash on the fire, or placing a piece of iron on the hearth. In Italy, at the Feast of the Epiphany, children hang up stockings for Befana to fill with gifts. She was once a deity of fate. In Germany the hearth is associated with Perchta, once a goddess of the hearth fire, home and marriage.

In the past, the hearth was the central focus of the home, providing warmth and food. It was the place of the fire, which meant the difference between freezing and surviving, eating and starving. As such it was sacred and the focus of many customs. The fire had to be kept burning, as it was, or represented, the living spirit of the home, and was only put out at certain times of year, to be re-lit from a sacred flame.

Because the smoke rose to the sky, it was a message rising to the spirits or gods, while below the hearthstone lay the underworld. Therefore the hearth was also a domestic cosmic axis via which the gods or spirits could enter the home and a shaman's spirit could travel out; this is why Father Christmas enters the house via the chimney.

Gateways

Gates on old roads and tracks are magical boundaries, and often the place where spirits are seen. In Wales it is said that a fairy sits on every stile. Cunning men often used field gateways as places to perform magical operations.

Bridges

A bridge is neither on land nor water, and therefore shares the magic of liminal places; a curse broken on a bridge will be washed away. Bridges are frequented by various types of spirits like the lovely White Ladies who ask passers by to dance with them. If the travellers are polite, the fairies will bless them. If they are rude and refuse the request, the spirits will toss them into the river to learn better manners.

On the Isle of Man is the Ballona Bridge ('Fairy Bridge') which no local will cross without offering his or her greetings to the little folk beneath.

In Sweden, people can visit bridges to meet with the water spirits called the Naecken to ask them to bestow the gift of music. A fiddle is hung beneath the bridge on three consecutive Thursday nights. On the last night, the seeker will find two fiddles hung there, and he must choose his own. If he does, he will become a great and famous musician, but should he choose the Naecken's instrument, the water fairy will take his soul.

Fords

Several spirits were encountered at fords, and there were special shrines for the traveller to invoke the ford spirits to allow him or her to cross the river, or to give thanks for being allowed to cross safely.

Wells

Well represent life force and always contain a spirit. They also act as entrances to the spirit world, where people can go to speak to the gods or spirits, perform divinations, or make offerings. Many wells, when excavated, have been found to contain numerous gifts of pins, pottery, bronzes and so on.

Water spirits have healing powers, and their help is still solicited in parts of Britain with offerings of coins thrown into wells. A well near Penrhos in Wales allegedly cured cancer. The sufferer would have to wash in the water, curse the disease, and drop pins into the well. Some special trees, called cloutie trees, which grow near holy wells and springs are hung with rags (clouties) to solicit blessings or healing from the spirits. As the rag disintegrates, the wish will be fulfilled. (Those people who hang up bits of plastic tape misunderstand the custom, and not only will they be disappointed in their hope, they will also anger the wildfolk by polluting the environment.)

In England, principally in Derbyshire, well dressing customs are still enacted every year, during which wells are decorated with pictures made of flowers. These were originally constructed to honour the well spirits, though the events now take place under the auspices of the local churches and the themes of the pictures are biblical ones. The wells which were once shrines of the spirits of healing waters have been re-dedicated to Christian saints with similar names like Anne (Anu), Brigit (Brighid) and Helen (Elen). Almost every English town has a well dedicated to a female saint that would once have been sacred to a healing spirit. Holy wells are more common in England, Ireland and Norway than elsewhere.

Water spirits are often described as beautiful women, though there are records of guardians taking the form of salmon, snakes and toads. There is an ancient healing spring at Acton Barnett, in Shropshire, England, where the guardian spirits of the well appear as frogs. The largest of the three is addressed as the Dark God.

In Germany, the fairy Frau Holda's realm is reached through the bottom of a well.

Lakes, Rivers and the Sea

Similarly, every body of water is inhabited by a spirit, or a number of spirits. Many rivers are still named after their indwelling spirit, like the Seine in France, after Sequana, the River Severn in England after Sabrina, the Boyne in Ireland after Bóann , the Danube after Danu, the Shannon after Sinend and so on. Names of the old spirits survive in other ways too. On the River Trent in England, the bargees used to say that when the river was flooding, 'Eager was coming'. The name is derived Aegir, the Norse sea god.

The sea is teeming with spirits such as mermaids, mermen, nymphs, elementals, and so on. They control the weather and the water, raise storms, and have the power to cause shipwreck, drowning and death. In ancient times, it was the practice to placate the spirits of the sea with a sacrifice before setting out on a voyage. Even today, we break a bottle of champagne over a new hull. If the sea spirits were denied their tributes, they would take another by sinking the ship and taking the souls of the sailors to dwell with them. For this reason, sailors have always taken many precautions so as not to offend the spirits. They often had tattoos of nymphs, tritons and mermaids, and would avoid saying the word 'pig' (an underworld animal) or swearing while on board. If this taboo were broken, they would have to stick an iron knife in the mast to avert the ill fortune. In honour of Rân, the queen of water spirits, sailors wore a piece of gold in the form of an earring. When bad weather threatened the ship, they would throw it in the waves to placate her. She was originally a Norse goddess, the wife of Aegir.

Any body of water is an entrance to the Otherworld, and there are numerous tales of fairy kingdoms under lakes or under the sea. People frequently made offerings to the spirits that dwelt there by throwing them into the water. Hoards of such offerings have been found in lakes and bogs, consisting of brooches, pins, swords, shears and so on, but all bent or broken, so that they have no use in the ordinary world, but are meant for the Otherworld. At the start of the Neolithic in southern Britain, people stopped eating fish though seashells occur in large quantities in Neolithic tombs- it was considered the food of the netherworld, not the ordinary world. The Neolithic dead were often placed in rivers which flow to the sea- the sea is part of the underworld.[73]

Crossroads

Crossroads are especially magical, since they form boundaries between four roads, and consequently between the human world and Otherworld, middle earth, the upper and lower worlds. Because of this they were dangerous places, presided over by a guardian spirit and frequented by spirits. In ancient Greece they were sacred to Hecate, the goddess of witches. In modern Greece, a spirit called Iskios manifests at crossroads during the time of the new moon. It appears in animal form, usually a dog or a goat.

In Germany crossroads are haunted by Wod, a Wild Huntsman who, mounted on a white horse and accompanied by his pack of ferocious hounds, accosts lonely travellers. He spares only those who remain in the middle of the path and show no fear. These he rewards with gold and silver. He is probably a folk survival of the god Wotan or Woden.

In Wales, the crossroads are the domain of the banshee the Gwrach y Rhibyn ('Hag of the Dribble'), a withered crone with black teeth, tangled hair and bat-like wings. She appears to those with relatives about to die, and shrieks their names.

Croatian spirits gather at crossroads. In Rumania, the Dinsele ('They Themselves') are strange vampiric spirits that look like large cats walking on two legs. They lie at crossroads awaiting human victims in order to suck their blood, but they cannot go into the middle of the crossroads.

In ancient Rome, special spirits called *Lares Compitales* guarded boundaries (a *compita* is the marker of a boundary). At important intersections, marble altars stood with temples housing statues of two *lares* accompanied by a *genius locus* (spirit of the place). Many boundaries run along a path or road and the lares compitales were worshipped at both rural and urban crossroads. Sometimes they were the chief deities of a hamlet.

Crossroads were traditionally places for contacting the Otherworld. The centres of the crossroads, which were often marked by small islands of planting or a tree, literally belonged to the spirits, a 'no man's land'. They were also places of execution and gibbets stood at crossroads, as the soul of the executed man would be hurried into the underworld by its spirits. Suicides and Pagans were buried at crossroads in Christian times.

Crossroads were marked by a post which stands for the World Tree, connecting the worlds of above and below. In Rumanian every crossroads is an image of the Sky Pillar (*Coloana Ceriului*). Witches were commonly believed to convene at crossroads, people were hanged there and suicides buried there. In Slavonic lore, witches gather there to spin and weave spells, and will bewitch any passer-by with sleep.

Islands

Islands are considered magical, neither land nor sea, but places between places. Spirits live on floating islands such as the Isles of the Blest, Lochlann, the Green Meadows of Enchantment, Ynis Gwydrin and Hy Brasil, which are only visible at certain times. Though humans have

THE PATH OF THE SHAMAN

sometimes visited them, they are notoriously difficult to get to. One thing is certain; a human visitor should not offend the spirits by taking iron or steel onto the island, or removing anything from it.

Edward Davies, writing in 1809, related the story of a lake near Brecknock associated with the Twyleth Teg, the Welsh fairy folk. Though an island stood in the middle of the lake it seemed small and undistinguished, but it was observed that no bird would fly over it and sometimes strains of music could be heard drifting over the water. In ancient times, a door in a nearby rock would open every May Day. Those who entered would find themselves in a passage that led to the small island, where they would be amazed to discover an enchanted garden, full of the choicest fruits and flowers, inhabited by the Twyleth Teg, whose ethereal beauty was only equalled by their courtesy and affability. Each guest would be entertained with delightful music and apprised of such future events as the spirits foresaw. The only rule was that the island was sacred, and nothing must be taken away. One day an ungrateful wretch pocketed a flower he had been presented with. This did him no good; as soon as he touched the shore the flower vanished and he lost his senses. The Twyleth Teg were extremely angry at this sacrilege, and the door to the island has never opened from that day to this. One man tried to drain the lake to see if he could discover the fairy kingdom, but a horrible figure arose from the lake and commanded him to desist.

One of the most famous fairy islands is Avalon, which means 'Isle of Apples', since the island is covered in fruitful orchards. Avalon is not just a place; it is more a state of consciousness that can be accessed when the veils that separate us from it are peeled away. Like all Otherworld places, it exists outside time and space. The island is inhabited by nine sisters, of which Morgan le Fay is the most beautiful and most powerful. In early Celtic legend the island could only be reached on a boat guided by the sea god Barinthus, and was a place fit only for the bravest and best.

Spirit Paths

Straight lines do not exist in nature, and have thus been considered supernatural. While nature is full of curves and bends, the straight is Otherworldly, associated with gods, spirits, fairies and ghosts. In many places, it is believed that spirits travel in straight lines. When travelling from mound to mound, the fairies use straight pathways between them. It is unlucky for any human to build on the paths between the mounds, and people have often gone to great lengths to avoid it. When a new runway for Shannon airport was proposed, workmen refused to construct in over a fairy path.

In China, bad spirits travel on straight paths, so it is thought that straight paths are dangerous for humans. In *Feng Shui*, straight lines in the landscape cause the *Qi* energy to become hyper-accelerated, causing disruption and draining good fortune and benign energy from a place.

In Europe, ancient burial mounds, old churches etc are laid out along straight lines. Straight lines are associated with death, trance and shamanic flight. Some of these lines are physical; others are spirits ways or roads of the dead. It is widely believed that the dead must travel by the shortest route and in a straight line. The German *Geisterwege* or 'ghost roads' run directly over mountains, marshes etc. They begin and end at a cemetery. In Iceland, the Vitki (wizard) goes to the crossroads at Midsummer Eve where four straight roads run to four churchyards. Wrapped in an animal skin he chants and concentrates on the edge of an axe. The ancestors travel along the roads and speak to him.

Though the theory of ley lines is usually dated to Alfred Watkins (1921) straight lines known as fairy paths or ghost roads were spoken of for several centuries previously. An Irish seer told Evans Wentz in 1911 that fairy paths were lines of energy that circulates the Earth's magnetism. While the straight alignments between ancient sites were only noted by scholars in the eighteenth century, tales of these straight fairy paths were current among the peasantry since time immemorial.

Labyrinths

Spirits are said to dwell in the various labyrinths of England. Labyrinths were ritual pathways used to retrieve the spring from the underworld, which lay at its centre, to revive the souls of the dead, and to perform weather magic. [74]

Stone Circles and Standing Stones

Wherever stone circles and standing stones exist, they have been connected with spirits. The Channel Isles were once thought to be fairy islands, because of the many prehistoric graves, stone circles and monuments there. Locals believed that they had been built by *Les Petits Faîtiaux* (the fairies) to live in. The prehistoric sites themselves were sometimes called *pouquelaie* or 'fairy dwellings'.

The beings that inhabit sacred sites are as old as time; they protect the holy places. In Brittany, for example, they are called the Korred and guard the ancient dolmens and the treasures that lie beneath them.

In Cornwall, the guardian spirits are called Spriggans ('Spirits').

They keep treasure beneath the old stones. One night a man tried to dig up the treasure buried under Trencrom Hill. As he neared the gold all about him went dark, thunder crashed and lightening streaked the sky. By its light, he saw a large number of spriggans swarming out of the rocks. At first they were small but they swelled in size until they were as big as giants. The man managed to escape, but without his treasure. He was so shaken by his experience that he took to his bed and never worked again.

Wreaths of eerie mist often surround the stone circles, and folklore has it that should you find a gap in the mist you will be able to pass through into the Otherworld. This is more likely at the magical 'times between times' of May Day, Halloween, or the Midsummer Solstice.

Forests

The grove was the centre of Celtic religion, the place where spirits were contacted, and the forest is alive with the chattering of the Otherworld, where messages can be heard in the whistling wind and the whispering of the leaves in the trees.

Vast numbers of spirits dwell in the forests. In Croatia, for example, the Sumske Dekle ('Woodland Maidens') are fairy girls, covered in hair. When humans leave food out for them they will return the favour by cleaning their houses. In Greece, the Sylvans are beautiful but dangerous, sometimes luring travellers to their deaths in the forests. In Hungarian fairy lore, the Vadleany ('Forest Girl') appears as a naked woman with hair so long that it sweeps the ground. When the forest rustles, it tells of her presence.

Among the southern and western Slavs, the Vile ('Whirlwind') dwell in woodlands, and ride about them on horses or on stags, hunting deer with their arrows and herding chamois. Some of the forest Vily are connected with particular trees in the manner of dryads and cannot venture far from them. In Dalmatia, they are described as the troop of Herodias, the witch queen. In Serbia they are called *divna* 'the divine', and it seems likely that they were originally Pagan goddesses, later associated with witch lore.

In both the orient and the occident, there are tales of spirits who inhabit trees. According to popular lore it is bad luck to cut down a tree, particularly those associated with spirits such as hawthorn, oak, birch and rowan. The Arabian Djinn sometimes live in trees, while in ancient Greece and Rome forests were the home of Dryads, Pans, and Centaurs among others. Various nymphs were associated with particular trees such as Rhoea with the pomegranate, Daphne with the laurel and Helike with the willow. In Scandinavia and Germany the forest spirits are often wild people covered in moss, or Moss Maidens.

Fairy Rings

These appear as bright green rings on the grass, or more likely a circle of fairy ring mushrooms (*Marasmius oreades*) which materialize on lawns and in meadows leaving a circular bare patch or later in the year a brighter patch of grass. They are said to be a favourite dancing place of the spirits. It is now thought that some of these rings are as many as 600 years old.

Be warned though, if you should join the fairies in their revels, you may become invisible to your companions outside the ring and find that it is impossible to leave, and be forced to dance until you collapse and die of exhaustion. Some have found that an evening spent in a fairy ring turns out to be many years in the human realm.

Mounds

Entrances to the Otherworld are often said to be through mounds, which occasionally open at the knocking of a witch, or at certain times of year, such as Halloween and May Day. These burial chambers, dating from the Neolithic period onwards, are found throughout Europe. There are upwards of 40,000 in Britain alone. They vary in size from a few feet across to over 300 feet in diameter. From Scandinavian to Celtic, Germanic and Slavonic lore, earth mounds are described as occasionally glowing or giving off a strange light.

Mounds are a link between the living and the dead, this world and the next. Both Saxons and Celts thought that fairies lived in mounds. Fairy mounds are also sometimes called 'Dane Forts', probably from *dun*, meaning a hill, as in dune, or from the Scandinavian *dáin*, meaning 'dead' referring to a spirit or ghost. Hill elves were known in Anglo-Saxon writings as *dunaelfen*. The name of the Dane Hills in Leicestershire, England - where the hag or witch Black Annis lives - probably has the same origin. Again, it may be that *dane* derives from the Celtic goddess Danu, widely known as the mother of the fairies.

The ghosts of the dead were widely believed to dwell in an underworld kingdom, along with the fairies, ruled by the Lord of the Dead, the Fairy King. In south Wales he is called Gwyn ap Nudd and rules the Welsh fairies the Tylwyth Teg. The entrance to his kingdom is through the Welsh lakes, or beneath Glastonbury Tor in England. In North Wales the King of the Fairies is Arawn, an ancient Welsh god of the underworld. In one story, he changed places with the human King Pwyll for a time. In Ulster myth, he is Finvarra ('White-topped'), King of the Daoine Sidhe of the west or Connacht, living in the mound of

75

THE PATH OF THE SHAMAN

Meadha. Finvarra was once a god of the dead and underworld, with some functions as a vegetation god since he is deemed to have the power of bringing good harvests.

Many burial mounds (as artificial earth wombs) are orientated so that the shaft of the sun, at the winter solstice, will strike a point in the underground chamber and trigger the rebirth of the sun, along with the ancestral spirits entombed there. Moreover, the dead had all the ancestral knowledge. Witches went to the underworld to converse with them and learn spells. For ordinary people, this journey was very risky.

Caves

Like burial mounds, caves are entrances to the underworld, long associated with spirits including a great many fairies, the best known being the dwarfs. Caves were the first temples of ancient man, who saw any entrance into the Earth as an opening into the fecund womb of Mother Earth.

Rainbows

The Leprechaun's pot of gold is found at the end of the rainbow. If you have ever tried to stand at the end of a rainbow, you will know that it is a place that cannot be reached physically, but only in spirit. For this reason, the rainbow is often thought to be the bridge to the world of the gods, the afterlife, or Fairyland. The Anglo Saxons believed that the Earth and Otherworld of the gods was connected by the Rainbow Bridge *Bifrost*, the Trembling Way of Fire.

Mountains

Mountains are powerful places, where people often felt that approached the realm of the gods and spirits. Particular mountains were considered especially sacred, and some are still revered to this day. Mountains are the dwelling places of numerous spirits, including the Bohemian Herr Johannes who lives on the wooded slopes of the Reisengebirge and is known as the Master of the Mountains. Among the Slavs, the Samogorska inhabits the high peaks and hilltops The Tennin are lovely fairy maidens of Buddhist lore, sometimes encountered on the highest summit of the mountains. In Slovenia the Vesna live in mountain palaces and influence the fates of both men and crops. Spirits were often encountered on the high mountain passes, and shrines were sometimes placed there.

THE PATH OF THE SHAMAN

Chapter 5
THE WORLD OF SPIRITS

Though they are called by different names, 'spirits' have been recognized in on every continent of the world, back into the most ancient of times. For the shaman, these are real entities, not merely psychological projections of the mind. Shamans see, hear, touch and smell a variety of spirits who may help with healing, teaching, divination and so on, or which may be entirely hostile. The principles of shamanic practice are remarkably similar through-out the world, and include the journeying to the Otherworld, speaking to the dead, healing and divination, all with the aid of helping spirits. For the shaman, there are two realities, the one we perceive with our five senses, and the Otherworld, only seen in an altered state of consciousness. The shaman can travel between these two realities by virtue of his enhanced knowledge and discipline in order to help others. He might become possessed by a helping spirit that would speak through him, or he might undertake a journey with the spirits, or a combination of the three.

For the shaman, everything has a soul, or spiritual essence. Many early religions were animistic in nature, sharing a belief that humans, animals, trees, plants, rocks, streams, rivers and places have *anima* or soul. As long as certain offerings were made and certain procedures followed, the spirits would remain friendly and beneficent. If they were neglected or offended, they would take their revenge. A river spirit might rise up and drown humans crossing his domain. The spirit of the corn might cause the crops to fail; an apple tree might refuse to be fruitful.

Before the advent of Christianity, all the peoples of Europe acknowledged a multitude of spirits that inhabited the Earth. The spirits were as much a part of the land as the animals that lived upon it, the birds that flew above it and the fish that swan in the sea, and equally essential for its life, wellbeing and growth. Shrines to these beings were scattered across the countryside. Special trees were protected by fences and decorated with garlands. People made offerings on stones, at wells and rivers. Every sacred place had a spiritual guardian.

However, in the Christian world-view, trees, rocks and stones have no spirit, no consciousness, and those who made offerings to the spirits within were deluded. Ælfric, an eleventh century inhabitant of the monastery of Cerne Abbas, denounced those who made offerings to 'earth-fast' stones, trees and so on *"even as the witches teach"*. The word he used for witches was Wiccan. [75] Missionaries destroyed Pagan temples and groves, and cut down sacred trees in an attempt to banish the spirits that dwelt there. The Church in

THE PATH OF THE SHAMAN

Britain continued to speak out against people who communed with spirits, from which we may infer that at least some people were known to do so. In 1548 the English Bishop John Hooper condemned those who sought the help of damned spirits and "*such souls as be departed out of the world, as Saul did*".[76] In 1659 the Bishop of Worcester railed against those used "*charms to cure men or beast; invocations of wicked spirits; telling where things are lost or stolen…*"[77] During the so-called 'Age of Enlightenment' Western science decreed that spirits did not exist and were therefore not relevant to scientific study. Later still, any experience of spirits was dismissed as hallucination or psychological aberration.

Both the ancient Celts and Anglo-Saxons believed in spirits, a faith that has had a lasting legacy up until the present day. The Celtic name for them is *sidhe*, a word that means a burial mound, hill or earth barrow, since this is where many spirits live. It is said that when the Celts invaded Ireland, the resident people, the Tuatha Dé Danaan who had supernatural powers, were forced to retreat into the hollow hills and were only occasionally seen after that, though people left offerings of meat and milk on their mounds. They are very tall and thin, eternally young and beautiful in appearance, and generally dressed in white. The Anglo-Saxon term for similar spirits is elf or *aelf*, a word meaning something like 'white spirit', or 'shining spirit'. They are tall and beautiful and shine with a kind of inner light. They also live in mounds, and people left offerings, called *elf blots*, of meat and milk on the mounds for them. It was difficult to banish a belief in spirits from the consciousness of the people who dwelt close to the land, who encountered them on a regular basis. The notions of the country people have survived the folk-lore and folk practice of Western Europe to the present day in the shape of a belief in fairies.

In these legends of fairies, we can trace the pre-Christian concept of nature spirits, along with the principles of dealing with them. Even into the nineteenth and early twentieth centuries, the good Christian farmers of Europe believed in spirits of land and water that could affect the growth of the crops and the fecundity of the land itself. There is plenty of evidence in Britain, Ireland and the rest of Western Europe that regular offerings were made to the fairies, of milk on the old standing stones, bread and salt in the corners of fields, cream in saucers left on the hearth, and were left part of the harvest. Special stones - called *dobby stones* in the northern counties - had shallow depressions for making offerings to them, and were placed by field gates or the farmhouse door. Spiritual guardians called the Ward gathered at dusk in their sacred places, still known as ward trees, ward hills and ward stones, to guard villages. The Wild Hunt rode out to collect the souls of the wicked.

79

Fairies could make the crops bountiful, animals hale and hearty, and they protected their favourite humans from harm, occasionally giving them great riches, beauty or magical powers. They could bestow the capacity to heal, or give a person the ability to make wonderful music or beautiful works of art and craftsmanship. Alternatively, fairies could blight the crops, make fields and animals barren, and steal the goodness from food. Fairies could also steal the spirit of the land itself - the fields appeared to yield a crop but the ears of corn would not fill out, the harvest would be slender and the animal fodder without nourishment. Fairies were thought to use elf bolts to cause harm, propelling them into humans or livestock. Deaths were attributed to them and it was thought they could induce paralysis; the origin of the word 'stroke' for paralysis is derived from 'elf-stroke'. Fairies also took the souls of animals and humans away to fairyland.

A kind of Pagan animism was mixed with an almost identical faith in the miraculous powers of Christian saints, their relics and charms, a mixture of beliefs that persisted at least until the Reformation, and evidentially far beyond. The average person knew very little of their avowed Christian religion, with the mass in Latin and no copies of the Bible in English, even for those capable of reading it. Many parish churches were without priests, and church attendance was poorer than is usually believed. In Elizabethan Wales, the Puritan John Penry claimed that thousands of people knew little of Christ *"and many who had never heard of him"*, but on the other hand fairies were held in *"astonishing reverence"* and the people dared not *"name them without honour"*.[78] In 1584 Reginald Scott wrote that people were more in fear of Robin Goodfellow and witches than God, and believed more in things that were not, *"than things that are"*.[79] In 1607 John Norden of Fulham claimed that people living in the hamlets of the New Forest were as ignorant of God *"as the very savages among the infidels."*[80] Certainly until the end of the seventeenth century, various writers throughout England wrote of a solid belief in fairies.[81]

Humble folk had their own complex system of beliefs and rituals concerning the supernatural. We often overlook how deep that belief in the paranormal was – people sincerely believed that dangerous demons lurked in the forest, and that they, their beasts and crops could be cursed by the evil eye of a witch or malicious intent of a fairy, that spells and magical formula could cure illnesses, that relics and amulets had magical power, and omens were everywhere. Seasonal rituals, which had nothing to do with Christianity, were necessary to ensure that the crops grew, and that spring, summer autumn and winter came in their proper turn, and that ill luck should be avoided. And lest we think that

THE PATH OF THE SHAMAN

these beliefs faded long ago, many of them were still very much alive during my childhood amongst the old people who were horrified by the wearing of green clothes, 'the fairies' colour', by stirring the cooking pot anti-clockwise, by bringing hawthorn into the house, and a hundred other superstitions. Modern historians often overlook how much these magical beliefs permeated everyday life.

In the practices and taboos surrounding fairies, there are direct parallels with shamanic cultures. The practices of wise women and cunning men had much in common with shamans and witch doctors around the world- a belief that we are surrounded by spirits and that we can commune with them, that the land is alive and must be honoured and cared for, that our actions affect the world around us and we must seek to live in harmony with it, that we are part of the ebb and flow of the seasons and must perform certain actions at the correct time.

When things went wrong, or relationships with the fairies broke down completely, it was necessary to call in an expert. These village shamans had many names including wise women, cunning men, blessers, witches, conjurors, fairy doctors and currens. Even after the coming of Christianity to Britain, the village wise women and cunning men cared for the bodies and spirits of those around them, telling their fortunes, treating their bodily ailments, dowsing their lost property, and physicking their farm animals, as well as dealing with the spirit world.

There are reliable accounts of many hundreds of such people in Britain from the Middle Ages until the beginning of the Twentieth Century when every village seems to have housed someone with a magical reputation of some sort. George Pickingill (1816-1909) was a well known cunning man who practiced his art in the Essex village of Canewdon. He traced his ancestry back to Julia the Witch of Brandon, who had lived in a village north of Thetford in Norfolk. He was a simple farm worker, yet the whole locality was in awe of his magical abilities. Anyone who crossed him fell ill, and could only be restored to health by the touch of his blackthorn walking stick. It is reputed that he established nine hereditary covens in Norfolk, Essex, Hertfordshire, Sussex and Hampshire, each with a leader that had proved his or her hereditary witch lineage.

Also in Essex, from 1812 to 1860, nearby Hadleigh was the home of James Murrell, called Cunning Murrell, the seventh son of a seventh son. He had a magic mirror for locating lost property, a telescope for looking through walls and a copper talisman which could differentiate between honest and dishonest clients. On December 15th 1860, Murrell predicted that he would die the next day, and the time of his death to the

81

THE PATH OF THE SHAMAN

minute. True to his prediction, he died and is buried in an unmarked grave in Hadleigh churchyard.

Witches and fairies were often thought to have the same powers: both use magic and both can bless and curse. In fact, the old Romany word for 'fairy' is the same as the one for 'witch'. The Irish believed that a witch was created when a young girl spent seven years in the Otherworld with her fairy lover, coming back somewhat aged, but with knowledge of herbs, philtres and secret spells. The famous witch Biddy Early insisted that her powers came from the fairies. She used a blue bottle, given to her by the fairies, for healing and prophecy. At her death in 1873 it was thrown into a lake so that no one else could attempt to use it. This belief that witches gained their powers from fairies is directly comparable to the tribal shaman gaining his power from spirits.

The old witches worked their magic in conjunction with fairy spirits, and there is plenty of evidence for this in the trial records; the accused often tried to explain that their powers came not from Devils, but from the fairies. Elspeth Reoch of Orkney confessed, in 1616, that she had met a fairy man who offered to teach her to understand and see anything she wanted. In 1566, John Walsh of Netherberry in Dorset said that he knew when men were bewitched because the fairies told him. When he wanted to converse with fairies he would go to the hills where there were mounds of earth, and speak to them between the hours of one and noon, or at midnight. In 1587 John Penry of Wales spoke of swarms of soothsayers and enchanters who professed to walk, on Tuesday and Thursday nights, with fairies, bragging of having knowledge of them. Fifty years later, a Caernarvonshire man claimed to speak twice weekly with the fairies, again on Tuesdays and Thursdays.

In the 1600s, in the North of England, a man was taken into court on charges of witchcraft. He claimed to use a powder to heal sicknesses, and offered to lead the gentlemen of the court to the fairy hill where he obtained the medicine. He had discovered the hill when he was destitute, and agonising about how to feed his wife and children. A lovely woman had appeared to him and advised him that if he followed her counsel, he would get a good living from it. She led him to a little hill and knocked on it three times. The hill opened and they went in, coming to a fair hall, where a fairy queen sat in great state, with many people about her. She gave him a box full of white powder, and taught him how to use it by giving two or three grains to any who were sick, which would heal them. The Judge asked whether the place within the hill, which he called a hall, were light or dark, and the accused replied it was like twilight. Being asked how he got more powder, he said that when he wanted it, he went to that hill and knocked three times, and said every time "I am coming, I am coming", whereupon it opened. Going in, he was conducted by the beautiful lady to the queen. The outraged judge said that if he were judged guilty, he would have him whipped all the way to the fairy hall, but the jury, since he had cured many with his white powder, acquitted him.

In 1623 Scottish witch Isobel Haldane claimed that as she lay in her bed she was taken forth and carried to a hillside, the hill opened and she entered inside. She stayed for three days with the fairy folk, until she was delivered from Fairyland by a man with a grey beard. Similar stories of witches gaining their powers from fairies were told over and over again all around Britain.

If people worked with fairies, it was considered that they had renounced their Christian faith, something often reiterated in the trial records. In 1670 Jean Weir confessed that she had performed a ritual at the bidding of a fairy so that all her troubles would depart. Afterwards she found that she had wonderful ability with spinning, but this made her afraid, and she stayed indoors for twenty days weeping, because she thought that what she had done in working with a fairy was, in effect, a renunciation of her baptism.

Shamans act on the principle that humans are part of the totality of nature, kin to animals and plants, and not superior to them. This is one of the reasons that indigenous shamans were persecuted by Western missionaries, who considered that man was the crown of creation with dominion over the natural world, and unrelated to it. Moreover, in Christian doctrine, any spirit that is neither saint nor angel is considered demonic in origin, and fairies are included under this heading. According to one Irish belief, those angels that were cast out of heaven for their pride became fairies. Some fell to earth and dwelled there long before man; others fell into the sea and became water fairies. Others fell into hell where the Devil commands them. They dwell under the earth and tempt humans into evil, teaching witches how to make potions, spells, and enchantments. King James I's book *Daemonologie* equated fairies with Devils in no uncertain terms and advised people who had them in their homes to get rid of them immediately. Writing in 1701 the Orkney vicar Rev. John Brand said that fairies were evil spirits seen dancing and feasting in wild places. English Puritan writers of the sixteenth and seventeenth centuries believed all fairies were Devils.

This association of fairies and witches goes beyond the British Isles and seems to have an almost universal resonance in other parts of the

83

THE PATH OF THE SHAMAN

world. For example, in parts of Eastern Europe, witches were called *vilenice*, which implies someone who deals with fairies (*vile*). During an investigation during the late seventeenth century, a young vilenica confirmed that her powers had been granted to her by a fairy who had shown her the properties of herbs, and who could be called upon by virtue of certain herbs picked together with their roots. As in other places, there were tales of children and adults disappearing into the mountains for months or years, and returning with magical powers granted to them by the fairies. In northern Croatia, the people said that on each Good Friday a vile flies down from the sky to teach women how to heal people and be of benefit to them. The women had to go with their hair unbraided into the green grove, where two had to climb the old trees with the vile, and eat yarn, to better remember what the vile was teaching them; in this way they became vilenice. [82]

Scottish witch trials in particular were often notable for their accounts of the Fairy Queen, or Queen of Elfhame ('Elf Home'). Isobel Gowdie said that she met the Fairy Queen when she went into the hollow hills, and learned all her magic from the fairies whilst there. She spoke of the wildfolk that waited upon her coven as Robert the Jakis, Sanderis the Reed Reever, Thomas the Fairy and Swain the Roaring Lion, but she was stopped from speaking further by the interrogators, as she often was when she spoke of fairies, as can be seen from the transcripts. The interrogators only wanted to hear of Devils and evil deeds.

In 1588 Alison Pearson was condemned for 'haunting and repairing with the Good Neighbours and the Queen of Elphame'. It seems that the Fairy Queen sent messengers to summon likely witches. In 1670, Jean Weir said that when she kept a school at Dalkeith a tall woman came to her house. She had a child upon her back and two at her feet. The woman desired that Jean should employ her to negotiate on her behalf with the Fairy Queen. This was how Jean first became involved in witchcraft. Her brother Major Weir offered himself up and was executed as a witch in Edinburgh, refusing all attempts to convert him. In 1576 Bessie Dunlop stated that as she lay in childbed, a stout woman came and sat down beside her, comforted and drank with her. The coven leader told her that it was the Queen of Elphame, his mistress.

The old British witches called their supernatural mistress the Fairy Queen and it was she who led the Sabbat. Similarly, many Italian witches believed in the historical existence of a woman (or goddess) named Aradia, who brought about a revival of Italian witchcraft, travelling the country and preaching the old Pagan religion of Diana, whom they called Queen of the Fairies. There was a Rumanian Pagan sect known as the Callusari who, during the Middle Ages, worshipped a mythical empress who they sometimes called "Arada" (possibly Aradia) naming her as Queen of the Fairies. The *Callu°ari* dancers were the followers of the Fairy Queen, and their dances were thought to have originated in the Otherworld. Similar Macedonian dance troops were called *Rusalia* or 'Fairies'. Like fairies, they were responsible for bringing fertility to the land.

The Italian carnival society of the Cavallino assembled under the banner of Erodiade, a name for the Queen of the Fairies, possibly synonymous with the witch goddess Herodias. The society grew to prominence in the Middle Ages, appearing in processions, pantomimes and healing sessions, but may have had a very ancient, Pagan origin. It was exclusively male, its members dressed in women's clothes and wore make up. They always gathered in odd numbers, such as seven or nine or eleven. The Catholic Church persecuted them as Pagans who worshipped the goddess Diana.

FAMILIARS

We are used to stories of witches having familiar spirits. What is not generally realized is that these familiars were often considered to be fairies, whether in the guise of humans, imps or animals such as fairy cats or dogs. Familiars often shared the common names of the local fairies- Robin, Jack, Tom, Hob, Jill, Peg and so on, though in the trial records they were also termed demons and Devils. Though familiar spirits are reported in a minority of witch trials, it is a significant minority, and the accounts of meeting the familiars and the witch's dealings with them, are remarkably consistent. John Beaumont, in 1705 (*Historical, Physiological, and Theological Treatise of Spirits*) wrote extensively of the popular belief in familiar spirits. Robert Kirk (*The Secret Commonwealth*) wrote about the common use of familiars by Scottish seers, and in 1654 Durant Hotham claimed that the familiar spirit was a standard magical aid:[83]

"...he was of the sort we call white witches, which are such as do cures beyond the ordinary reasons and deductions of our usual practitioners, and are supposed (and most part of them truly) to do the same by the ministrations of spirits."[84]

Reginald Scot wrote that the witch would heal by means of her charms and familiars. [85]

In 1646 John Winnick confessed that one Friday he was in his barn when a black shaggy spirit appeared to him, with paws like a bear, though it was smaller than a rabbit. The spirit asked him why he was so

THE PATH OF THE SHAMAN

unhappy, and John replied that he had lost a sum of money, and the spirit agreed to help him. Stories of gaining a familiar often have similar, common elements- people in trouble or sick people are visited by a fairy who promises them a gift which is then faithfully delivered. The gift is usually one of knowledge- the power to cast spells, make herbal potions and cures and so on- in other words, the power to become a witch.

There is always a price to pay for possessing a fairy familiar. The Belvoir witch Margaret Flower, tried in 1619, said that she promised her familiars to fulfil their needs, in return for which they fulfilled her desires. The desires of fairies ranged from bowls of milk and offerings of bread, to human company, music and even human blood.

Familiars were often said to drink the blood of their witches, sometimes by nipping or scratching, sometimes from specially formed 'teats' on the witch's body, known as the 'Devil's Mark'. Ellen Shepherd, a Huntingdon witch, in 1646 said that she had four familiars in the shape of grey rats, which she fed with blood from her hips, and in return, they granted her 'all happiness'. In 1645 Thomas Everard, a Suffolk with, said that something like a rabbit asked for his allegiance, and when he gave his consent, it scratched him under the ear and drank his blood.[86] The Suffolk witch Elizabeth Hubbard (1645) said that three things in the likeness of children said that if she would cleave to them, she would want for nothing. They then scratched her back to make the marks, and afterwards sucked from them.[87] In 1582 Margery Sammon was given two familiars by her mother, two toads called Tom and Robin. Her mother advised her to feed them on milk; otherwise they would want to suck her blood.[88] In 1644, a Yarmouth witch claimed that a tall man came to her door in the moonlight, and asked for her hand, and pricked it with a knife so that the blood flowed, and the mark remained for some time afterwards.[89]

The Irish always advocated leaving out water for fairies at night; otherwise they would be angry and suck sleepers' blood. In one story from Glen Rushen, on the Isle of Man, the fairies went onto a house one night to do some baking. The family had put no water out for them; they were heard to say, "We have no water, so we'll take blood out of the toe of the servant who forgot our water." From the girl's blood they mixed their dough and baked their cakes, eating most of them, and poking the rest up under the thatch. The next day the servant-girl fell ill, and remained ill until she was given a piece of the fairy cake that was hidden in the thatched roof.

On other occasions, familiars were simply fed with ordinary food, such as milk, water and chicken. Margaret Moone fed her twelve imps with

THE PATH OF THE SHAMAN

bread and beer, and Elizabeth Francis fed her familiar on bread and milk. This has direct parallels with the feeding of a shaman's spirit allies in other cultures. In Malaysia, for example, a Bajang (a spirit/fairy) can be kept as a familiar by a magician who feeds it on eggs and milk.

This is reminiscent of the many stories of fairies being fed in return for their help. Bowls of fresh milk and cream were left by the hearth for brownies and other house fairies, like the German Chimke. Robin Goodfellow's standard fee was a mess of white bread and milk. Before setting out on a journey, offerings of bread and milk were made to the *Fridean*, Scottish fairies that guard the roads. In Gotland, offerings of milk, beer and flax seeds were made to the *Disma* by being poured into a fairy ring.

ANCESTRAL SPIRITS

The dead are considered to be free to move through the Cosmos mediating between its levels, and this is their power. The shaman who associates himself with the dead is placed at the point of transition between the worlds. In Neolithic burial chambers, shamans performed rituals with the cremated remains of the dead. The tombs formed a cosmic axis; the dead moved up through the capstone into the sky where they consorted with the gods. Painted motifs in the tombs guided the souls on their way. At Newgrange, at the winter solstice, the light from the sun illuminated the chamber containing triple spirals, looped upwards to the corbelled vault and exited the top of the mound to rejoin the sun, the route the dead themselves followed.[90]

The Celts made no distinction between the spirits of fairies and the spirits of the dead, the ancestors. Both were believed to roam the earth, and were seen feasting together. In Irish myth, one young man was imprudent enough to go out on All Hallows Eve and encountered King Finvarra and his Queen Oonagh. Their company was full of merriment and passed around much food and wine, but *"for all that they were the company of the dead"*. He recognised a neighbour who had died many years before. The fifteenth century *Orfeo* talks of Fairyland as the Land of the Dead.[91] In the original story of Cinderella, the fairy godmother was the spirit of her dead mother. In the seventeenth century, philosopher Thomas Hobbes said that fairies were spirits and ghosts that inhabit the darkness, solitary places and graves.[92] Robert Kirk wrote that a local Scottish seer said that fairies were departed souls.

A Cornishman called Noy met his dead sweetheart among the fairy hoards.[93] One day he set out for an inn but when three days had passed and he hadn't returned home his servants went to look for him. He was discovered in a ruined barn and was amazed to discover that he had been missing for three days. He had got lost on the moor trying to take a short cut, but had discovered a farmhouse where they were holding a Harvest Home supper. Inside hundreds of richly dressed people were feasting, but they all looked rather small. He was staggered to recognise his former sweetheart, Grace Hutchens, dead four years. He knew then that the company inside the house were fairies. Grace warned him not to touch her, eat the fairy food, or drink the cider, or he would be unable to leave. Mr Noy believed he knew a way to rescue them both and took his hedging gloves from his pocket, turned them inside out and threw them among the fairies who vanished, taking Grace with them.

Every country in the world has legends of the wandering spirits of the dead, and in many places these have been incorporated into fairy lore. Some tales speak of fairies as the souls of unbaptised children, such as the Will o'the Wisp, or the Mexican Jimaninos who dance at the Festival of the Dead. The Highland Sluagh are human souls, the hosts of the unforgiven dead, Cornish Spriggans are the ghosts of humans and the Dunters are the souls of the victims of the Picts.

The Norse *Dísir* (*Idis* in Anglo-Saxon) was the female ancestral spirit who was honoured as a guardian of whichever person, family or clan that lived on her territory. The Dísir were sometimes simply referred to as 'dead women'. She had her own shrine at the farm where prayers and offerings were made, and she was given a sacrifice every autumn, since she influenced the fertility of the land and its inhabitants. In addition special temples called *Dísasalr* were dedicated to particular Dísir. The Dísir appear in folk-lore as female fairy godmothers or house fairies.

Entrances to fairyland are often said to be through burial mounds and most British, Irish and continental fairies are said to live in the hollow hills in an underground country where the summer never ends. This is comparable with many ancient ideas of the afterlife. The Greeks believed that the souls of the good dwelt in Elysium, which means 'apple-land' or 'apple orchards'. It was a happy realm of perpetual day and the inhabitants could choose to be reborn on earth wherever they elected. The Celts believed that the afterlife was lived in a permanent summer, a land of the ever young; an apple orchard where the trees were always in fruit. In fairy land the passage of time bears no relation to time in the real world as might be expected in a realm inhabited by souls after death.

People who are taken to fairyland are warned not eat the food there, or they will never be able to return to the human realms. This echoes ancient Egyptian mythology where the goddess Amenti was associated with the Land of the West, or underworld. She welcomed all deceased people to the land of the dead with bread and water. If they ate and drank they could not return to the land of the living. In Greek myth the goddess of spring Persephone was captured and taken to the underworld where she ate six seeds of a pomegranate. Because of this she was forced to spend six months of each year there, which is why the earth has winter in her absence. In Celtic lore red food was the food of the dead and was forbidden to mankind.

The Druids taught that after death, the human soul was not extinguished, and it did not go to heaven, but instead entered into a new born baby, a newborn animal, a tree and so on. According to Nigel Pennick:

"Thus the individual is not a separate being, but part of the great continuum of all things. This is expressed in the traditional relationship of humans to their heimat, *where family, life and place are indistinguishable. The ancestral dead are part of family and place, and the non-human spirits and deities of the place acknowledged equally. The ancestors played an important role in the everyday spiritual life of the common people."*[94]

SPRITS OF PLACE

A *Genius Locus* is the guardian spirit or soul of a specific place. Every location has its own spirit, not only the well known sacred sites. It was once the custom to honour these guardian spirits with offerings and seasonal rituals. As long as this happened, the spirits would remain friendly and beneficent. If they were neglected or offended, they might take their revenge. Sometimes, neglected spirits drift away, sometimes they are deliberately driven away, and when this happens the land becomes spiritually barren. Sometimes the land is inhabited by unfriendly, inimical spirits that just want to be left alone. If you enter such a place you may sense a bad atmosphere and feel decidedly unwelcome.

Many fairies are described as protecting individual localities such as certain groves, ancient sites and bridges. These fairies are often described as 'white ladies' and there are many of them throughout the world from the African Shamantin to the Irish Banshee. A large number of white ladies appear in northern Europe including the Sibelle, Fainen, Witte Juffern and Weisse Frauen. In Normandy, they are the fairies of ravines, fords, bridges and other narrow places. They ask passing travellers to dance. If the travellers are polite, all is well, but if they are rude, the fairies toss them into the ditch to learn better manners. They are usually well disposed to humans, and may help travellers find their way, aid women in

THE PATH OF THE SHAMAN

childbirth, prophesy the future, make cows give milk, show miners rich veins of precious metal, turn pebbles into precious stones and bestow wonderful gifts on their favourites.

A white lady appears in the Arthurian myths: Guinevere means 'white phantom', which indicates that she may have been of fairy origin, the guardian spirit of a place, maybe Albion itself. Perhaps if Guinevere was the guardian spirit of Albion, Morgan Le Fay was the *Mor Gwyn* ('white lady') of the Otherworld, Avalon, the magical island outside time and space where illness, old age and death are unknown.

White ladies also manifest near holy wells, streams, borders and bridges, and may once have been the patron deities of the locality. Many wells have a fairy guardian in the form of a salmon, trout, snake, frog, toad or nymph. These fairies are particular to the locale. Sometimes the resident fairies have to be placated with offerings of pins or coins.

These legends may derive from the ancient belief that nymphs or goddesses guard wells and other waterways. Such places were holy and veneration of them still persists today. They were believed to have healing or cursing powers, the ability to bestow luck or take it away, and were presided over by Pagan deities, many of whom were later transformed into Christian saints, such as Brighid, or passed into folklore as 'white ladies' or 'green ladies'.

HEARTH SPIRITS

Every house has its own spirit, which should be honoured in the proper way. In bygone Rome this spirit was called the *Lar familiaris* ('household lar') and was given daily offerings of food and monthly gifts of garlands, all placed on the hearth shrine. Legends of similar house spirits are found throughout the world, from the Hawaiian Menahune to the British Brownie, the Spanish Duende, the German Hausmänner, the Russian Igosha, the Finnish Kodin-Haltia, and the North American Shvod and Cambodian Àràk.

The first thing that people did when they moved into a new house was to greet its resident spirit. For example, the Deduška ('Grandfather') is a Russian house fairy who appears as an old man covered in hair, often in the likeness of a family patriarch. He wears a red shirt, cloak and a red belt. He lives behind the oven or near the threshold of the house, in the cupboard, or in the stable, sometimes with his wife and children. He will protect the family, their home and their livestock from bad luck, keep the servants in order and do all kinds of chores about the place while everyone is sleeping. He is especially keen on spinning. To keep him happy he should

THE PATH OF THE SHAMAN

be given something from each meal and white linen should be placed in his favourite room. The family that pleases its fairy will prosper in all things but the family that fails to do him honour or uses bad language in his presence will suffer his anger. He will revenge himself on the crops and cattle or leave the house altogether. The unprotected family will then fall ill and die.

Brownies are solitary fairies found in southern Scotland and the northern counties of England. They become attached to particular houses or families and while the humans are asleep, they work about the house or farm, cleaning, tidying up, or help with the brewing. When the cock crows it is to let the brownie know it is time to go to bed. The only reward they ask is a bowl of cream or best milk.

MUSES

Surviving Celtic poetry and stories are full of visits to the Otherworld, and tell us that poets found their inspiration there. The bard Taliesin described a period spent in the Otherworld where he gained his poetic spirit. The story of the bard Thomas the Rhymer tells of his time in fairyland, where he was given the apple of truth and initiation. Some of the ancient poets and bards, like the famed Carolan, learned their craft by sleeping on fairy hills and mounds, allowing the magical music to enter their hearts and souls as they slept.

In Celtic lore, the nine hazel trees of poetic art grow about a stream or well in the Otherworld. There, poets drink and are thus inspired and refreshed. This may have some connection with the many magical cauldrons which appear in Celtic myth. The nine muses blew upon the cauldron and each imparted a gift.

There are many clues that tell us that the Celtic bard was much more than a story teller: that he was, in fact, akin to an initiated shaman who gained his knowledge and inspiration from the Otherworld. His poems describe experiencing other realities, such as becoming various animals, he describes an initiatory drink, and there are descriptions of the provoking or experiencing of a shamanic crisis. He speaks with the spirits of the Otherworld (fairies and so on) and he mediated with, and interpreted, the spirits on behalf of others

He used magic and made prophecies. The Irish word for bard, *fili*, meant 'weaver of spells'. The function of the poet was a magical one. Like shamans in other countries, Irish poets wore swan-feathered cloaks called *tugen*. The bards carried wands or branches to denote their profession and status. It is thought that these had small bells on, which would be rung to call for silence when they were about to perform. The

91

silver branch had another meaning; in several tales a silver branch is given to mortals by Queens of the Fairy, and it allows them to enter the Otherworld. Sometimes the branch has fruit and blossoms on one stem. Other branches had silver apples upon it, and these would ring to enable the poet to have a vision of the Otherworld - in Celtic myth the apple is the fruit of the Otherworld, the sustenance of its inhabitants and the food of the dead.

VEGETATION SPIRITS

Early humans were hunter-gatherers, but during the Neolithic period became food growers, dependant on the yearly cycle of planting, germination, growth and harvest. In winter, the spirit of vegetation seems to die, to go down as seed into the underworld womb of the Mother Earth until it is resurrected the next spring. Ancient religion was largely concerned with entreating the gods and nature spirits to provide the corn. Many fairies are associated with vegetation, crops and the fertility of the land, with the power of either blessing or blighting.

The German Kornböcke causes the crops to ripen; the Russian Polevik grows with the corn and after the harvest shrinks to the size of the stubble. The Russian Rusalki cause the corn to grow when they move through it. These fairies may be directly related to ancient vegetation spirits. In Britain, this spirit is still portrayed on May Day by the Green Man. Green, of course, is the colour of growing things; after winter, the spring returns with a flurry of fresh growth. Green is therefore a symbol of regeneration, the spirit of vegetation, hope, beauty, harmony, and eternal life. Fairies are very much associated with the colour green. They are often described as wearing green clothes, or as having green skin. Most fairies haunt wild places, especially ancient woodlands and forests, which they protect. Often it is dangerous for human beings to enter these places and they will be attacked by fairies or be pixie led. Fairies like Puck and Robin Goodfellow play tricks on those who enter their domain.

In lore, the good fairies like Puck and Robin Goodfellow - who might be seen as representing the powers of summer, growth and life - retire from sight after Samhain, the start of winter, until spring returns. Evil fairies, representing the powers of blight, winter and death, such as the Scottish Unseelie Court become very active. They are capable of stealing the spirit of the land, so that ears will not ripen on the corn, or cattle fatten. Good fairies re-appear again with the spring.

Evergreens like holly and ivy preserve the green vegetation spirit though the winter. In England there is a saying that "the little elves fly away on the brown oak leaves," meaning that they disappear for the winter, like the vegetation spirits. elves and fairies were both thought to be happy to take part in human family gatherings at Christmas, and greenery was hung at that festival so that the elves could take shelter in it from the wintry weather. This may be directly descended from the Druidic custom of hanging up evergreens in the winter as shelter for the vegetation spirits during the dead time of the year.

TREE SPIRITS

In both the orient and the occident, there are tales of spirits who inhabit trees. According to popular lore it is bad luck to cut down a tree, particularly those associated with fairies such as hawthorn, oak, birch and rowan.

Some fairies are associated with particular types of trees. The Albanian Aerico and the Lithuanian Kirnis guard cherry trees. The English Oakmen, the Italian Salvanelli, and the German Wood-Wives protect the Oak. The Ash falls under the safekeeping of the Scandinavian Askafroa, and the Polish Vile. In Ireland the Lunantishee guard the blackthorn, in England and Denmark the Elder Mother safeguards the Elder, the Russian Leshie is associated with the Birch and in Western Slavonic certain fairies take up their abodes in Willows. In Africa, Huntin lives in the silk cotton tree, while Kakua Kambuzi inhabits incense trees.

Trees were objects of veneration in ancient times. While the life span of humankind is short, trees can live for many centuries. When all else fades in winter, evergreens remain changeless in a changing world, strong enough to resist the death time. Thus the tree became identified with the power of the deity or was seen as a deity itself. Representations of sacred trees are found in Chaldean and Assyrian temples, and in ancient Egypt several deities inhabited the sacred sycamore (*Ficus sycomorus*) which marked the boundary between this world and the Otherworld. In the Old Testament, altars were set up in groves or beneath particular oak trees. The cypress was the symbol of the Persian Abura Mazda, while in Greece Artemis was represented by the willow, Apollo by the bay laurel and Athene by the olive. Sticks or wands were (and still are) carried by elders, kings, heralds, and military leaders as a symbol of god given authority, derived from the sacredness of the tree.

As symbols of the god, or a god in actuality, trees were associated with fertility. At the festival of Dionysus anyone with a tree in the garden would dress it up to represent the god. At various other harvest and fecundity festivals trees would be decorated with wreaths and otherwise honoured. From this connection of the tree deity with virility comes the

THE PATH OF THE SHAMAN

custom of carrying tree sprigs in a wedding bouquet and such May Day observances such as the leaf-clad Jack in the Green dancer.

Many people instinctively feel that a tree has a spirit or consciousness. In the early days of Buddhism this was a matter of some controversy and it was decided that trees do not have souls like humans, but had certain resident spirits called dewas who spoke from within them. Among the Hindus these dewas are gods. Occultists use the term 'devas' to describe the resident spirit of a tree or other plant. We still honour the spirit of the tree when we decorate the evergreen Christmas tree and place the fairy, which represents its living spirit, at the top.

WATER SPIRITS

Every body of water, from the smallest stream to the vast ocean, has its own protective spirit, living below the surface. In Wales, maidens called the Gwragedd Annwn dwell beneath the lakes. They are exceedingly beautiful and occasionally venture ashore to take human lovers and husbands. One such Lady of the Lake, called Vivienne or Nimue, appears in the stories of King Arthur, supplying him with Excalibur, a magical fairy sword.

The sea is as densely populated with spirits as any place on earth. In its depths dwell mermaids and mermen, nymphs, and others. These spirits control the weather and the water, raise storms, and have the power to cause shipwreck, or keep a ship safe. Like the sea, many sea fairies are personified as lovely and seductive, but treacherous. The best known of these is the mermaid. It is possible that the legend of the mermaid has its origins in the goddesses who rose from the sea, like Venus/Aphrodite, or the fish tailed Atargatis and Derceto. The sea is associated with the Great Mother Goddess whose names include Maia, Mary, Mara, Marian, Maria, and Miriam; all names derived from a root word for sea. Sea goddesses are usually also goddesses of love and the moon, drawing the tides, rivers, dew and flow of human life. Ancient mariners would have a tattoo of a star to honour the goddess Venus as they steered by her star. She was also the prototype of the ship figureheads.

Some water spirits are unfriendly and dangerous. Jenny Greenteeth lives in the River Ribble in Northern England. When green weeds wave in the flowing water, it is a sign that Peggy is lurking beneath the surface, ready to take another victim. She haunts the stepping stones near Brungerley and every seven years claims a human life by grabbing some hapless traveller and pulling him beneath the water to drown. Children are warned not to go near the water, or Jenny Greenteeth will take them.

Water has often been considered to be a living thing, or certainly to have the power of sustaining, bestowing and even restoring life - as well as being capable of taking it. Every ancient society honoured springs, wells, and water sources as sacred. The Celts and others sacrificed treasure to lake and river spirits. Rivers were worshipped by the Druids and were believed to each have their resident water spirits that required sacrifices to be made to them.

Water is a universal symbol of cleansing and regeneration. Some bodies of water have healing powers, like the Chalice Well in Glastonbury. Water heals; especially water that flows east to west is empowered by the rising sun at the vernal equinox, May Day and Midsummer. Any stream that runs north to south has magical properties as does the place where two streams meet; these were often the places for magic and Otherworld contact. Pools and lakes are magical entrances to the Otherworld. Where three streams meet was always considered to be a especially potent place for magic where people gathered to drink the water as it had magical properties.

EARTH SPIRITS

The earth has many guardian spirits, such as the Icelandic *Landvættir* ('Land Wights') who protect the land itself, and live within the stones, streams, trees, rivers, and features of the landscape. There was a legal requirement that Icelandic long ships had to remove their dragon head carvings when approaching home to prevent them frightening away the Landvættir. A multitude of Landvættir in various forms chased away a scout of King Harald's invasion fleet. Certain areas were not settled at all, but reserved for the Landvaettir. Ceremonies were performed in their honour and offerings left for them.

What we do to the earth, we do to ourselves, since we are connected with it. We must be rooted in the physical realm; it connects us to who we are, to the past, to our ancestors, to our land. Any plant disconnected from its roots will wither and die.

When Australian aborigines visit a new place they first sing up the land, to greet it and announce their visit in a respectful way. When visiting or working with a new site, you should approach in silence and with deference, demanding nothing- this is not your right. Some places welcome you with open arms and are happy to work with humans on all sorts of levels; other places will permit certain activities but not others. Some may be protected by elemental spirits and barrow wights that do not welcome human contact, and who will cause accidents to drive people away.

AIR SPIRITS

The word 'spirit' is derived from *spiro*, 'I breathe'. 'Wind', 'breath' and 'spirit' were believed by many peoples to be identical. In Egyptian mythology, the god Knef was a wind god, and his name means 'wind', 'breath', and 'spirit' or 'the air of life'. In Memphis, the chief god was Hershef, who breathed from his nostrils the north wind, which gave life to every living being. Breath is a divine gift, returned to the giver at death. The secret of breath is part of the magic of air. We take air into us which contains vital energy that some call *prana* and others *chi*. When we breathe in deeply we inhale this life force.

Inhaled air is the sustaining breath of life, while exhaled air carries the words, poetry, and song that communicate human ideas and knowledge. In many myths creation is brought to life when a god breathes into it. It was often thought that spirit could be blown into or out of people; demons were blown out of people. The soul of the shaman is often said to leave his mouth on his exhaled breath, or in a yawn. He blows a lost soul back into the chest of its owner.

The voice of the air spirits is heard in the wind. There were many sacred groves where the voices of spirits were heard in the breeze whispering in the trees. The head of the alder was used as whistle so that the spirits might speak through it.

FIRE SPIRITS

As well as the many house fairies that live in the hearth or behind the stove, there are spirits that represent the fire itself. In Northern European countries, they were called drakes, salamanders or dragons. They are said smell like rotten eggs, and their presence is usually only betrayed by the stench, though they are sometimes glimpsed as a flaming ball. They only take on the character of fire when they fly, when they look like streaks of flame or fiery balls with long tails. The bond is between the male head of the house and the male drake, and is a serious pact, often written in blood. The drake takes care of the house, barn and stables, making sure that the pantry and money chest are well stocked. They can travel the world in a split second, and bring their masters a present back from far away places. In return, the master keeps the drake fed and treated with respect.

There are many other fire spirits. The Arabian Djinn, for example, are composed of fire without smoke, with fire in their veins instead of blood. Will o' the wisps are bog fairies that appear as curious lights, usually seen flickering in the distance over swamps and marshes. They jump and dance along with the aim of leading travellers astray. Perhaps the most

THE PATH OF THE SHAMAN

common name is Jack-a-Lantern or Jack O'Lantern. In Wales the will o' the wisp it is called *ellyldan* meaning 'fire fairy'. It can be seen dancing about on marshy ground, into which it may lead a hapless traveller.

There is a connection between trades that use fire and magic. The magical reputation of the smith persisted in Europe into the nineteenth century and is still extant in India and Africa. In Britain, it was believed that smiths were blood charmers (healers) and could foretell the future. Even the water the smith used to cool metal had magical properties and was much sought after for healing purposes. A smithy-forged nail, hammered into a tree, was thought to transfer the illness to the tree. Smiths also possessed the secret of the Horseman's Word which, when whispered into the ear of the wildest horse, would calm it. People swore oaths by the smith's anvil and in some places; he had the authority to marry couples, as at the famous Gretna Green in Scotland. In fairy stories smiths often protect people and animals against malignant fairies, evil spirits, witchcraft and the evil eye.

Fire is wild and untameable, dangerous; it can burn those around it. This is true of the fire spirits too. They are intense, impatient of human ignorance; they can be intolerant of our failings, and capable of infernos of rage and intemperance. Rituals connected with fire spirits are necessarily concerned with placating the spirits, availing ourselves of their gifts while averting disaster.

Fire is an agent of transformation- the food in the cauldron is changed as it cooks, raw ores and metals are altered into useful objects on the blacksmith's forge, and it transforms the materials it consumes into ashes. Fairies and other spirits were attracted by these fires and circled round them, and sometimes had to be placated so that they would not cause trouble and steal the feast. Fire spirits are agents of purification. Cattle were driven over the ashes of the Beltane and Samhain fires to purify them, and flaming torches were carried around the crops at Mid-summer to protect them.

TUTELARY SPIRITS

A spirit that helps, protects or instructs a shaman is often called a tutelary spirit. Often a shaman will have his own special spirit helpers or guides, with whom he develops a close relationship. Sometimes such a teacher might even be an ancestor of the shaman or his clan. Any communication or instruction that passes between the two happens while the shaman is in an altered state of consciousness. The shaman might also have a variety of spirit allies who aid him in his work, and these may take the form of animal powers.

97

THE PATH OF THE SHAMAN

SPIRIT MARRIAGES

The shaman's relationship with his tutelary spirit is often an intimate one. The Goldi shamans of Siberia explain the relations between the shaman and his *ayami* as a complex sexual emotion:

> *"Once I was asleep on my sick-bed, when a spirit approached me. It was a very beautiful woman. Her figure was very slight, she was no more than half an arshin tall. Her face and attire were quite as those of one of our Goldi women. Her hair fell down to her shoulders in short black tresses. Other shamans say they have had the vision of a woman with one half of her face black, and the other half red. She said: 'I am the ayami of your ancestors, the Shamans. I taught them shamaning. Now I am going to teach you. The old shamans have died off, and there is no one to heal people. You are to become a shaman.' Next she said: 'I love you, I have no husband now, you will be my husband and I shall be a wife unto you. I shall give you assistant spirits. You are to heal with their aid, and I shall teach and help you myself. Food will come to us from the people."* [95]

This idea of a spirit spouse is frequently encountered in both shamanic tradition and fairy lore. There are many stories of humans who have married or become the lovers of fairies. These relationships always have conditions and taboos imposed on them, such as the fairy should never be struck or touched with iron, or seen on a certain day. Should the fairy spouse leave for any reason, usually because of the breaking of a taboo, then the human partner will pine away and die.

According to the Welsh fairy legend of the Lady of Llyn Y Fan Fach, a young man was grazing his cattle on the banks of Llyn y Fan Fach when he saw a lovely fairy maiden sitting on the shore, combing her hair. He thought that he had never seen a woman as beautiful, and tried to entice her to come to him by offering her gifts of bread. She smiled and shook her head, but this only made him more determined. Eventually, after many attempts, he persuaded the fairy to marry him. She warned him that if he should strike her more than twice, she would vanish forever. As her dowry, her father bestowed upon the couple many fairy sheep, goats and cows, which all emerged from the lake at the call of the fairy woman.

The couple were married, and for many years lived happily on a small farm near Myddfai and had three lovely sons. One day, the couple were preparing to go to a Christening, and the man asked his fairy wife to get the pony, while he fetched something from the house. On returning, he found her still standing in the same spot. Fearing they would be late, he tapped his wife on the shoulder and told her to hurry up. She turned and looked at him with a sad expression, for he had struck her once.

THE PATH OF THE SHAMAN

A few months later they went to a wedding, and the fairy burst into tears. Embarrassed, the man struck her on the shoulder and bade her be quiet. She turned to him and said 'I am weeping because their troubles are just beginning, and so are ours, for you have struck the second blow.'

This frightened the farmer, and he took care not to strike his wife again in the years that passed, until one day they attended a funeral and his wife burst out laughing. Enraged, he tapped her on the shoulder and asked what the matter with her was. She replied that 'When people die, their troubles are over, and so is our marriage, for you have struck the third blow.' With that, she disappeared into the lake, taking all her fairy animals with her. The farmer never saw her again, but she returned occasionally to instruct her sons in the art of herbs and medicine. They became the famous physicians of Myddfai.

One human who married a fairy was Kirwan of Castle Hackett, the great Connaught chief. A Fairy King asked his help against a hostile fairy tribe that had invaded his territories. This was granted and men and fairies together plunged into the lake and defeated the enemy. The Connaught men were rewarded with presents of gold and silver while Kirwan received a fairy bride. All of his female descendants were noted for their unearthly beauty.

In Irish and Manx tradition, the *Leanan Sidhe* ('fairy love') seek the love of mortals and if the mortal refuses, then the fairy must become their slave. However, if the mortal consents, they are bound to the fairy and cannot escape, except by finding another to take their place. As a lover, the leanan sidhe is very passionate, but their human partner pays the price of the relationship with a short life. The embrace of the fairy draws life and breath from them while the fairy becomes bright and strong. A leanan sidhe is also a muse who gives inspiration to her poet or musician lover. She sometimes takes the form of a woman to inspire men in battle with her songs. Those she favours have brilliant careers, but die young. [96]

A MacLeod called The Forester of the Fairy Corrie, who served with the Earl of Argyll's troops in 1644, had a *leannan sith* who followed him everywhere in the shape of a white fairy hind. Its presence irritated the earl and he ordered the forester to kill it. MacLeod told the earl that he would obey; though it meant his own death. As the shot hit the fairy, it gave a shriek and disappeared, while the forester fell down dead.

A leanan sidhe inspired the poetess Eodain and it was she who helped Eugene, the King of Munster, to gain victory over his foes. After this he gave himself up to a life of luxury and went to Spain for nine years where he married the king's daughter. Then he returned to Ireland with a

99

band of Spanish followers to find his kingdom ruined and drunkards and
wastrels feasting in his halls. The nation blamed the king for neglecting his
duties and would not listen to him or help him. So he sent for Eodain to
give him counsel. She told him to govern like a true hero, as it is by strength
and justice that kings should rule. Heartened by her words he overthrew his
enemies and brought peace back to the land.

It was rumoured that fairies and humans often mated; preachers
even denounced human and fairy liaisons from the pulpit. Marriage to a
fairy unites the two realms and from it a magical child will be born. Such
children are always wild and strange, their beautiful eyes and bold, reckless
temperaments betraying their fairy blood. Many famous people are thought
to have had one mortal and one Otherworldly parent, including Alexander
the Great, the Queen of Sheba and Merlin. Even Shakespeare was said to
have been part fairy. People with fairy blood are passionate, sensitive and
psychic, and if they find their true path may develop into the artists, poets,
seers, shamans and witches of our world: indeed, the heritage is sometimes
called the 'witch blood'.

THE PERILS OF THE OTHERWORLD

To encounter the world of spirits, you must first realise that the whole
world and everything in it is alive, animate, conscious, and infused with
spirit; it is sacred, it is holy. This includes trees, rocks, stones, animals, even
city streets and hearth fires.

The walker between the worlds has duties and obligations. Visits
to the Otherworld are fraught with danger. Once you have entered the
realm of spirits, nothing will ever be the same again. Fairy lore is full of
warnings about people who have visited Fairyland and ever afterwards
pined for its glory.

Time flows differently in the Otherworld; a person may think that he
has spent many years in the Otherworld, but has been absent from the
mundane world for only a few minutes. This occurred in the case of the
Pembrokeshire shepherd who joined a dance in a fairy ring and found himself
in the Otherworld. He lived happily for several years among the fairies, feasting
and drinking with them in their lovely palaces. However, he was warned that he
must not drink from a magical fountain that stood in the centre of the gardens.
Inevitably, he eventually broke the taboo and plunged into the water. He
instantly found himself back on the hillside, with his flock of sheep, having
been absent for only a few moments of ordinary time. Many shamans describe
being in the Otherworld for days or years, when their journey has taken a matter
of a few hours or even minutes.

These distortions in time are experienced by anyone who visits the Otherworld, whether in trance, through ritual or some other discipline. When, as a witch, I cast a circle, I create a place that exists between the worlds. The circle is not a barrier to keep things out, or a container to keep the power in, it is an interface between the worlds, where all the worlds can be accessed. We sometime think that we have spent an hour or two inside the circle, when six or seven hours have passed ion the everyday world.

The Otherworld has a habit of breaking through into this world to contact us, if we only have the eyes to see it and the ears to hear it. If you approach a numinous place with an open heart and heightened awareness, you may be astonished at what you experience. There are a wide variety of exercises you can follow to help make you more aware, and some of them are detailed in this chapter, but Nature herself is the greatest teacher in this quest.

Contact from the Otherworld may be spontaneous and surprising. You may become aware of synchronicities; things that seem coincidental but are not. You may come across a piece of information that answers your immediate questions, a book that comes to hand containing knowledge that you need and so on. You might become aware that the same bird greets you each morning, and reappears throughout the day for several weeks. These types of omens are very individual, and you won't find them in any dictionary of dreams or divination. It is important not to over-analyse them and look for related symbolism, since spirits rarely use symbolism to communicate with us. Their messages usually mean 'look at what I'm showing you' or 'listen to what I am telling you'. Contact with spirits may trigger all sorts of memories, abilities and understanding that you never knew you had. You may be pixie-led on our journeys, taken from the worn path on to a new way. You may feel lost at first, but you will arrive at the place you most need to be.

The spirits have their own courses and objectives; their reason for existence is not to be your teacher, and they are certainly not there for your entertainment. Any contact with spirits is on their terms, and offending them will have dire consequences. It should be remembered that there are both munificent spirits and malevolent spirits - both kinds demand a price for their assistance. Spirits will trap, exploit and eventually destroy dilettantes, pleasure seekers, the greedy, the selfish and those of evil intent.

Chapter 6
ANIMAL POWERS

Working with animal powers formed part of my early magical training and has been an essential part of my work ever since. Shamans and traditional witches all over the world work with animal spirits. These spirits often represent a species as a whole: not a bear, but Bear. Through this connection, the shaman can call upon the strength of the bear, the swiftness of the horse, or the far sight of the eagle and so on. The animal protects the shaman, may instruct him, and becomes a vehicle for his soul in the Otherworld.

Most of these spirits take the form of untamed, rather than domesticated animals, usually wild game, such as bear, elk, seal, wolf, hare, deer etc. Wild animals come from the Lord of the Animals and are imbued with a mystical strength not possessed by tame animals, and it is this potency that shamans draw on to reach the Otherworld. Amongst tribal societies, hunting is more than the acquisition of meat, it is the gaining of supernatural energy, and is encircled with ritual observances and taboos. Wild animals have spiritual counterparts that can become guides and helpers in various ways. Shamans are often thought to be able to guide animals into hunter's ambushes, for example. The San of South Africa had several types of shaman, one of which was the Shaman of the Game who wore a springbok cap and the deer were thought to follow the wearer of the cap. A San shaman explained how she kept a spirit springbok tethered; her heart's springbok, and therefore she 'owned' all the springbok.[97] The incarnated animal spirit was the symbol of her power.

While some shamans seek alliances with the jaguar, the leopard, the wolf or lion, others seek relationships with deer, bison, birds and so on. The bond of the shaman with his animal allies is an entirely personal one, and is not shared by any group or family, though others in a group may have the same power animal. A shaman of South East Australia described encountering spirit animals:

> "…my father pointed to a Gunr (tiger-snake) saying 'That is your budian; it is mine also.' There was a string tied to the tail of the snake…He took hold of it, saying, 'Let us follow him.' The tiger-snake went through several tree trunks, and let us through. Then we came to a great Currajong tree, and went through it, and after that to a tree with a great swelling round its roots. It is in such places that Daramulun lives. Here the Gunr went down into the ground, and we followed him, and came up inside the tree, which was hollow…After we came out again the snake took us into a great hole in the ground in which were a

THE PATH OF THE SHAMAN

number of snakes, which rubbed themselves against me, but did not hurt me, being my Budjan. They did this to make me a clever man, and to make me a Wulla-mullung. My father then said to me, 'We will go up to Baiame's camp.' He got astride of a Mauir (thread) and put me on another, and we held by each other's arms. At the end of the thread was Wombu, the bird of Baiame. We went through the clouds, and on the other side was the sky. We went through the place where the Doctors go through, and it kept opening and shutting very quickly. My father said that, if it touched a Doctor when he was going through, it would hurt his spirit, and when he returned home he would sicken and die. On the other side we saw Baiame sitting in his camp. He was a very great old man with a long beard. He sat with his legs under him and from his shoulders extended two great quartz crystals to the sky above him. There were also numbers of the boys of Baiame and of his people, who are birds and beasts.'[98]

Witches call these spirit animals familiars, while in North America they are called power animals. The animal fetch or *Dyr-Fylgja* of Norse magicians was thought to accompany everyone through life. In Siberia an animal familiar is termed the *Kyla* or *Chargi* (animal soul).

In South America, familiars are known as *nagual* animals. To find his ally, an Aztec might go to the forest among the wild animals and enter into a trance. When he awoke, he would see his own animal spirit and seal a pact with it. Afterwards, he could assume the shape of the animal and travel long distances in its form. [99] It is said that Aztec priests took morning glory seeds to release the nagual from within. Amongst the Maya, People could sleep in sacred incubation temples called *Uaybil* (from *uay* or 'animal soul'/ 'dream') to encounter their power animals in a dream. [100] Even gods possessed a nagual; Quetzacoathl was the Quetzal bird with lovely plumage; Tezcatlipoca, the god of night and magic, had the jaguar as his nagual; his spotted pelt represented the stars.

The cult of the jaguar is found all across Central America. Among the Mayan peoples, the word *balam* signified both 'jaguar' and 'magician-priest'. These shamans were believed to turn into spider monkeys, owls, jaguars, coyotes and humming birds.

The word *totem* is different and implies a blood relationship or kinship between a person, a family or tribe and an animal. Those so related would be forbidden to hunt or kill their totem, or to marry a person with an inimical totem. Celtic tribes and individuals adopted animal totems, and were forbidden to kill or eat their animal kin. There are several tales of a hero being born with an animal twin who is bound up with his or her destiny, and having a *geis* (taboo) against killing or eating such an animal. If the

THE PATH OF THE SHAMAN

taboo were to be broken, then his downfall was assured. Personal and clan totems evolved into the heraldic devices featuring animals that were used all over Europe in later periods.

The magician might have an animal helper that stays with him throughout his life or the animal may change as he changes. Some stay for years, others only a few weeks. He might have more than one:

(The ayami) *has given me three assistants-the jarga (the panther), the doonto (the bear) and the amba (the tiger). They come to me in my dreams, and appear whenever I summon them while shamaning.*[101]

Traditionally, the shaman's costume represents his animal helpers. The Nganasan shaman's costume, for example, symbolizes an elk. It is sewn of elk hide with a metal figure of a hartshorn on its back. There are two bears on the costume, a she-bear and a he-bear, which the shaman 'hitches to a sledge' to take him into the Otherworld. There are also six goose head figures which take the shaman to the upper world, and three bird tails which help him dive beneath the waves to the realm of sick spirits which are held there, which the shaman will free, setting them on the bird-tail and tying them there so that they won't fall off on the journey home. [102]

Kathy tells me that birds often appeared as her allies, appearing spontaneously when needed. Once, as we meditated together, I had the sensation of something tugging at chest. Afterwards, Kathy told me that her eagle ally had appeared and used his beak to remove blockages in my heart centre.

One of the most important functions of a familiar or animal ally is to help you journey to the Otherworld, the mysterious realm beyond normal waking consciousness, and the journey would be dangerous without the help of the spirit ally. For example, a shaman might be led by a fox into tunnels beneath the ground to experience the underworld, or a bird familiar might take him on a spirit flight through the treetops, showing him things he couldn't see from the ground, or beyond, into the heavens.

Many Celtic heroes only succeeded in their quests when they turned to animals for help. During their quest to find the Mabon, Arthur's messengers conversed with the five oldest animals: an eagle, an owl, a stag, a blackbird and a salmon. Other heroes learned how to speak the language of birds, and thus were warned of dangers, or were told secrets by their feathered allies. By virtue of their special abilities, animals had access to the realms of the gods, and often served as their messengers. Other animals guarded sacred places and the entrances to the Otherworld.

The ancient Celts believed that everything contained spirit, whether human, animal, plant or place - nature was sacred. The Celts saw no great

104

divide between humans and the rest of creation. In the Otherworld, human souls and animal souls dwelt together with the gods. Because animals possessed spirit, or soul, permission had to be sought from the gods before they were killed, and ritual reparation made. The Celts believed in transmigration of souls, which meant that the next life might well be lived in animal form.

Celtic gods are rarely depicted without their animal attendants, like Epona with her horse or Nodens with his dog. Other deities were shown with animal attributes such as horns and hooves as in the case of the Gaulish Cernunnos, or the ram horned British war gods Belatucadros and Cocidius.

Celtic religion and magic seems to have been intimately bound up with the powers of animals. Some creatures were considered so Otherworldy that sorcerers were needed to herd them- Celtic swineherds were also powerful magicians. Animal powers were deliberately sought and used in a manner we would describe today as shamanic. A character called the Wild Herdsman appears in Celtic tales as the Lord of the Animals, the guardian of beasts, a huge black man who had one foot, one eye in the centre of his forehead and a massive iron club.

Dreams of animals were thought to be prophetic. Arthur dreamed of dragons the night before his bastard son Mordred ('Sea Dragon') was born, and again on the night of his last battle. Oisin dreamed of a hornless fawn pursued over the waters of the sea by the red and white hounds of the underworld- the fawn was his own soul and the dream heralded his death. The Druids formalised the experience of prophetic dreaming, utilising animal powers, into a variety of rituals. One such rite involved the use of a bull's hide, spreading out the hide of a sacrificed animal, raw side up, on wattles of rowan wood (a plant of divination). The Druid lay down to sleep on the skin, and awaited whatever dreams should come.

Animals that appeared in strange circumstances, or that behaved in an unusual way were often considered messengers from the gods. The actions of ordinary animals were interpreted as oracles. The Druids closely watched the flight of birds and made predictions from the type of birds involved, and the direction they flew from. This is the origin of the children's magpie rhyme 'one for sorrow, two for joy etc.' The activities of other animals were also considered in the light of symbolic messages. The warrior queen Boudicca divined the outcome of a battle from the movements of a hare she loosed from her cloak.

SUMMONING ANIMAL SPIRITS

The shaman's animal familiar must be summoned before he attempts to journey into the Otherworld, and there are various ways of doing this. The Australian aborigine *me* (shamans) summon spirits with a bullroarer, the so-called voice of spirits. Others do it by playing a drum, its rhythms reflecting the animal in question: ponderous and heavy for larger animals, lighter and quicker for a deer and so on. Pipes and flutes might be used to summon bird spirits.

In several Indian tribes, both in North America and South America, it is compulsory for the shamans to acquire imitating skills during the initiation period. Uttering the cries of animals and birds draws those spirits, though the sounds may be abstracted beyond the real-life sound, transformed into songs or music played on instruments. In some languages the words 'magic' and 'song' (especially bird song) are the same. In Germanic tongues, the word 'magic' is *galdr* from the verb *galan* meaning 'to sing'.

A shaman may also imitate the movements and sounds of his animal helpers with rhythmical dances, during which the he transforms into his spirit helper. For example, bird flight is imitated by moving the extended arms up and down. Riding on a draught animal is imitated by bumping along, as when riding the real animal. In the diary of his travels to Siberia in the 1840s, Middendorff gave a detailed description of the Samoyed ceremony in which bear movements were imitated, accompanied by grunting and coughing, which was the sound of the bear. [103]

Once the spirits are present, the shaman can begin his journey, transforming his soul into his bird or animal depending on where he wants to go. Imitating the animal, the shaman tries to find the path he needs to travel. Sometimes his assistant will hold a tether fastened to the back of the shaman to guide him back from the Otherworld when his journey is done.

When the shaman returns from his journey, he sits down and relates what he has seen, releasing the spirits that have accompanied him. Sometimes he may make another journey and yet another straight away, using different helpers and going to different places. He may change from bear to goose and back to bear again in the process. Afterwards, he gathers all his helping spirits together and sends them back to their appointed places.

SHAPESHIFTING

The shaman is said to possess the ability to shapeshift. The shamans of the Malay Peninsula, for example, are empowered by the Tiger Ancestor.

THE PATH OF THE SHAMAN

Candidates go into the forest, and in a vision encounter a tiger and travel on its back to the underworld, the land of the *Kadang Baluk* or tiger-men. There, they are magically killed and resurrected by the Tiger Ancestor, and when they return they have the ability to shapeshift into tiger form. The Buryat name any shaman's guardian spirit *khubilgan*, meaning 'metamorphosis'.

Celtic legends are replete with stories of people who shapeshift into animals for a time. In one famous story, the goddess Ceridwen lived on an island in the middle of a lake. Her children were Creirwy ('Dear One'), the most beautiful girl in the world, and Afagddu ('Utter Darkness'), the ugliest boy. Ceridwen decided to help Afagddu overcome his disadvantages by brewing a potion for him that would contain all the wisdom of the Three Realms of heaven, earth and underworld. The herbs were ritually collected and the cauldron brewed for a year and a day, stirred by a blind man and warmed by the breath of nine muses. A little boy called Gwion was given the job of feeding the fire beneath it. One day three scalding drops fell from the cauldron onto his finger, which he put into his mouth to ease the pain. Instantly he was at one with all things, past, present and future.

Furious that he had stolen the magic intended for her son, Ceridwen pursued Gwion in the form of a black hag. Gwion, using his new powers, changed himself into a hare but Ceridwen turned into a greyhound to catch him. Gwion jumped into a river and became a fish, while Ceridwen proceeded to change herself into an otter and swam after him. He then flew from the river as a small bird and Ceridwen became a hunting hawk. Hoping to elude her, Gwion transformed into a grain of wheat on the threshing floor of a granary, but the goddess, becoming a black hen, ate him. For nine months, Gwion remained in the womb of the goddess, until at last he was reborn as a beautiful boy child. Ceridwen immediately snatched him up, sewed him into a leather bag and threw him into the sea. He was rescued by Prince Elphin, who adopted him, renaming him Taliesin ('Radiant Brow'). Taliesin went on to become a great bard and seer.

In Norse myth, whenever Odin wished, he lay down as though he were asleep or even dead, and changed into a bird, beast, fish or dragon, and could travel in an instant to far off lands. The *fylgja* is the guardian spirit or animal double of the Norse shaman, whom it protects through magic. The term may be connected to *fulga* which means a caul, since people born with cauls were thought destined to become sorcerers.

Seiðr-witches could shape-shift into sea creatures or land creatures associated with Freyja, such as a cat, boar, or falcon, a practice called *gand-reið* or 'riding the gand' ('chant/ enchantment'). In *Kormáks Saga,* the seið-witch Þórveig's spirit appeared as a walrus, while her body remained in

THE PATH OF THE SHAMAN

trance on the shore. When the walrus was injured, she died.[104] Gand riders also rode broomsticks, staffs, distaffs and wolves. The witch was also called *hamhleypa*, '*hamingja*-leaper', or 'shape-changer'. [105] *Hamingja* is the shapeshifting force of a sorcerer; *Hamr* means 'skin' or 'shape'. There are several related terms: *Hammrammr* means 'shape-strong' and describes an accomplished shapeshifter; *Ham-hleypa* means 'skin-leaper' and *Ergi Einhamr* means 'not of one shape'. [106]

Warriors in some cultures were said to take on the ferocity and form of wolves, bears and other animals. The Beserkers, Fianna and Einherjar were said to be shapeshifters, inducing a state of magical fury in which the soul left the body and assumed the form of an animal to engage in spectral combats. The Iranian Clan of the Haomavarka ('Haoma Wolves') used *haoma* (soma) to enter a trance. In Norse myth, Bodvar Biarki, while battle raged, lay down in his tent and sent out his animal spirit in the form of a great bear to join the fight.

Warriors were often associated with wolves, and donning a wolfskin meant assuming the adult warrior's role. The Irish hero Laignech Faeland turned into a wolf. It is probably that such warriors were shamans, existing outside normal society, roving in bands at one with the ghosts and beasts of the underworld, regarding themselves as wolves, and identified with the dead who inhabited 'the other side'.

There are many tales of witches turning into animals. *Discours des Sorciers* by Henri Boguet (1590) mentions witches who changed into wolves by the use of an ointment.[107] The shapeshifting ability of shamans may be the origin of the tales of werewolves.

European witches were said to prowl in the form of cats. In the 1830s, the Burnley witch Sally Walton visited a farmer in the form of a black cat, sitting at the foot of his bed. He threw a knife at her, and the next day, Sally was seen with a bandaged arm. In 1711 Jane Walham, the wise woman of Walken, was accused of changing into a cat when a man saw a cat with her face. A seventeenth century Staffordshire with song declared:

"And we shall follow as black tom-cats,
And chase thee through the corn and vats,
And we shall go in our master's name,
Aye to fetch thee home again."

Witches were also said to change into hares. In 1662, Isobel Gowdie described how she changed into a hare by chanting:

"I shall go intil a hare
With sorrow and such and mickle care,

THE PATH OF THE SHAMAN

And I shall go in the Devil's name,
Ay, will I come home again.'

Flying ointment contained such hallucinogenic (and potentially deadly) ingredients as nightshade, henbane, datura, plants known to engender images of body transformation. Other potions included fly agaric and liberty cap. In 1606 Richard Rowlands (*A Restitution of Decayed Intelligence*) mentioned that werewolves were certain sorcerers who anointed their bodies with an ointment, and putting on an enchanted girdle took on the shape and nature of wolves, seeming so to onlookers, as long as they wore the girdle. Nigel Jackson (*Compleat Vampire*) states that the girdle had to be three fingers wide, with a nine tongued buckle, inscribed with crooked and sinister runes.

The Red Sects of Haitian voodoo cultivate the *Point Loup-garou* (werewolf point) to travel forth at night, ambushing travellers to force them to join in their rituals, as well as drinking their blood. The werewolf point is conferred by the god Ogu-je-Rouge. A loup-garou witch lights a candle marked with three notches before leaving to travel the night, and must return before the last notch is reached. The wrists, neck and ankles are anointed with a herbal preparation which removes her old skin, fire streams from her anus and wings unfold from her shoulders. She travels the sky in the form of a comet or fire trail. [108]

Joan Halifax (*Shamanic Voices*) said that all of the Cosmos is accessible when the art of transformation is mastered.[109] It is only when the shaman transforms his soul into his animal fetch that he can travel the Otherworld.

Let's be clear, it is the shaman's *soul* that transforms into his animal, and journeys and is sometimes seen in this form by others. Here in the West, where people tend to be materialistic and take things literally, people have the mistaken belief that his *body* transforms. All sorts of explanations have thus been put forward as to how this might be possible, such as the manipulation of the etheric template, the layer of the aura that determines form, but the body does not enter the Otherworld- only the soul can. However, though we could say that turning into a wolf might be simply an hallucination, this is only true on the surface. The shaman learns what it is to be a wolf through direct contact with the spirit of Wolf.

THE LESSONS OF THE ANIMALS:

Every animal has its own powers and abilities, along with its own lessons to teach. The bull was admired for its strength and virility, the dog for its loyalty, the eagle for its gift of flight, the horse for its swiftness and so on.

THE PATH OF THE SHAMAN

Whatever a human could do, there was an animal that could do it better; animals possessed knowledge that no human could possibly imagine.

Kathy says that she uses animal powers in a variety of ways: *"Thinking on the butterfly, for example, one can understand that everything has its stages and times. I had encountered butterflies in meditations, and these were about the Higher Self. I had also read about the stages of the butterfly in the Medicine Cards, how it metamorphosed into the next stage, and related to the egg stage as the idea and so on. Basically, Butterfly is telling you to take things slowly and concentrate on what you are doing at the moment and not get a mile ahead of yourself, which is what you do when you are worried. It allows you to assess what stage you are at and can help in the simplest of situations, like just working your way through a project to assessing recovery from an illness. You think about the future and 'what if'? I decided to use this way of thinking, it appealed to me. There are all sorts of ways that the animals can help you. You can read about how they behave and apply that way of thinking as a mental tool. You can identify with an animal, such as a wolf or a snake, and absorb its lessons."*

Badger

The badger is a robust creature the size of a small dog, with a distinctive black and white striped head and grey body. Equipped by nature for digging, badgers build extensive underground dwellings called setts, typically covering a thousand square feet (300 metres), with tunnels linking chambers that are lined with grass, moss and bracken. Some setts are hundreds of years old, and are passed on through the family, giving badgers the title 'the oldest landowners in Britain'. Badger is peaceful and home loving, continually improving and tidying his sett. As inheritors of ancient dwelling places, badgers are keepers of ancestral knowledge.

Badgers were admired by the Celts, with badger skins found buried in the graves of chieftains. The badger is still called brock in many parts of Britain; a nickname derived from its old Gaelic name of *brocc* (or *broch* in Welsh). The seventh century *Life of Columba* refers to Pictish Druids as *Brokan* or *Broichan* meaning 'badgers'[110]. This is probably because the badger lives under the ground, or is associated with prehistoric mounds, the dwelling place of gods and ancestral spirits. If he lives with them, then he must be privy to their secrets, including the mysterious germination of life that takes place in the underworld. The badger is one of the sacred animals of the goddess Brigantia and a totem of the Imbolc festival (2nd February), when Celtic women gathered together to celebrate the rebirth of the spring, symbolised by the badger emerging from beneath the earth, just as new growth emerges from the ground.

THE PATH OF THE SHAMAN

The Celtic shaman or Druid knew that the underworld was the source of wisdom. When the five sons of Conall dug into the fairy mound of Cnoc Greine, the goddess Grian turned them into badgers for their crime, perhaps because they sought the secrets they were not entitled to as men, but which were suitable for *Brokan*. Nevertheless, they were hunted, killed and eaten by Cormac Gaileng. In the Welsh tale of Pwyll's courting of Rhiannon, a badger is mentioned as a guide during dreaming- a suitable shamanic guide to the secrets of the Otherworld.

The badger is very strong and powerful, with a muscular wedge-shaped body and short strong legs with long claws. The cruel and illegal practice of badger baiting pitted the badger against several dogs which struggled to overcome the sturdy creature. From this, we get our phrase 'to badger' which means 'to tease or annoy by superior numbers'. There was an old game called 'badger in the bag' which involved a youth running the gauntlet between two lines of boys armed with sticks, originally a trial of courage and fortitude.

Badger is one of the strongest woodland animals and even when set upon by several dogs can hold his own against them. If it sometimes seems that the whole world is against you, turning you into 'the badger in the bag' then listen to the lessons of Badger. His defences are his fortitude and his indomitable will, even against overwhelming odds. He doesn't waste time on blame or regret, but stands his ground, tenacious and unyielding. If you feel powerless and angry, stop blaming other people: they can only make you feel what you allow them to. Go within yourself and find the power of Badger, centred, grounded and unshakeable.

Because of the badger's innate power and courage, Celtic warriors thought that badger grease made the best cure for wounds, working by a kind of sympathetic magic. Similarly Scottish clansmen wore sporrans made from badger skins and the MacIvor Clan wore badger heads and skins to invoke the beast's strength in battle.

Badger is single minded, dogged and determined, patiently removing obstacles that fall on the path he is accustomed to walking each and every day. He reminds you that these qualities are needed to progress or complete a task. Hard, mundane work will be needed to turn creative dreams into a reality.

Bear

Though it is hard to imagine today, the brown bear once dwelled in Britain. It was hunted out of existence in England and Scotland during the Middle Ages, earlier in Wales, while in Ireland there is no evidence of bears at all

111

during historical times, though prehistoric remains exist. Nevertheless, bears were once numerous and during Celtic times their skins were exported; Scotland sent large numbers to the Circus in Rome.

The bear cult is maybe the oldest religion in existence, featuring in the lore of all the countries of the north and far older than the type of shamanism of the cave temple period, which is reflected in the cave paintings of France and Spain. Alpine grottoes have been discovered, dating from around 100,000 BCE, which contain cave bear skulls and ceremonial hearths.[111]

The bear is one of the most revered animals in the world, venerated by all hunting peoples, and believed to have enormous powers, able to hear things from great distances, and to remember and avenge the smallest slight. It was often thought to be a god incarnate, a visitor from the realm of spirits, and the killing of a bear was a ritual act.

The Celts certainly venerated the bear, and had several bear gods and goddesses. The words *art* and *artos* or *math* and *matus* mean 'bear' in the various Celtic languages. Thus we find the goddess Andarta ('Powerful Bear') and Arthur (from the Welsh *Arth Vawr* meaning 'Great Bear'). [112] The Gaulish bear god was Artaios, worshipped at Beaucroissant. Gaul also had a bear goddess called Arduinna, who gave her name to the Ardennes. She was a deity of hunting in the manner of the Greek Artemis. The goddess Artio ('Bear') was venerated in Switzerland, worshipped by the Helvetian tribe near Bern (which also means 'bear') and a bear still appears on the city's coat of arms. He protected wayfarers.

As the bear is a fierce and powerful fighter, its name was also adopted by kings and warriors, while other legendary characters were designated 'son of the bear', implying that they had bear-like power, or perhaps that they were descended from a bear god. These include the Welsh Arthgen and Artigan, and the Irish Artigenos.

The bear hibernates in the winter, entering a cave or some quiet, secluded place. It emerges in the spring, with the female often having given birth in the meantime, and appearing with cubs in tow. This led to the bear being associated with regeneration and rebirth, adopted as a solar symbol. The ancients believed that the sun sickened as the winter progressed, getting weaker and weaker as the hours of daylight diminished. Finally, at the winter solstice (the shortest day) it died and went into the underworld. At dawn it was reborn, emerging from the womb of the Mother Earth via a cave mouth, then growing stronger with each passing day. Many sun gods are said to have been born in a cave at this time. It seems likely that Arthur was originally a sun/bear god, with the solstice being called *Alban Arthur* or 'Arthur's Time' by modern Druids.

THE PATH OF THE SHAMAN

The constellation of the Great Bear is known in Wales as 'Arthur's Wain' i.e. Arthur's wagon. The seven main stars of the Great Bear look rather like an old fashioned plough (which gives it its alternative name) with a crooked handle. The right hand side of the plough has two stars that point to the pole star Polaris, the last star in the tail of the Little Bear, and these are called 'the Pointers'. The Pole Star was used as an aid to navigation by travellers on both sea and land as the nearest star to the celestial 'north pole', around which all the constellations appear to turn.

Following the Great Bear is the constellation of Boötes, the herdsman, with its brightest star Arcturus meaning 'Bear Keeper', a star held sacred by the Celts. When it first rises over the eastern horizon in January, it is a sign that spring is on its way. Arcturus is known as 'The One who Comes', rising not long after the winter solstice each year, just as Arthur is known as the 'Once and Future King' who sleeps until the day of his promised return.[113] The Celtic goddess Brighid was styled 'daughter of the bear', because her spring festival of Imbolc follows the rebirth of the sun and rising of Arcturus.

The mythology of the bear is thus inextricably linked with its winter retreat into hibernation, going into the underworld, and its apparent renewal in the dreaming darkness. Bears are rarely represented in Celtic art, and when they are, they are usually connected with burial goods. Jet amulets in the form of bears were found in northern Britain from the Romano-Celtic period; one was buried with a child at Malton in Yorkshire, and another at Bootle in Lancashire.[114] The bear seems to have been considered a protective spirit in the Otherworld realms of dreams and death.

Bear withdraws from the living world and goes into hibernation, seeking stillness and solitude in the dreaming world of the deep unconscious. She is associated with winter, darkness and death- ideas that frighten most human beings, but it is in the winter, in the gloom, that she finds renewal, just as it is during the most frightening and blackest times of our lives that the greatest spiritual growth occurs. Only then do we truly become aware of the infinity of possibilities that lie within us. When logical thoughts provide no answers, the path of inner knowing is illuminated. Remember that all life emerges from the darkness, as the seed grows form the earth, the child from the womb, and the creative idea from the unconscious mind.

Bear protects travellers on the road to wisdom. She teaches the value of stillness and silence inside, where all true knowledge begins. The lesson of Bear is that strength comes from within- not from what you own, what you wear, what you say or even what other people think of you.

113

Boar

Wild boars once roamed freely through the forests of Britain and Ireland, and a legacy of this remains in the many places named after them such as Boarshill, Boarhunt and Wild Boar Fell. They became extinct in Ireland during pre-historic times, but not in England and Scotland until the seventeenth century. Today, they have been re-introduced in some counties.

Representations of boars in Celtic art tend to emphasise the erect bristles as a sign of aggression; indeed, the bristles were viewed as the seat of the creature's power and thought to be poisonous. The wild boar is tremendously strong, with a tough hide and curving tusks from both upper and lower jaws. It is capable of short bursts of high speed and has been known to attack pursuing horses, dogs and humans. Boar hunts were therefore very dangerous, a test of both skill and courage. Most Celtic tales of boars concern a hunt where the bravery and resources of the hero are challenged to the utmost, and during which he may be led into the Otherworld, or meet a supernatural character who demands his help.

A boar hunt is featured in the story of Culhwch, who was the son of a woman called Goleuddydd. She was struck with a sudden madness soon after he was conceived and ran off to the forest to live as a wild-woman. As she gave birth her sanity returned and though she was surprised to find herself in a pig sty in the company of a swineherd, she decided to name her son Culhwch, which means 'Pig Run'. Sadly, she died soon afterwards, and it was some time before her husband was ready to remarry. When he did, his new wife wasn't happy at being saddled with an unwanted stepson, and hatched a plan to be rid of him. She set a *geis* (taboo) upon him that he should only marry Olwen, the daughter of the giant Yspaddaden ('Hawthorn'). On hearing the name 'Olwen' the young man fell instantly in love, and set off to ask her hand. Now the giant knew that when his daughter married, he would die, so he resolved to set the young suitor several impossible tasks before he would consent to the wedding. One of these was the capture of the comb and scissors that lay between the ears of the monstrous boar Twrch Trwyth. After many adventures, the boar was forced into the River Severn where the comb and shears were taken from him.

It is possible that the giant needed the comb and scissors to cut his hair and beard, an ancient token of the loss of virility that would have necessitated the relinquishing of his kingdom to a younger and fitter man. On the other hand, in the magical *ogham* alphabet the comb and scissors are a cipher for spiritual knowledge and transformation. This is perhaps clearer in the Irish version of the story, in which the boar is called Torc Triath, the King of Boars, and is the companion of Brighid the goddess of poetry. She was supplanted in later times by the god Ogma, who was said to have invented ogham.

Boars were officially hunted in October, the fall of the year, associating them with dissolution and death, and the turning of the season into winter. In many legends it is a wild boar that kills the summer vegetation god: in Egyptian myth Osiris, lover of the goddess Isis; in Greek myth Adonis, the lover of the goddess Aphrodite; while in Irish myth a boar slew Diarmuid, lover of Grainne. Diarmuid's mother committed adultery and gave birth to a son, who was killed by her jealous husband. However, her lover took the corpse and turned it onto a dark green boar, linking its destiny with that of its half brother Diarmuid, who was put under a *geis* never to hunt boar.

When Diarmuid reached manhood, he joined a band of warriors called the Fianna, led by the ageing Finn MacCumhal. Unfortunately, Diarmuid fell in love Finn's betrothed, a lovely young woman called Grainne who returned his affection in full measure. Together they eloped, but the enraged Finn gave chase across the length and breadth of Ireland. Eventually the gods interceded, and Finn pretended to forgive the pair. Then one day he saw a means of exacting revenge, and invited Diarmuid to join him in a boar hunt at Samhain (October 31st). The boar they killed was Diarmuid's half brother, so the young man was doubly damned. Finn asked Diarmuid to pace the length of the beast, and in doing so, the young man stepped onto a poisoned bristle which pierced his heel, killing him. Note the time of year- Samhain, the start of winter when the vegetation god is destroyed by the forces of winter, represented by a wild boar.

The Celts venerated the boar and the pig as sacred animals connected with prophecy and magical powers; swineherds were considered magicians and were highly honoured. King Bladud himself tended a herd of pigs that led him to the healing springs at Bath in southern England, where he founded a city. Some grades of Druids were called 'pigs' and the flesh of certain red pigs was chewed in a divination rite called *Imbas Forosnai*.

Though pork or boar was the favourite meat of the Celts it was not part of their everyday diet, but seems to have been reserved for special feasts, especially winter festivals like Samhain and Yule. In Scotland, it was rarely eaten, and some tribes would not eat it at all. This may have been because of its association with death and the underworld; joints of pork were buried with nobles for use in the afterlife. The first herd of pigs was a gift from Arawn, the king of the underworld. There are many accounts of pork being served at feasts in the Otherworld, with magical beasts being killed, roasted,

THE PATH OF THE SHAMAN

eaten and found alive the next morning. The 'good god' Dagda carried two pigs, one alive and one roasted, which never decreased in size, no matter how much was eaten. The sea god Mannanan had a whole herd of pigs that could be served in a similar manner. He explained that the meat would not boil in the cauldron until a truth was spoken for each quarter. Whoever ate them gained immortality. Thus, the boar was associated with truth, spiritual sustenance, resurrection and immortality.

Boars are ferocious, strong and courageous, so much so that only the bravest and most skilful hunters could kill them. When a boar appears in a Celtic tale, the hero is always presented with a challenge: a task that must be accomplished. He must be able, clever and brave- all the qualities of the boar itself. Boars prefer to run in straight lines, going straight for their goal without veering to the right or left. They are capable of bursts of great speed, short-lived, but incredibly powerful while they last. They don't vacillate, but go straight to the heart of the matter and tackle it head on.

In the story of Mannanan's pigs, the meat will only cook in the cauldron if a truth is spoken for each quarter. The cauldron is a vessel of transformation, and the pork is spiritual sustenance, which can only be gained through truth. To lie or take the easy option is not the path of the hero, who must show both personal and moral courage when faced with a difficult trial.

Bull

For many ancient societies, the strong and powerful bull was the supreme symbol of earthly might, vitality and fertility. Though it can be combative, the mythological bull it uses its aggression against the forces of negativity, barrenness and winter.[115] In Celtic symbolism, horns always represent power. There are even images of bulls with three horns, possibly indicating supernatural power, including one on a bronze mace discovered Willingham Fen in Cambridgeshire, showing a god with a wheel accompanied by the head of a three horned bull. Several others have been discovered at healing shrines both in Britain and on the Continent.

The solar deity Beli was called 'the loud roaring Beli', indicating bull-like attributes. In Celtic myth, the cart that pulled the sun across the sky was pulled by three oxen. The Druids revered the sky god as the potent father bull because he showered fertilising rain upon the earth mother, visualised as a nurturing mother cow. These concepts are paralleled in other mythologies. The Canaanite Baal took the form of a bull to mate with his sister who was in the form of a cow, while the Greek Zeus took the form of a bull to mate with Io, transformed into a bovine form. This association

THE PATH OF THE SHAMAN

of bull and sky god goes further, with the sound of thunder supposed to be the hoofed feet of the god storming across the heavens.

Like the bull, the oak tree was sacred to sky divinities all over Europe, especially those who had control over thunder and lightning, such as the Celtic god Taranis. The sky god seems to throw his lighting at the oak more than any other tree, so many old oak trees are known as 'bull oaks'. When the Druids cut the mistletoe from the sacred oak at the Winter Solstice, they sacrificed white bulls. They believed that when the leaves fell from the oak in autumn, all of its power was transferred into the white mistletoe berries that represented the potent seed of the god.

The bull symbolises the masculine, solar, generative forces of the sky gods, and their earthly representative, the true king. The emblem of the bull is intimately bound up with the rites of kingship. A bull ceremony figured in the choosing of a king in ancient Ireland. At the *tarbhfheis* ('bull-feast') a white bull was killed then a Druid consumed some of its meat and soup, and went to sleep. Four other Druids sang a charm of truth over him to enable him to dream of the man who was to be the rightful king.[116] For example, on the night before she was to marry the king of Tara, the princess Mes Buachalla was surprised in her bedchamber by the arrival of a bird. She was even more amazed when the bird threw off its feathers and became a man who made love to her. She married the king as arranged, but gave birth to the son of the bird-man. The child was called Conaire and put out to foster parents. When the king died, the Druids held a bull-feast to discover who should be the new king. They received a vision of a naked man at daybreak on the road to Tara, holding a sling with a stone ready in it. Meanwhile, Conaire's bird father appeared to him and told him to go straight away to Tara, not even delaying to get dressed. The Druids discovered him on the road and hailed him as the true king.

The change from nomadic hunter-gatherer to a settled agricultural lifestyle began in the Age of Taurus, from 4000-2000 BCE. This seems to have led to an association of the bull with vegetation deities. In earlier times, Taurus and not Aries was the first sign of the zodiac. Virgil said that 'the white bull with his golden horns opens the year', making the bull a symbol of the springtime. In the Northern Hemisphere, the constellation of Taurus disappears from the midnight sky from March to August (Old Lughnasa 12th August). The latter is a time associated with several vegetation gods with bull attributes, such as the Sumerian Dumuzi, the Wild Bull who is sacrificed and dies for his people, and the Egyptian corn god Osiris, and the 'bull-footed' Dionysus, the Greek vine god. A bull was certainly concerned with the Celtic Lughnasa festival, which marked the start of the harvest. At Loch Maree in Scotland, and Cois Fhairrge in Ireland, bulls were sacrificed at Lughnasa in honour of the ancient god Crom Dubh ('Dark Crooked One') as late as the eighteenth century. The hide of the bull would be preserved after the sacrifice, and sleeping in it was a rite of divination according to several Irish and Scottish accounts.

There appears to be a hidden meaning concerning a fertility or corn god in a tale which occurs in the Irish Ulster Cycle there the story of two bulls (actually two transformed men) over which a great war was fought. They met in battle with the dark one killing the white one and scattering its remains by dropping the parts from its horns. This recalls the scattering of the parts of the dismembered corn god. The Romans would sacrifice a bull and send the parts to different parts of the land

In Celtic myth, the bull is a creature of masculine power and potency, symbolic of the return of springtime and the fertility of the land. The bull is a creature of earth; he is grounded in the physical world, and acts powerfully within it. The bull knows who is he, where he has been, and where he is going. He sets off on his path with determination and energy, pursuing his goals until they are achieved. This sense of self and physical presence gives him his power. His stance is firmly rooted on the earth, feet spread wide, giving him unshakeable strength and stability. The bull is no follower of the herd, but a determined leader. He goes his own way.

Bull is a masculine influence in counterpoint to the feminine influence of the cow. He typifies fatherhood in all its aspects, perhaps especially in the sense of the guidance or mentoring.

Butterfly

Butterflies and moths both belong to the order of insects known as *lepidoptera,* a Greek word meaning 'scaled wing'. Lepidoptera have a five-stage life cycle: first an egg, then a caterpillar, followed by a pupae that matures into a chrysalis which, after a dormant period, breaks to reveal the butterfly. The ancients marvelled at the amazing transformation from a crawling worm-like creature that seems to 'die', become en-tombed, and then emerges as a glorious butterfly that spreads its wings and flies. Perhaps it isn't surprising that the life cycle of the butterfly, with its many transformations, became an allegory for the existence of a human, who at first crawls on the earth, dies, and emerges from the mortal shell as a transfigured soul. Depicting a creature with butterfly wings marked it out as a creature of spirit, and this is why angels and fairies are often depicted with butterfly wings.

THE PATH OF THE SHAMAN

The Celts suspected that butterflies might be human souls in actuality, and wore butterfly badges as a mark of respect for their ancestral spirits. It was said that the soul of a newly dead person could sometimes be seen hovering over the corpse in the form of a butterfly, and this was a good omen for the fate of the soul. However, in some cases the butterfly might be the soul not of a dead person, but of a dreamer or shaman, flying free while the body slept, and some say the soul-butterfly's ability to leave the body in sleep accounts for dreams. In any case, it was taboo to kill a butterfly, since it might mean destroying a human soul.

The Celts saw the butterfly as symbol of renewal and rebirth. At the festivals where all torches and lights were extinguished and re-lit from a central bonfire (such as Samhain or Halloween), the brand was called a 'butterfly'.

Butterfly never appears as a personal power animal, but can be a wonderful spirit helper that shows the way to personal growth. She indicates a total transformation in your life. This might be very frightening, as we tend to cling to what is known, what feels secure. However, movement and development are necessary if you are to grow beyond what you are at this moment in time. If the caterpillar did not surrender itself to a painful change (paralleled by the shamanic crisis), it could never achieve its ultimate glory as a butterfly and take flight. You should not try to remain in any life phase forever, but recognise when the time has come to move on.

It is important to accept that life has cycles and stages, some active and expanding, some passive and contracting. Sometimes you might experience rapid change, at other times nothing may seem to be happening but it is important to realise that, as deep within the chrysalis, radical alterations are taking place, even though you can't see them. Remember that it isn't possible to have everything at once, but each thing comes in its own time and season. Every stage of your life has its purpose and its own rewards. You need to understand what this phase is teaching you, and how you can use that knowledge to progress. You are not only sum of your life experiences, but also of how you have used the knowledge with which they presented you.

Cat

Cats were not usually sacred animals for the Celts, though there are numerous references to them in stories. But don't be fooled, these tales do not relate to the domestic moggie, which only arrived in Britain with the Romans, but to the wild cat, a larger and more aggressive creature with tabby markings that prefers to live in dense forests, hills and moor land.

119

THE PATH OF THE SHAMAN

Though wild cats had become extinct in England and Wales by 1850, they are still found in the Scottish Highlands. We still use one of the Irish Gaelic words for cat, or 'puss'.

In Celtic narratives, cats are mysterious, often supernatural, and usually ferocious. The most powerful was Cath Palug, born in Anglesey of the magical white sow Henwen (an aspect of the hag goddess Ceridwen). It wreaked havoc about the land until King Arthur and his foster brother Cei destroyed it. Even now unearthly cats appear all over Britain, with newspaper reports of large cats frequently frightening the population.

Legendary cats often hail from the Otherworld. The Knowth fairy mound was the home of Irusan the King Cat, who was as large as a plough-ox and once bore away the chief poet of Ireland in revenge for a satire against him. The Celts held that looking into cat's eyes would enable you to see the fairies, or see into the Otherworld. This strange supernatural reputation of felines may arise from their association with the moon. Cats' eyes change according to the levels of light, imitating the waxing and waning of the moon. Along with their nocturnal hunting habits, this made the cat a creature of the moon goddess. The Roman naturalist Pliny said that a she-cat would bear a total of twenty-eight kittens during her lifetime- the same number as the days of a lunar cycle.

Cats are sometimes the guardians of Otherworldy places. Maeldun set sail with several companions to avenge the death of his father. After many adventures, they arrived at a small island. Everywhere was deserted, but as they entered a house, they discovered a table set with wine and roast meat, piles of clean clothes and comfortable beds with warm coverlets. The only occupant was a little cat who played on top of four pillars. Maeldun saluted the creature, and asked if they could eat and drink, but the cat ignored him, making no sign as they ate their fill, and lay down to sleep for the night. Then, just as they were about to leave in the morning, Maeldun's foster-brother helped himself to a piece of jewellery from the wall. Instantly, the cat transformed into a fiery arrow which pierced right through the man, turning him to ashes in seconds. Maeldun was careful to apologise to the cat for his brother's churlish and ungrateful behaviour, which ran contrary to all the laws of hospitality, and returned the jewellery to the wall. The cat's house was plainly in the Otherworld from which nothing should ever be removed if the inhabitants are not to be angered.

Because cats had a connection with the powers of both the moon and the Otherworld, they were considered oracular. At Clogh-magh-righ-cat in north western Ireland there was a shrine where a black cat lay on a throne of silver, uttering prophecies. The Irish Druids performed a ritual known as *Imbas Forosnai*, in which the raw flesh of a cat was chewed. Even today, old country folk view cats as predictors of the weather: if a cat washes its ears or sneezes, it is sure to rain

Cats have two associations with fertility. Firstly they can produce several litters a year, and secondly they prey on the rodents that can devastate the pantry or grain stores, thereby protecting both the home and the harvest. In some places, the cat was a representative of the corn spirit, and children trampling cornfields were warned the phantom cat would get them.

The cat was a totem of several Celtic and pre-Celtic clans and individuals. The Highlands was the centre of two Pictish clans, the Orcs (boars) and the Kati ('cat people') who lived in Kataobh ('cat country'), which is now called Caithness. The Mac Pherson clan is descended from cat clan ancestors and the chief's crest shows a wild cat with claws ungloved and the motto 'Touch not the Cat but a Glove'. In this case 'but' is a contraction of 'beout' - a warning not to touch the dangerous cat without a glove. The Chieftain of Clan Chattan is called *Mohr an Chat* ('the great cat') and there are many places in the Highlands that take their name from cats. One Irish King was called Cairbre Caitheann (Cathead) and ruled over the Milesians who were the Celtic invaders of Ireland. He was said to have the ears of a cat, which may mean that he had a cat totem, or wore a helmet or hood of cat skin. There is an Irish legend of an island inhabited by men with cats' heads. The hero Finn mac Cumhail fought a clan of "cat-headed" (or cat hooded) people.[117]

The cat is a creature long associated with magic, from the sacred cats of ancient Egypt to the archetypal storybook witch with her cat familiar. Aloof, knowing and mysterious, the cat's eyes seem to promise secrets- no wonder the Celts thought you could see fairyland by gazing into a cat's eyes. We all need a little magic in our lives.

Cat is a paradoxical creature, capable of intense concentration when stalking her prey, but who also knows how to relax completely, curling up before the fire and falling asleep in seconds. She is a wild and bloody huntress, but can be playful and kittenish, a home loving lady who insists on high standards of personal hygiene. She is a sensuous creature who might purr at your feet or turn and scratch you. You might as well try to fathom the enigma of the moon goddess who is both virgin and crone, who creates and destroys, or understand the eternal mystery of woman, who is all of these things and more. She is much more than she seems. Cat reminds you that deep within you is a secret self, untamed by the world and its experiences, complex, individual, and needing to be fulfilled.

THE PATH OF THE SHAMAN

Whatever it is that you are hunting, whether it is a job, a lover, or knowledge itself, you can learn from Cat. She does not waste energy chasing here, there and everywhere- she might miss the clues that reveal her true target. She listens to every whisper on the wind, sniffs the air for every scent, and watches carefully for the slightest movement. She waits quietly until she sees what she really wants, and when it is within her grasp, she moves like lightening, and with one graceful pounce clasps it within her paws. Cat tells you that there is power in stillness, and beauty in dignity.

Cock

Introduced into Britain by the Romans, cockerels were quickly adopted into the mythology of the Celts. Julius Caesar reported Celts would not eat hare, geese or chickens as these were considered sacred animals. The name of ancient Gaul itself is derived from the Latin *gallus*, which means 'cock'. This designation was probably bestowed on the Gallic Celts because they were as fierce and aggressive as fighting cocks. The cock is still the emblem of France.

The magic of the cock lies in its famous dawn call. As well as being a kind of natural alarm clock signalling that it was time to wake and begin the business of the day, it was believed to chase away darkness, ghosts and the hidden powers of the night. This theme is echoed in many folk songs and stories where the cock-crow drives away visions of a dead lover, nightmares, magic spells and mischievous fairies such as the Welsh Tylwyth Teg. The Celts held their festivals from dusk until cockcrow, indicating that during the hours of darkness occult powers were strongest, and dispersed by daylight.

This ability to drive away evil made the cock an emblem of protection. The traditional weathercock represents a vigilant cockerel spirit placed on the highest part of the roof. To safeguard the newly harvested corn, a straw figure was fashioned in the shape of a 'corn cock' and placed on top of the rick. At harvest time a cock was killed with a sickle and buried in the fields to ensure the survival of the corn spirit, and its blood was mixed with the new seeds.

Because it is credited with the power of driving out harm, the cock was also believed to have healing abilities and was associated with healer gods, particularly when those gods were also solar deities. It was held that a cockerel rubbed on the body and then cast out of the district would take the illness with it. Until quite recent times in many parts of Britain, medicine taken at cockcrow was believed to be more effective, showing the persistence of Pagan ideas.

THE PATH OF THE SHAMAN

Julius Caesar wrote in *The Gallic Wars* that the Britons kept chickens for sport, rather than meat. Despite its small size, the cock is a fierce and aggressive fighter (we still call slightly built boxers 'bantam weights' after a species of chicken). Put two cocks in a pen together and they will fight for dominance. Cockfighting was a popular pastime over most of the ancient world, with birds being specially bred for aggressive qualities. It was a cruel pastime, with sharp artificial spurs or small knives often attached to the birds' legs before the contest.

The sacrifice of a cock and a ritual cockfight was part of the Imbolc (2nd February) festivities in honour of the pan-Celtic goddess Brighid. Cockfighting was a part of the West Highland's celebrations at Candlemas (the Christianised version of the festival) well into the nineteenth century. Boys would take cockerels (called stags) to school and *Coileach Buadha* or 'victorious cock' was elected Candlemas King. The cock and hen seem to have been paired at the early spring festivals with the solar cock sacrificed at Imbolc to disperse the powers of winter and darkness, while at the vernal equinox hen's eggs were dyed red represented the new dawn sun.

As a solar creature the cock is also a bird of augury - daylight uncovers hidden secrets. A number of omens were derived their behaviour: if a cock behaves unnaturally, it is a very bad omen. If a cock crows early in the evening it means bad weather; when a cock crows at midnight a spirit is passing; in England it is a death omen if one crows three times between sunset and midnight. Crowing at other times is often a warning against misfortune. If a cock crows while perched on a gate, or at nightfall, the next day will be rainy.

Cock is a solar animal, greeting the dawn, banishing night, and uncovering all that the darkness has concealed. He is a herald of healing, renewal and the positive energy of the light. His magic is a powerful force against negativity, whether this comes in the form of bad luck, depression or ill health; hidden secrets, worries and grievances brought into the light lose their power and become easier to deal with.

With a determined yell, he shakes his feathers in the sun, calling upon you to recognise that a new era has begun and that it is time wake up and to get on the business of life, to move forward and embrace the future with enthusiasm.

The cock is definitely not a team player, he is arrogant, noisy and aggressive, and demands that he should be the one and only male within his territory; two cocks in a pen together and they will fight to the death. He is the epitome of the macho man, whom we still call 'cock of the walk'-

123

THE PATH OF THE SHAMAN

just watch the way he behaves among his own private flock of hens. Remember too that we use the phrase 'cocky' to describe someone who is over confidant and heading for a fall.

Cow

In Britain, before the coming of the Romans, the main tracks across the country were cattle droves. When ancient peoples abandoned a hunter-gatherer life for pastoral and agrarian practices, cattle became immensely important. They played a vital role in the economy of the Celts as the source of meat, milk and cheese, of hide, bone and horn, while oxen pulled wagons and ploughs. Cattle were a measure of status and wealth, with the bride price and the price of slaves being set in cows. In Britain and Ireland, cattle raids were a common way of ensuring riches and power, and were not even considered wrong, but rather something of an occupational hazard. The Dagda ('Good God') had a cow called Ocean who could call all the cows in Ireland to follow her, which enabled his people, the Tuatha de Danaan, to recover all their stolen cattle.

The two great Celtic festivals of Beltane and Samhain centred around the needs of cows. At Beltane (May Day) cattle were driven through the ashes of the Bel fire to purify and protect them, before being taken up to their summer pastures. At Samhain (Halloween), they were brought down to sheltered winter feeding grounds, and any surplus animals were slaughtered, with black puddings and oatcakes made from the blood. Beltane fell when the seven stars of the Pleiades rose in the constellation of Taurus the Bull, and Samhain when the Pleiades set below the horizon.

For the Druids the bull represented the fertilising power of the heavens, while the cow was the productive abundance of the earth. The cow is a symbol of plenty, nourishment and nurture and is an attribute of many mother goddesses. Even the stars in the sky were thought to be droplets of milk from the Mother's breasts; in Lancashire the Milky Way is called 'the Cow's Lane'. In Welsh myth, the great mother was Madron, often depicted as a matronly woman holding a cornucopia (cow's horn) filled with fruit and grains. A Gaulish goddess called Damona ('Great Cow') was a mother goddess of healing and fertility. She seems to have had two husbands, Borvo and Moritasgus, both gods of healing springs.

In Ireland, the cow was connected with the water goddess Boanne ('She of the White Cattle'), and was one of the four sacred animals of Brighid (the others being a wolf, a snake and a bird of prey). Brighid was a goddess of inspiration, healing, craft and fertility, with a cult centre in Kildare. She was born in the house of a Druid and raised on the milk of fairy cattle. Her cows were milked three times daily, providing an endless supply of milk. To invoke the female power of regeneration at Brighid's festival of Imbolc (2nd February), an image of a cow was made, and the person to be 'regenerated' (i.e. given spiritual or physical healing), was enclosed inside the image, later emerging from it in a ritual act of rebirth. Brighid's Christian replacement St Brigit was the patroness of cattle and dairy work, and is still prayed to for fertility and healing.

The Great Mother is also the harvester, the goddess of death, and the cow is also sacred to her death aspects. The Irish battle Morrigan once took on the form of a red cow to approach the hero Cuchulainn. She again appeared to him in the guise of a hag milking a cow with only three teats, and as a female charioteer dressed in red, driving a cow before her. In all these guises, she heralded his death, signified by the colour red, an emblem of the Otherworld. The cow is sometimes a psychopomp (a being that conveys souls into the Otherworld). Some believed that if a man gave a gift of a cow to the poor, at his death the spirit of the animal would return to guide him to the Otherworld.

According to Irish myth, the first cattle came from the Otherworld, the Land of the West. Otherworldly cattle are also common in British lore, recognised by their red or round ears. Sometimes a fairy cow would join human herds and would supply amazing quantities of milk, unless it was offended by some mortal slight, in which case it would return to the sea or lake from which it came. Cattle formed the dowry of the fairy lake maiden of Llyn-y-Fan-Fach in Wales, who married a poor shepherd. When he lost his temper and struck her, she returned to the lake taking all her cattle with her. However, the sons of the marriage became the legendary physicians of Myddfai, so here again we have the connection of cattle, healing and water.

Like her mate the bull, the cow is also associated with divination and prophecy. In the Mabinogion tale of *The Vision* of *Rhonabwy* a sleeper saw a vision of the court of King Arthur whilst lying on the skin of a yellow heifer.

In Celtic lore the cow represented Mother Earth who provides everything her children need- nourishment, love and protection.

Crane
The Crane was an important bird in Celtic mythology. Sadly, it no longer lives in the British Isles as it was hunted out of existence in the seventeenth century. The stork and heron share much of the lore of the crane, but only the heron is still found in Britain.

THE PATH OF THE SHAMAN

The Celts associated marsh birds with the supernatural; dwelling as they do in a misty 'place between places' that is neither land nor water. Liminal sites were deemed possible entrances to the Otherworld, such as Bri Leith, the fairy mound of Midir, where three cranes warned travellers to 'keep out'. They were sentinels at the castle of the sea god Manannan on the Isle of Man. It was commonly believed that the crane was the epitome of vigilance, standing on one leg and holding a stone in its raised foot; if the bird fell asleep, the stone would drop, waking it. The one-legged stance is also associated with shamans in Celtic lore.

Standing on the threshold of the Otherworld, cranes were counted birds of augury, foretelling events and heralding storms and rain. They were emissaries of the gods of death and might summon a human soul to enter the Otherworld. On church carvings, they were portrayed as sucking the breath (or spirit) from the dying. In Welsh legend Pwyll, the Lord of the underworld, took the form of a crane. Cranes were sacred to gods and goddesses who presided over the mysteries of death and rebirth.

Flying cranes are sometimes said to be the souls of the dead, or mark the death of the old year. The mating dance of cranes was once thought to be a magical ritual and the movements were imitated by human dancers. It was performed round a horned altar and represented the labyrinth- the twisting path into the Otherworld.[118] In Greece, the crane dance marked the start of the New Year and the death of the old.

Cranes are solar birds, and when they returned in springtime, they were thought to bring the sun back with them. Standing by the waters, cranes and herons are among the first birds to greet the dawn. They catch many small fish to feed their young, and have the curious habit of laying them on the bank, tails together, in the form of a wheel. The wheel is the symbol of the sun and its passage through the year.

Cranes were very much associated with the hag goddess and her hoary wisdom. Miadhach, daughter of Eachdhonn Mor, was transformed into a crane. She lived to become one of the oldest animals who possessed all the ancient knowledge between them. In the tale of the 'Hag of the Temple', an old woman appeared with four cranes, the Cranes of Death, her sons transformed. They could only be released from the enchantment by the blood of a bull owned by the Cailleach Bheara ('Hag of Beare'), a harvest goddess. Only the power of the Taurus the Bull and the return of spring could transform the Cranes of Death.

This association of the bull and crane is a common thread in Celtic mythology. A monument from Paris shows a large bull that stands before a willow tree, with two cranes on his back and one on his head,

THE PATH OF THE SHAMAN

pecking at his pelt. A woodcutter hacks at the willow. The inscription over the bull reads *Tarvostrigaranus* ('The Bull with Three Cranes') and above the man is *Esus* ('Lord'). The willow is the tree of the hag goddess, lady of winter and death; who sometimes takes the form of a crane, while the bull represents virility, spring and life. It is possible that the monument depicts a seasonal allegory, with the cranes diminishing the bull's power (earth fertility) in the hag's season.

Two girls called Aoife and Iuchra both fell in love with Ilbrec, the son of the sea god Mannanan. Iuchra deftly rid herself of her rival by turning Aoife into a crane. In this form, Aoife lived on the Isle of Man for two hundred years, and when she died, her skin was made into a bag for Mannanan. It became one of his most important possessions, as he kept five magical items in it. Some suggest that these were the five letters of the ogham alphabet.[119] The Druids kept their ogham lots in a craneskin bag, from which they would cast them to perform rites of divination.

The Celtic god Ogma was said to have invented ogham after watching the flight of cranes, the shapes of the birds against the sky giving him the idea for the angular letters. The same story is told of the Roman Mercury, the Greek Hermes and the Egyptian Thoth; it is interesting to note that as well as being gods of communication and writing, all these gods have a role as psychopomp, conveying souls into the Otherworld after death.

Crane keeps the secrets of magical writing. For our ancestors, the act of writing was far removed from what it is today. To write a character was to connect with the thing that character represented, and to call it into being. Many early alphabets were angular in appearance, since they had to be carved into stone, or scratched onto bark. The legs of the crane in flight are said to resemble these characters. For the Druids Crane Knowledge referred to secrets of the ogham alphabet and all that entailed. Each character was assigned a tree, plant, animal, bird and colour, each embodying a wealth of lore and learning. The god Manannan owned a magical bag made from crane skin. It contained the shears of the king of Scotland, the helmet of the king of Lochlainn, the bones from Assails's swine, the hook of the smith Goibne, a shirt and a strip from the back of the great whale. These were the vowels of the ogham alphabet and the strip of the whale represented the horizon, the stave on which ogham was written.

In Ireland, the sudden appearance of a crane heralded the cessation of hostilities in a war. If a warrior on his way to battle chanced to see one, he was doomed, since the sight of it would rob him of his courage. For this reason, cranes were often engraved on shields and pieces of armour to strike terror into the enemy. The crane was a hallowed bird and its meat was forbidden. Breaking this taboo would result in ill fortune, the loss of courage, illness, or perhaps even death. This prohibition was preserved in folklore well into the seventeenth century when Scotsmen would get rid of unwelcome guests by inviting them to eat the flesh of cranes.

Dog

Dogs have a long history as loyal companions to humankind. The Celts had several kinds of dogs, including deerhounds and greyhounds for hunting, wolfhounds for war, terriers to control vermin, and small lapdogs for house pets. The latter were considered so valuable that their export was strictly forbidden.

Many Celtic warriors and kings included 'hound' (*cú*) in their names, such as Curoi ('Hound of Roi') and Cunobelinus ('Hound of Belinus' or 'Hound of the Sun'). Perhaps the most famous of all is Cuchulainn ('Hound of Chulainn') so called because he once killed the dog of the blacksmith Chulainn, and had to take its place for a time. For the rest of his life, he was under a *geis* (taboo) not to eat dog flesh. This was all very well, but he was also under a *geis* never to refuse hospitality. When three crones offered him a meal of roasted dog flesh, he had to eat it. Immediately, his strength and skills deserted him and he was defeated in battle.

Various solar deities are accompanied by a dog: Arthur had a hound called Cabal, and the pan-Celtic god Lugh had a hound which could not be beaten in combat, and whose bath water turned to wine.

Celtic mother goddesses were sometimes depicted with little lap dogs, and offerings of tiny dog images were dedicated at their shrines. In Britain, a goddess with a lap dog was worshipped at Canturbury and in Essex. The Gaulish goddess Aveta was given offerings of clay statuettes of dogs, swaddled babies or ladies with fruit, implying that three were all connected with fertility and abundance. This theme is echoed in a relief from Cirencester that shows the Three Mothers (*Deae Matres*) seated on a bench, the central figure with a lap dog; the others hold bread, grapes and a human baby. A god of nature and fertility was worshipped in Gaul, and along with hammer and wolfskin cloak attributes, he was portrayed with a dog seated at his feet.

Dogs seem to be able to cure their wounds with their own saliva. Because of this, they were associated with healing.[120] Representations of dogs are often found at Celtic healing shrines, or they are illustrated in the company of gods and goddesses of healing. In Britain, dog images were found at a cult site overlooked the river Severn in Gloucestershire, which

THE PATH OF THE SHAMAN

was sacred to the god Nodens, and which had a shrine for healing sleep. The sacred curative spring at Mavilly in Burgundy was presided over by a god who was depicted with a dog, a raven and a suffering pilgrim. This unnamed god appears to be analogous with Mars, the god of war, who had aspects as a powerful healer among the Celts. At Nettleton Scrub in Wiltshire, a healing sanctuary to Cunomaglus ('Hound-Lord') was found.

In the Netherlands, the coastal Morini tribe revered the goddess Nehalennia, shown with baskets of fruit and a dog at her feet, watchful and protective. She safeguarded merchants and other travellers. Early Christians regarded the dog as a symbol of vigilance, an adjunct of the good shepherd. In monuments, a dog was placed at the feet of women to signify affection and fidelity, while at the feet of a man it exemplified courage and magnanimity. At the feet of a Crusader, it showed that he had followed the standard of Christ as faithfully as a dog follows its master.

Dogs are associated with death and the underworld, perhaps because they feed on carrion, or because they accompany the hunter in the death chase. They featured in ceremonial sacrifices connected with the underworld powers and in early burial rituals. Dogs have been discovered inhumed in deep pits, perhaps as offerings to the spirits of the underworld.[121]

As well as being a mundane guardian of home and farmstead, dogs were also considered to be guardians of the threshold- the boundaries between the worlds- standing at the portal of the underworld, like the three-headed Greek Cerberus. The Welsh underworld god Gwynn ap Nudd had a hound called Dormath, meaning 'Death's Door'. *The Black Book of Carmarthen* relates that Gwynn, mounted upon his pale horse, would be present wherever there was slaughter with Dormath at his side. He did not encourage the killing; he merely collected the souls of the dead. The shaman travels to the underworld in search of knowledge. To do so he must pass the dog that guards its gateway. Here your self-created demons dwell: your deepest fears, prejudices and feelings of self loathing, buried maybe, but that nevertheless, influencing your behaviour and outlook.

Ghostly dogs and phantom black hounds haunt the northern and eastern coasts of Britain. This may be a folk memory of the Viking invasions, which brought with them the stories of the Hounds of Odin. The mud flats of East Anglia are haunted by a phantom dog known as Black Shuck, a name derived from the Saxon word for the Devil, *succa*. He is variously described as having a single eye set in the centre of his head, or having glowing red eyes, or even as being headless, yet having glowing eyes suspended in front of him.

THE PATH OF THE SHAMAN

Legends of Britain and Continental Europe also tell of the Wild Hunt, a pack of ghostly dogs who fly through the night sky to pursue their quarry. The leadership of the hunt has been ascribed to Herne the Hunter, King Arthur, the Devil, Charlemagne, Gwyn ap Nudd, Odin and Woden. The prey is variously a white stag, a white boar, white-breasted maidens or the souls of the damned.

Eagle

The eagle's Gaelic names suggest the high regard in which it was held: these include *Iolair* ('Guide to the Air'), *Suil-na Graine* ('Eye of the Sun'), and *Righ na h-Ealtain* ('King of the Bird World').

In Wales, it is said that when there are high winds the eagles are creating whirlwinds on Snowdon. Eagles were believed to bring storms with them, and so were associated with sky and thunder gods, depicted on plaques and altars in the company of deities such Taranis, who was shown holding a wheel and a lightning bolt. This association was also prevalent in other mythologies; an eagle accompanies the Greek Zeus and the Roman Jupiter, for example.

The eagle is a bird very much associated with the sun. It was a commonly held belief that eagles could look at the sun without blinking and that parent birds would initiate their fledglings by taking them close to sun to stare at it; those who blinked were unworthy and fell to their deaths. The Celts thought that the eagle was very long lived, renewing itself periodically by flying to the sun and scorching its feathers, before diving into the sea and emerging as a young bird. In the Bible's *Book of Psalms* is the phrase "Thy youth is renewed like the eagles'". In an Irish legend called *The Voyages of Maeldun,* the travellers visited the Island of the Eagle. One evening, a large bird appeared from the south west, carrying a branch on which were red berries, which it began to eat. It was a ragged old bird, with hardly any strength, so the men came out of hiding to look at it. Some of them ventured to eat the berries it dropped. This went on until two eagles arrived to preen its feathers and improve its appearance. The hoary old bird was starting to look better. Eventually, on the third day, the bird became much stronger and younger looking, and it rose up into the air before diving headlong into the lake. One of Maeldun's companions decided to try the remedy for himself, and despite the warnings of his fellows, he jumped into the water. When he swam to the shore he found that all his aches and pains had disappeared, his eyesight was perfect, and his loose teeth were firm in his jaw once more. For as long as he lived, he never knew another day's illness.

In the *Mabinogion* story that tells of the search for the young god Mabon, the eagle was second oldest animal on earth and pointed the way to

THE PATH OF THE SHAMAN

the oldest, the salmon, who knew where the young god was. Both animals were considered repositories of ancient knowledge stretching back to beginning of time.

The eagle is often associated with kingship, and represents both temporal and spiritual power, appearing on crests and heraldic devices throughout Europe. The Sacred King's soul was said to leave the king's body in the form of an eagle while the souls of lesser men might leave in the form of butterflies. A Roman knight claimed to have seen the Emperor Augustus's soul rise from his body in the form of an eagle, thus proclaiming his deity, and was rewarded by his widow, Livia. Ganymede rose to heaven in the form of an eagle, or in another version was carried off by an eagle to become Zeus's cup bearer. In the Welsh tale of Llew and Blodeuwedd when Llew was struck him a fatal blow, instead of dying, he turned into an eagle and flew away.

The motif of the solar or celestial power of summer in conflict with the serpent or sea dragon forces of winter and the underworld are expressed in the many stories of eagles fighting snakes. In Norse myth an eagle sits at the top of Yggdrasil, the World Tree. It is at war with the serpent at the trees roots. In Hittite myth the eagle with the serpent in its talons symbolised the strife between the weather god and the serpent Illuyankas. The Aztec eagle of the sun ate the serpent of darkness. The Hindu Vishnu rides an eagle when he is at war with the Nagas or serpents. Some species of eagle actually eat serpents and can sometimes be seen carrying them off: it is an expression of the tension between the sky and the underworld, between summer and winter, between light and darkness.

As Eagle circles high in the air, riding the thermals, he sees the whole landscape spread out before him, but his sharp eye can pick out the tiniest detail below. This viewpoint gives him the ability to relate the particulars to the bigger picture.

Fox

The fox is a very ancient inhabitant of Britain, though not Ireland, the Orkneys or the Hebrides. It is probably more common today than it ever was, since most of its predators, such as wolves, are extinct in Britain. It is a highly adaptable creature, and feels at home in many diverse environments, whether woodlands, pasture land, moorland, cliffs or even towns and cities, where large numbers of foxes survive on what humans throw away.

The best known attribute of the fox is his cunning and devious nature. Foxes are supposed to hunt well away from their own dens to lay the blame on other foxes, and be able to blend in with the background or follow

THE PATH OF THE SHAMAN

twisting and turning tracks to divert hunters. The Venerable Bede compared the wily fox with Pagans: "*The nature of foxes accords well with the ways and the words of heretics, for they are exceedingly deceitful creatures who lie hidden in dens and caves, and when they do come out they never run on a straight course but follow devious paths.*" This might be unflattering, but the fox's abilities were much admired by the Celts. In Taliesin's song of his origins, he claims to have assumed the shape of a satirising fox, a reference to his artfulness.

Foxes are gregarious creatures who meet frequently and communicate by sense and sound; they were once thought to be holding counsels. 'Fox' formed part of the name of men who were known for their skill in counsel: one Gaulish chieftain was called Louernius, or 'Son of the Fox' and Ua Leochann, a king of Scotland, was nicknamed *An Sionnach* or 'The Fox' for his adroitness.

There is a widely circulated story that foxes have an ingenious method of ridding themselves of fleas. Taking a piece of wool retrieved from a barbed-wire fence, the fox holds it in his mouth and swims into a pond or stream. As he goes deeper and deeper, the fleas scramble to stay above the waterline, going up to the shoulders, then the head. Finally, the fox ducks his head beneath the surface and the frantic fleas migrate into the wool. When he has achieved this objective, the fox lets go of the wool, and all his little problems float away. Some people say this story is apocryphal, but I have met many a countryman who swears he has witnessed it.

Foxes were interred in ritual burial sites in both Britain and France, often in the company of deers or stags. Like the dog, the fox is associated with the underworld, probably because during the winter both dog fox and vixen spend most of their time sheltering in subterranean earths within their territory. Fox earths, like badger setts, can be very ancient. Like other burrowing animals, the fox is thought to be a shamanic guide to the chthonic realms.

The red fox emerging from his burrow at the winter solstice is symbolic of the rebirth of the sun. Its red colour also associates it with the element of fire and the strengthening of the sun at the spring equinox.

Because of its underworld connections and its place Pagan religion, Christians associated the fox with the Devil. It was said to be a favourite shape changing form of witches. Its reputation was so evil that its bite was thought to be fatal; any person bitten would die seven years later.

Very old foxes are said to have magical pearls in their heads, which may represent their accumulated wisdom.

If Cat represents intuition, then Fox typifies analytical intelligence. Fox is cunning, a word that comes from the old Scottish word

THE PATH OF THE SHAMAN

kenning, meaning 'to know' and possibly connected with the Gaelic *cu* or 'hound'- meaning that the fox has innate hound wisdom. Clever Fox can camouflage himself and outfox his pursuers by taking devious paths, and it is this that that helps him elude the hunter, not his strength or speed.

Foxes are not promiscuous like dogs, but mate for life. They are devoted family animals, and both male and female animals look after the cubs. According to a number of folk songs, it is the male who ventures out to hunt for food to feed his family, and who goes to look for missing cubs.

Frog

The Celts often identified frogs with the spirits that they believed inhabited every spring, pool or well, particularly those at healing shrines.

Frogs were thought to be in such close contact with the spirits of water that they could summon the rain with their croaking. They are only vocal during the mating season, in late February and March, which is a particularly rainy time in Britain. The Celts thought that the frogs invoked the rains in spring in order to cleanse and renew the face of the earth after winter, regenerating and transforming it, watering the sleeping seeds so that they could burst into life. In a similar fashion, the water at the healing shrines could wash away illness, purify the body and stimulate health.

The frog itself is very much associated with healing. Gypsies recommend frogspawn as a cure for rheumatism, and the famous Welsh physicians of Myddfai used frogs in many of their remedies. Warts could be removed by rubbing a frog over them: when it died the warts would disappear. A dried frog, worn in a bag around the neck warded off harm, while the eyes of a frog cured blindness. A frog was held to the mouth to cure trenchmouth or a cough.

The frog has another ability that connects it with healing- an ability to metamorphose itself which is second only to the butterfly. It begins life in the jelly-like eggs known as frogspawn, hatches as a legless tailed tadpole, then gradually changes into a frog, growing legs and shedding its tail. Though the tadpole needs to live in water, the frog leaves the pond as soon as its transformation is effected. Contrary to popular supposition, the frog spends most of its life on land, though it prefers damp, marshy places. This power of metamorphosis associates the frog with magic, the power of shapeshifting, and the ability to transform the self.

Everyone is familiar with the story of the princess who dropped her golden ball into a well. The ugly frog agreed to retrieve it for her, but only in return for a kiss. At first she refused, but when she relented and placed a kiss on his unprepossessing head, the frog turned into a handsome prince.

133

THE PATH OF THE SHAMAN

This teaches us not to judge by appearances: the ugliest exterior may conceal a soul of pure gold. In a society where the surface is accounted supremely important, we can easily forget, and fall into the trap of being superficial.

There are several stories where the frog is a man in disguise, usually the unwilling victim of enchantment, but these tales might well be related to the shapeshifting abilities of the shaman.

The association of the frog with creation appears all over the world: it is thought to resemble a foetus. The Sheela-na-gig ('Old Woman with Vulva') may be derived from early images of a frog goddess. Depictions of a frog or toad goddess with a human vulva have been found dating from the earliest times; sometimes they have a woman's head. The vulva represented an opening to the underworld womb of the earth goddess. Both frog and toad are also associated with the goddess of death and regeneration, the mirror image of the birth goddess.

There is an ancient connection between the frog and the horse. 'Pad' means frog or toad, otherwise called paddock. 'Paddock ride' means frog spawn, while paddock pipes is another name for marsh horsetail. A frog or toad bone gives power over horses, and is said to resemble a mark on the underside of a horse's hoof called 'the frog'.

Frog is a fertility symbol representing the creative power of the waters, the primal source of all life; she has a moist skin, which contrasts with the dryness of death. Water flows, nourishes and replenishes the earth. The power of Frog is concerned with cleansing and purifying, and with the free flowing of emotional energies.

Hare

Unlike rabbits, hares are native to Britain. Rabbits were introduced by the Romans and the lore of the two animals is very different, as are their habits- the rabbit is a sociable animal, living within large groups, whereas hares are solitary creatures.

Julius Caesar reported that they were among the most sacred animals of the Celts, so much so that killing and eating them was taboo. This restriction was lifted in the spring, when a ritual hunt and consumption was made. Indeed, until the end of the eighteenth century an annual hare hunt took place near Leicester, led by the mayor and corporation together with hunters and hounds. This hare was an attribute of Black Annis, a fearful hag who was said to live in a cave in the nearby Dane Hills, and the hunt was once perhaps the ritual expulsion of the winter goddess. In Europe, the white or arctic hare (the earliest indigenous species) symbolised snow and the white goddess of winter.

In contrast, the brown hare represented the coming of spring and the return of the flowering summer goddess after the earth's long winter sleep. The hare is usually a nocturnal creature that remains hidden during the hours of daylight. However, this is not the case during the mating season when hares can be seen abroad in daylight, behaving in a most peculiar way. They may be witnessed leaping into the air or boxing (it was once thought that the male hares were fighting for mating rights, but it is now believed that the behaviour is due to female hares repulsing unwanted male advances) giving rise to the expression 'the mad March hare'. Some say they resemble a coven of witches dancing.

The hare has a reputation for lusty sexuality and fecundity. It is a prolific breeder, even - as observed by Herodotus - conceiving while already pregnant. It is closely associated with the Saxon hare-headed fertility goddess Eostre, who carries an egg and gives birth to the whole of creation from her egg shaped womb. The terms oestrogen and oestrus are both derived from the name of this goddess, as is the name of the festival of Easter. All originate in the old Norse *austr* which means 'east'- the direction of the newly risen sun at the spring equinox. Mythologically, the hare is connected with the east, dawn and Ostara (the spring equinox festival of Eostre), and with light bringing or messenger gods. An ancient belief that the hare lays eggs like a bird is behind the once popular Easter pastime of Hunting the Hares' Eggs. Even now, the Easter Bunny is said to distribute eggs in springtime.

The hare has another connection with fertility; in Europe, the hare is also associated with the corn spirit. Hares hid in cornfields until the final few sheaves were reaped; the last sheaf was called 'the hare' and its cutting 'killing the hare', 'cutting the hare' or 'cutting the hare's tail off'.

Apart from the breeding season, the hare is only seen at night, by the light of the moon. Should he be disturbed by a nocturnal predator, such as a fox, he will use his great speed and manoeuvrability to escape, zig-zagging rather than running in straight lines.

The hare, like the moon, stands for birth, growth, reproduction, death and rebirth. It is sacred to gods and goddesses of the moon and the patterns in the full moon are sometimes thought to resemble a hare. Celtic hunting and moon deities were often shown holding hares in their hands. The moon shines in the darkness and is thus connected with intuitive knowledge and insight, powers thought to be shared by the hare. Young hares are born with their eyes open and never again close them - or so the Celts believed - even to blink or sleep. Boudicca, the warrior queen of the Iceni, released a hare from beneath her cloak while making an invocation to the goddess Andraste ('Victory'), to predict the outcome of her battles against the Romans.

The hare is the commonest witch familiar in Europe, with witches reputed to turn themselves into the creatures. The hare was denigrated and reviled by the Christian church because it was quick, clever, mated where it willed and did all the things humans would like to do, but dare not. Hare breaks free of restrictions and is unconventional. The March hare is touched by a divine madness that urges him to express his inner passions. His is the anarchy that overturns dogmatic tradition and restrictions.

Horse

Horse cults existed in Britain long before the coming of the Celts. A Stone Age carving found in Derbyshire shows a man in a horse mask. There are several chalk horse hill-figures in Britain, the oldest being the one at Uffington in Oxfordshire, dating from 1400-600 BCE. The horse represented the spirit of the land itself.

It is no exaggeration to say that the domestication of the horse changed the face of the world. Horses were invaluable creatures that enabled people to travel much further and improve communication between distant places. The Celts were expert cavalrymen, and the horse no doubt aided them in their westward journey of conquest across Europe.

Among the Celts horses were status symbols, and were never used as lowly beasts of burden; rather they were the mounts of chieftains and warriors. Eating their flesh was taboo (as it still is in Britain). Its value made the horse a favourite tribal totem or god of the Iron and Bronze Ages; Wales is named after the horse god Waels or Waelsi. Other possible Celtic horse gods include Rudiobus from Loiret, Segomo ('Victory') from Burgundy and Mullo ('Mule') who was invoked at Rennes and Allonnes in New Gaul.

The horse was considered a solar creature. Celtic coins depict the horse with sun or wheel emblems. On the Jupiter Columns set up in eastern Gaul and the Rhineland, Celtic sky gods were depicted on horseback, brandishing thunderbolts or sometimes a solar wheel, and riding down a semi-serpentine monster- the forces of the sky in opposition to the chthonic forces of the earth and underworld.

Epona was the British and Gallic horse goddess, usually depicted between two horses, or riding side-saddle. Her worship was adopted by Roman cavalrymen, who often carved niches for a statuette of Epona in their stables. For the non-military sections of society, she was a mother goddess, an emblem of fertility, shown with mare and foal. Images of her

THE PATH OF THE SHAMAN

have been found in Celtic graveyards, dedicated by relatives of the deceased, showing that she was also a protector and guide of the dead. She carried a key which unlocked both the stable door and the gates of the Otherworld.[122] Horse goddesses also rule as Queens of the Dead. They ride between the worlds at will. The Celts believed that the dead rode to the afterlife on horseback. As a shamanic ally, Horse facilitates journeys to the Otherworld, with the shaman visualising him or herself riding on the horse's back as it gallops between the realms. Sometimes too, the drum the shaman uses to induce trance is made of horse-skin, and this is another meaning of 'riding the horse'.

Epona's Welsh counterpart was Rhiannon, who married Pwyll, the ruler of Dyfed. At the winter solstice she gave birth to a son called Pryderi ('Anxiety') but during the night, the child vanished and the attendants, afraid that they would be accused of its abduction, killed a dog and smeared the sleeping Rhiannon with its blood, accusing her of eating the child. All the evidence pointed to her guilt, and she was given the punishment of carrying all the visitors to the castle on her back, like a horse. Meanwhile, some distance away in Gwent, a man called Teyrnon Twrf Liant ('Lord of the Raging Sea') was attending his mare, which was about to give birth. Every year at Beltane she dropped a foal, but every year a great hand snatched it from the stable and spirited it away. This year Teyrnon was ready with a hatchet. As the giant hand reached in, he hacked it from the arm, and the foal fell to the stable floor, and with it was a human baby. He and his wife raised the boy, and the boy grew as quickly as the foal. After seven years, the plight of Pwyll and Rhiannon came to his ears, and it occurred to him that the child bore a remarkable resemblance to Pwyll. He duly presented him at the castle, and the child was recognised as Rhiannon's son.

In Irish mythology, the horse goddess was called Macha. She married a poor man called Crunnchu MacAgnoman and soon became pregnant. However, Crunnchu was a foolish man and boasted that his marvellous wife could outrun the king's horses. King Conchobar was enraged and sent for Macha and, despite her pregnancy, he forced her into a race. She won the contest, but fell down dying on the finish line, giving birth to twins. With her dying breath, she cursed the men of Ulster that they should become as weak as women in labour during their hour of greatest need.

Like the other horse goddesses, Macha represented the land itself and the power of sovereignty. Her golden hair was the corn at harvest time and her feast day was Lughnasa (1st August). In early Ireland, a white mare was instrumental in the bestowing of kingship. An account as late as the twelfth century CE described the making of a minor king and how he must be symbolically reborn from a white mare in a patently shamanic ceremony. Stripped naked he had to crawl on all fours to the mare, like a foal. The mare was then slaughtered and cut up, the pieces boiled in a cauldron. The king got into the cauldron to eat pieces of the meat and drink the both. Finally he stood on the inauguration stone, was presented with a white wand and turned three times to the right, then three times to the left 'to honour the trinity'- in the original rites the trinity honoured would have been the sovereign triple-goddess of the land.

The kind of interaction that takes place between horse and rider is an instinctive partnership. A solitary horse will happily spend its time eating grass, but in coalition with a human will willingly pull a plough, a carriage, or carry a rider long distances. The strength of one aids the wit of the other, and of such alliances, perfect partnerships are made.

Lizard

Britain has three native lizards, the common lizard *(Lacerta vivipara)*, the slow worm *(Anguis fragilis)* which has no legs and is sometimes mistaken for a small snake, and the sand lizard *(Lacerta agilis)*, which is only found in certain isolated areas in Northern England.

All lizards have a residual third eye and in some species, this is capable of detecting changes in light conditions. This mystical third eye has given the lizard associations with inner or psychic sight, whether through visions, divination or dreams. In Greek Hermetic tradition, it was associated with Hermes-Thoth who had a chariot drawn by lizards, thus showing its association with supernatural methods of discovering secrets. The ancient Greeks watched the movements of lizards on a wall as a form of divination.

The tradition that associates lizards with the world of dreaming is widespread. Native Americans believe that it guards the gate of dreams, while the ancient Greeks associated it with Hypnos the god of sleep who communicated with humankind through dreams. Throughout the ages, dreams have been seen as many different things, including omens and messages from the gods. It was a common practice to visit a healing shrine and undertake 'temple sleep' in order to receive a restorative dream, sent directly by the deity. Shamans believe that one of the gates to the Otherworld lies through realm of dreams, guarded by the lizard. This make the lizard a sought-after shamanic ally.

For the Celts, the lizard was an animal of the sun, a representative of midsummer magic. Its name in Welsh *(lleufer)* and Gaelic *(luachair)*

THE PATH OF THE SHAMAN

associate it with white light. The creature is sun loving, seeking out warm places to bask in sunshine. For the Celts, its pursuit of the light symbolised the soul's search for enlightenment. Lizards were carved on corbels on mediaeval cathedrals, such as Southwell and Wells, to symbolise the illuminating power of the gospels.

Lizards are also emblems of resurrection. Some ancient authorities thought that they hibernated during the cold winter and re-emerged in the spring when the weather got warmer, going blind during this period and remaining sightless until they climbed an east facing wall and looked east to the sunrise, which restored their vision.

Another ability of the lizard associates it with regeneration: it is able to break off its tail to escape predators. As the tail is writhing it distracts the predator long enough for the lizard can make its escape. Unfortunately, a lizard can only do this once because the tail grows back cartilage instead of vertebrae. And like the snake, the lizard sheds its skin, and grows a new one. Perhaps because of this ability, it is a creature of healing. The Irish once believed that a person who licked a lizard all over would be able to heal sores with his or her tongue.

Otter

In every Celtic tongue the otter is called 'water dog', and shares some symbolism of the dog. There are numerous stories of otters befriending humans, with a loyalty akin to that of the dog. In the Irish story of the voyages of Maelduine, the crew alighted on the Isle of Otters. It was inhabited by a solitary human, cared for by numerous otters that fed him each day on the salmon they caught. The association of the dog with the otter is also seen in the Irish story of Cuculain who was under a *geas* not to eat dog meat. When he broke the taboo, he was killed, and an otter appeared to lick his blood.

The Celts prized otter skin very highly and used it to make waterproof items. The otter has rich, thick fur with two distinctive layers; the top layer is long and coarse, while the under-fur is fine and glossy, so thick it can't be parted. This inner coat traps a layer of air bubbles that prevent water getting in, and gives the otter its distinctive silver colour while it is swimming. Otter skin constituted the traditional bag for the Celtic harp and was also used as a lucky lining for shields, since it had a considerable reputation as a magical protector. This reputation persisted into later ages, when soldiers believed an otter skin would preserve them from bullet and sword, while a small piece of the skin kept a house from fire and made a powerful charm against drowning.

Otters are skilful hunters, and the Celts were particularly impressed by the speed with which the otter caught the salmon, a symbol of wisdom. Because otters are such dextrous hunters, clothing made from otter-skin was worn by human hunters as an act of sympathetic magic. Killing an otter was a magical act, undertaken with a three-pronged spear, the symbol of the water god.

Though it spends much of its time in the water, the otter rests and breeds on land, with several resting places along the river called 'holts'. This dual nature, taken with its fluidity and deftness made the otter a popular form for shapeshifting magicians, and it was one of the forms taken by the goddess Ceridwen during her battle with Taliesin.

In European myth, the otter sometimes surfaces with a pearl or stone in its paws, the object of a quest. The otter often appeared as a guide to those undertaking voyages or quests.

Owl

Owls are very vocal in November and then fall silent until February; thus, they are believed to be the servants of the Crone Goddess of death and winter. In Scotland the owl is known as *Cailleach* which means 'Hag' and is called the *Cailleach Oidhche* ('the Hag of the Night') and *Cailleach Oidhche Gheal* ('Hag of the Night Moon'). It is linked to the *Cailleach Bheur*, the blue faced hag who strides across the land after Samhain, bringing the snow and frost. It is also the death bird, ' the Bird of the Corpse'.

Chaucer called the owl *'prophet of woe and mischance'* and Shakespeare, in *Macbeth*, called the owl *'the fatal bellman which gives the stern'st good night'*. All over Britain, the owl call was believed to be a death omen, especially if it was heard during the day, or for three nights running. An owl hooting at the birth of a child signified he would lead an unhappy life. In Wales it was said that when an owl hooted a girl was about to lose her virginity. In Ireland, the call of a screech owl foretold the death of the king.

Owls are thought of as ghostly creatures. They attack from behind and fly silently; sometimes people who have been foraging too near an owl's nest receive a sharp smack on the back of their heads and think they have been hit by a ghost. In most of Europe owls were associated with witches, who were thought to be able to turn themselves into the birds, so owls were often killed as a precaution. Owls had such a fearful reputation that people would not even touch a dead one.

In the Welsh *Mabinogion* tale, the faithless Blodeuwedd was turned into an owl, and Blodeuwedd is a Welsh name for the owl- some say that the face of an owl resembles a flower.

As well as its association with ill omen, the owl is a symbol of wisdom, linked with goddesses of wisdom, such as the Celtic Sulis, the Greek Athene and the Roman Minerva. The Celts believed that it was one of the five oldest beasts on earth (with the blackbird, stag, eagle and salmon), and thus possessed much ancient knowledge.

For a human, the night is a frightening place; its darkness representing all that is hidden, all that is unknown. Owl has keen sight and hearing that enable her to thrive in a nocturnal environment, detecting her prey with ease. She can see what is concealed from human sight, piercing through the shadows that surround her. Owl's wisdom recognises the dark side: night, winter, the underworld, illness, old age and death. These things are a needful balance- without winter we would not have summer, without darkness, we would not know light, without decay, there would be no new growth. These things are not evil, but part of the cycle of life, which must be understood and accepted as a whole. This is the realm of the Crone, the goddess of wisdom who points the way to true enlightenment.

Raven
In early stories, the raven is interchangeable with other members of the crow family who all have dubious reputations. Ravens feed on carrion, and it was once a common sight to see them feeding on gibbet corpses. After a battle, they would descend on the field to feast on the flesh of the slain. The Celts believed that the raven was a bird of death, associated with death and the battle goddesses such as Morrigan, Badb and Nemain who could all take raven form, especially on the battlefield. As late as 1014 CE Badb was seen hovering over the Battle of Clontarf.

The raven's carrion habits made it a natural attribute of deities of death and the underworld. Like other mother goddesses, Nantosuelta had a death aspect, depicted at Sarrebourg near Metz, and at Speier in Germany accompanied by a raven. Small images of ravens were placed in wells and graves.

The raven's croak is distinctive, and the bird has been known to mimic human speech giving it an association with prophecy and oracular utterance. The Irish phrase 'raven's knowledge'; meant to discover secrets. The raven was thought to be the most prophetic of birds, having knowledge of public and private events and people are still spoken of as having 'the foresight of a raven'. The Druids took omens from the flight of ravens; for example, if ravens were seen flying towards each other it was an omen of war. Ravens warned the Irish god Lugh of the invasion of the Formorians, and ravens are said to have foretold the deaths of Plato and Tiberius.

Celtic bards, being privy to many secrets, were occasionally called 'ravens' and their conversation 'the motley jargon of ravens'. The affinity also comes from the fact that ravens were associated with inspiration and prophecy, as shown in the tale of Ceridwen's Cauldron of Inspiration, which was brewed for her ugly son Afagddu ('Utter Darkness') who was also known as Morvran, or 'Sea Raven'.

The raven's association with shamanic vision is demonstrated in the Irish story of Da Choca's Hostel (an entrance to the Otherworld) where King Cormac met Badb, in the guise of a red-clad hag who was washing the trappings of a chariot; the water ran red with blood. The crone, noticing the king, stood on one leg, closed one eye and pointed with one finger, declaring that she was washing the armour of Cormac, a doomed king. This posture is the classic pose of the shaman, who closes one eye to gain inner vision, and stands on one leg, so that he is between the worlds.

The raven is allied with the Welsh god Bran ('Raven'). After his death, Bran's head was taken to the White Mount in London, where it continued to prophesy and to protect Britain from invasion. King Arthur removed the head as a sign that he was solely responsible for safeguarding the realm. The Tower of London now stands on the site, and Bran's ravens still live there. It is said that if they ever leave the tower, Britain will fall to invaders. Naturally, they are well looked after.

Arthur has several connections with the raven. In several areas of Britain, he was said to have taken raven form after his death and countrymen

THE PATH OF THE SHAMAN

tipped their hats to the birds in consequence. To kill one was a crime, and insulted Arthur. The Spanish writer Cervantes reported *'No Englishman would shoot a crow for Arthur's sake'*

Raven is the teacher and protector of seers and clairvoyants. His clear sight pierces the veils of past and future, and discovers the secrets of the present. However, Raven is not purely a bird of instinct; he is also very intelligent and uses his resourcefulness to adapt tools for his use.

Salmon

The resourceful salmon is most famous for its strenuous journey upstream to its mating grounds, against seemingly impossible odds; it even leaps up waterfalls. Salmon's ability does not rely on blind courage- his determination is allied with wisdom. Instead of battling against the prevailing current, clever Salmon uses a reverse current to swim upstream. But the cost can be very high. Not all the salmon make it, and of those that do manage to mate, none return; they die in the breeding grounds, having made the supreme sacrifice. Their eggs hatch and after several years the young fish return, and the cycle begins again.

This determination is mirrored in the story of the fledgling warriors who applied for training at the school the warrior woman Scathach. One such was Cuchulain, who travelled overseas to find her, crossed the Plain of Ill Luck, escaped the beasts of the Perilous Glen and eventually arrived at the Bridge of Leaps beyond which was the land of Scathach. There he saw many young warriors and princes of Britain and Ireland, including his friend Ferdia. He asked Ferdia how he could cross the bridge, but Ferdia replied that none of them had yet managed it, as the last two skills that Scathach taught were the leaping of the bridge, called the 'hero's salmon leap' and the throwing of the Gae Bolg.

Cuchulain waited until evening, recovering his strength after his travels, before trying to try to leap the bridge. Instead of trying to jump across in one go, he decided a series of leaps would be more effective. With his fourth leap, he stood in the centre and with another, he had crossed it. Scathach was impressed and took him on as a pupil. For a year and a day, he stayed with her, learning everything she could teach of the arts of war.

This story also demonstrates the other quality the salmon was admired for- its wisdom. In Irish myth, the salmon that swam in Connla's Well were said to gain their knowledge by eating the Nine Hazels of Wisdom that fell from the Tree of Knowledge into it. With each nut they ate, another red spot appeared on their backs: those with the most marks

143

THE PATH OF THE SHAMAN

were the cleverest fish. The hazel is the tree of wisdom, and the nuts represent knowledge in a concentrated form. If a person were to catch and eat one of these salmon, the wisdom would be transferred to them. The idea that eating fish can increase cleverness is still with us; we continue to call fish 'brain food'.

One wise salmon was called Fintan. The giant Finegas hunted it along the banks of the Boyne for seven years, eventually catching it and setting it to roast, watched by his pupil Fionn mac Cumhal. Fionn chanced to burn his finger on the hot flesh and put in into his mouth to cool it. But as soon as he tasted the salmon, he acquired all of its wisdom. Afterwards he had only to place his thumb in his mouth to have foreknowledge of events.

The Celts considered the salmon to be the oldest living creature, as old as time itself. One of Culhwch 's tasks was to find the imprisoned god Mabon. He asked many birds and animals, each older and wiser than the last and in the end came to the salmon of Llyn Llyw, the most ancient of all, who told him where the child of light was hidden.

The salmon was a popular form amongst Celtic shape-changing magicians. Taliesin became a salmon in his battle with Ceridwen. In a similar story Tuan Mac Carill was eaten in salmon form by the wife of the king of Ireland and was once again reborn as a human from her womb. These are metaphors for a shamanic initiation.

Particular salmon were considered to be the guardians of the wells or pools where they lived. Some say that if one of these were to be killed and removed from its domain, it would later revive, and make its way back to it, perhaps adopting human form to do so.

Like most water creatures, the salmon is associated with healing, particularly with the god Nodens who had many healing shrines at sacred springs and rivers. All traditions regard water as the element of life. The primordial waters are chaos, but contain the potential of all life forms, and therefore fishes are associated with fertility and creation. They were eaten at the feasts of the mother goddess on her sacred day, Friday.

Snake

The snake was an important animal for the ancient Celts, and far from being the symbol of evil that it became amongst Christians, it was a creature that represented both goddesses and gods, fertility, healing and renewal, and linked the three realms of the shaman-priest.

The snake was an obvious symbol of the fertility of the god: even the shape looks vaguely phallic, while the male snake has a multiple penis. Its

shape also associated it with sky and storm gods, with lightning known as the sky-serpent or lightening-snake: the phallic thrust of the Sky Father that fertilised Mother Earth during the thunderstorms of summer.

Snakes were companions of goddesses of healing, fecundity and abundance. Celto-Germanic mother goddesses were invoked on dedicatory stones decorated with snakes. The underworld womb of Mother Earth was regarded as the source of all life and the tomb into which all things were laid at death. The snake usually lives within the earth, inside the body of the mother, and was considered to be aware of all her secrets. The coiled serpent represented her vagina.

All the waters of the earth came from the womb of the earth goddess. Water is one of the basic necessities of life, and its sources were usually treated as shrines. Snakes were depicted with deities of healing springs and wells, such as Brighid. Because the snake sheds its skin each year and appears renewed, it was thought to be immortal, and the epitome of healing and renewal. Its movements are sinuous and wave-like, like the course of a river. A river goddess called Verbeia, the spirit of the River Wharfe, was worshipped at Ilkley, in northern England, represented by a woman grasping two snakes, which fall in zigzag lines from her hands.

In several stories, a monster snake appears as a trail that must be overcome by heroes such as Cuchulain, Fionn and Conall Cernach. It was a symbol of the underworld, depicted on the Jupiter Columns of Gaul as a representative of the chthonic forces (winter, darkness, death) at war with

THE PATH OF THE SHAMAN

the solar powers (summer, light, birth). This may be the origin of later dragon slaying myths such as that of St. George, though in earlier stories, the dragon would rise again every year, with the powers of winter and summer ruling in turn. A ram-horned serpent was shown in conjunction with Cernunnos, the horned god, a symbol of chthonic and solar powers combined. Ram horned snakes also accompanied the Celtic Mars, a god of healing who combated barrenness and disease.

The snake was a powerful guardian spirit and was encouraged in temples and homes to keep down vermin, and often kept as a pet. The theme of the guardian serpent appears in Celtic legends such as the tale of Conal Cernach, who had a serpent coiled around his waist which helped him in battle.

The snake has long been associated with sagacity, cunning and divination. It was commonly thought that having your ears licked clean by a serpent would enable you to receive oracular wisdom. The Druids were known in Wales as *Nadredd* or adders.[123] Taliesin declared "*I am a wiseman, I am a serpent*". When St. Patrick boasted that he had driven all of the snakes out of Ireland, he meant the Druids. We know that the Druids used amulets called *gloine nathair* ('serpent glass') for healing and divination. These may have been adder stones (holed stones) or blown glass, though it was claimed that they were formed by snakes in a process described by the Roman naturalist Pliny. He said that in the summer, countless snakes entwined themselves into a ball, held together by spittle and a bodily secretion. The resulting ball was thrown up into the air by the snakes, and must then be caught on a cloak, so that it should not touch the ground, if it were to remain effective.

Because it sheds its skin and emerges renewed, Snake is as a symbol of life, death and rebirth into a new consciousness. Yogic principles tell us that the *kundalini* is the serpent fire that lies coiled within the root chakra at the base of the spine. The awakening of the *kundalini* snake, through careful practice and preparation, causes it to rise through the chakras, bringing with it enlightenment. The forced awakening of the *kundalini* in one who is not ready is extremely dangerous. Snake magic should be treated with care: its power concerns the deepest mysteries of life.

A snake with its tail in its own mouth represents the circle of eternity and the oneness of the universe. This tells us that all aspects of life and creation stand equally, even those things viewed as unpleasant and poisonous. If they are accepted as part of the whole, within the Dance of Life, they can be assimilated and transmuted to positive benefits. Initiation rites

THE PATH OF THE SHAMAN

around the world have often included being bitten by poisonous snakes or ingesting 'snake' plants. The candidate was expected to survive by transmuting the poison into a learning experience. Those things which are 'poisonous', frightening and unpleasant, whether mental, physical or spiritual can be assimilated and transformed if one has the proper approach and mental attitude: acceptance with focused Will.

Spider

The spider is the archetypal spinner and weaver, its web representing the pattern of life itself. It was associated with all spinning and weaving goddesses, those twisters of fate who spin the thread of human destiny, as well as the world, the stars, the Cosmos and the web of energies that joins it all together. Such weaver goddesses were believed to have absolute sway over human destiny, and neither prayers nor pleas would move them; even the gods could not alter the decrees of the Fates. They were usually depicted as a triad with one who span the strand of life, one that measured its length, and one who cut the thread, the death goddess 'she who cannot be stayed'.

Sometimes the weaver was a solitary creatrix, as in Welsh legend, where she appeared as Arianrhod ('Silver Wheel'), the mistress of Caer Arianrhod, the Spiral Castle which is located in the circumpolar stars that circle the Pole Star. The castle reflects the spiralling skein spun from her wheel, which is the revolution of the stars. Like other such goddesses, she has aspects as a goddess of death and the Otherworld. Souls resided in her castle between incarnations, while poets and shamans, seeking inspiration, journeyed there in spirit.

The spiral shape, which is the basis of the spider's web, is an ancient and almost universal symbol of the spiral maze of life, which travels inwards towards death and the centre where death (or initiation) takes place, then outwards again in rebirth. Arianrhod is comparable with the Greek Ariadne, who led Theseus out of the underworld maze of the Minotaur by means of a thread.

A number of Celtic gods were depicted with wheels, and wheels decorated altars and tombstones. They represented the cycle of life, and the turning of the year. Spiders have eight legs representing the eight solar festivals, the four winds, the four directions and the symbol of infinity.

Because the spider is associated with powerful goddesses, it is unlucky to kill one. It preys on flies, symbol of corruption, evil and disease: *If you wish to live and thrive, let the spider run alive.* The golden money spider (signifying a gold coin) confers riches to anyone it runs over. It is considered

147

very lucky if a spider drops from a ceiling onto your face. The spider is the model of industry and perseverance. In 1305, Robert the Bruce was inspired by the persistence of a spider that tried six times to spin its web before it eventually succeeded on the seventh attempt. He took this as an omen, and went out to rebuild his forces, eventually making himself virtual master of Scotland.

The spider was believed to contain a health giving stone, like the toad. Mediaeval cures for gout, ague and whooping cough sometimes included spiders and webs. The seventeenth century antiquarian Elias Ashmole claimed to have cured his ague by hanging three spiders round his neck. Spider's webs were used to staunch wounds and cure warts.

Spider patiently spins her web with the skill of a craftsman, sometimes trying repeatedly until she has it right. She is the mistress of weaving, taking disparate stands and integrating them into a single design. She reminds you that with every action, you are weaving the shape of your life. Look carefully, and you will discern its pattern.

Spider is concerned with the twisting of fate, the turning of the wheel of fortune, and cycles of change. But don't misunderstand the word fate. Nothing happens in isolation, but is connected to events that came before, and to events that will follow. You may be an individual, but you are nevertheless connected with the planet on which you live and the other life upon it through the Weaver Goddess's web of power. Your every action vibrates the web, affecting all that lies along the connecting thread. Through the web, every action will eventually return to you amplified, for good or ill. In other words, you construct your own fate, and are the instrument of your own justice.

Stag

The red deer and roebuck are indigenous to Britain, while fallow deer were introduced by the Romans. The stag was one of the most sacred animals of the Celts and has played an important part in the religion of many parts of the world. The earliest representations of the stag god- or of the shaman wearing stag horns- date from round 12000 BCE, the most famous being the 'sorcerer' of Les Trois Freres. Stags appear on Old Stone Age paintings and carvings. Antlers have been found buried at Newgrange, Glastonbury, Stonehenge and a set discovered at Star Carr, Pickering, Yorkshire were adapted for use as headgear.

The Celts considered all horned beasts to be sacred, counting the horns as powerful emblems of fertility. On a practical level, antlers were amongst the earliest tools used to till the soil, while powdered stag antlers are among the best fertilisers known. On a symbolic level, they represent the potency and strength of the male animal. The aggressive clashes of the stags during the rutting season were much admired by Celtic warriors. Horns were placed on helmets to signify such might, and all sorts of creatures were depicted with horns to imbue them with vigour, including those that did not possess them naturally, such as birds.

Unlike that other influential horned symbol, the bull, stags shed their antlers each year, just as deciduous trees shed their leaves. The stag is a solar animal, with its antlers sometimes shown curving like the rays of the sun. The growth of the antlers represents the sun's increase in summer and the shedding the loss of the sun's 'virility' in the winter. This made the stag a symbol of passing of the seasons, reflected in the life cycle of the stag. They clean their new antlers in August and September, rubbing off the velvety coating on the branches of trees. The rutting season begins from then on, often going on into November, driven to greater ferocity by the frosts. Then, in the early summer at Beltane, the roebuck acquires his new red coloured coat.

King Arthur's knights took part in a yearly hunt of the white stag, and its head would be presented to the fairest lady in the land. This may be a seasonal tale in which the white solar beast is killed. It was once thought that the 'King Stag', the leader of the herd, should be ritually hunted and killed every year to ensure the return of summer. The king or royal stag was a beast with twelve or fourteen points on his horns (a stag would have to have to be seven years old to have twelve points). In Celtic myth, the stag or hind often symbolises the soul, usually the soul of a king or hero. As the stag was considered to be a royal beast, its hunting was often the preserve of the nobles, perhaps originally only the priest-king. In mediaeval times, it was death for anyone but the king to hunt deer.

King Arthur seems to have had several dealings with magical stags. In one Irish story, Arthur and his knights were beguiled into the Otherworld by a deer-woman called Ailleann. She persuaded Arthur's men to take fairy wives, and married Arthur herself. This legend may be derived from an even older tale where Arthur marries the lady who represents the sovereignty of the land, and becomes the stag king.[124] The stag was identified with the sacred king, whose sacrifice was necessary: it is the fate of the antlered king to be hunted and betrayed, it is this that gives the cuckold his horns. Guinevere betrayed Arthur and this led to his death.

Stags, especially white ones, frequently appear as spirit animals that entice heroes to the Otherworld. Pwyll, Prince of Dyfed, was out hunting one day when he chanced to meet Arawn, the Lord of the

THE PATH OF THE SHAMAN

underworld, who was hunting a stag. He failed to give way, which was a breach of hunting etiquette. He apologised and offered to make amends. Arawn agreed that he should swap places with him for a year, and at the end of it fight his enemy Hafgan ('Summer') for him. So Pwyll ruled the underworld for a year. The tale is plainly one of the solar forces of summer in yearly conflict with the chthonic forces of winter. The stag Arawn was hunting was Pwyll's soul.

The stag is inextricably linked with gods and goddesses of the hunt. A sculpture from the sanctuary of Le Donon in the Vosges shows a god who is both hunter and protector of the forest and its creatures. He stands, carrying pine cones, nuts and acorns in an open bag under his arm. He wears a wolf pelt cloak, boots ornamented with animal heads, and carries a hunting knife, axe and spear. He rests his hand on the antlers of his companion, a stag. Other hunter gods have the same ambivalent position in relation to their prey. A figure usually taken to be Cernunnos is portrayed on the Gundestrup cauldron, dating from 300 BCE, as a seated figure with antlers growing from his head. He holds a snake in one hand and a torc in the other, showing that he is a god of winter and summer, sky and underworld, death and resurrection. He is surrounded by the animals of the forest. A secondary illustration shows him as Lord of the Animals, holding aloft a stag in either hand. Cernunnos was an intermediary between the animal kingdom and man, a guardian of the gateway to the Otherworld. The stag god is at the same time the divine huntsman, the Lord of the Animals, and the god of the dead and keeper of souls.

Remnants of the ancient stag cult may be discerned in the legend of Herne the Hunter, possibly a British stag god equivalent to the Gaulish Cernunnos. Herne the Hunter haunts Windsor Great Park and rides out with the Wild Hunt at the midwinter solstice. He is described as a mighty, bearded figure with a huge pair of stag horns on his head. He wears chains, carries a hunting horn and rides out on a black horse with a pack of ferocious hunting hounds.

According to the Mabinogion story of the hunt for the child of light, Mabon, Arthur's messengers sought the help of the five oldest animals, which included the stag of Rhedynfre. Though he couldn't tell them where to find the young god, he advised them to ask the Owl of Cwm Cawlwyd, who was older than him. The owl directed them to an older creature still, and so the story went on, until eventually the Mabon was located.

Stag was one of the chief sacred animals of the ancient Celts. Its life cycle reflected the changes of the seasons, the fertility of the earth and the forest, symbolised by the yearly growth and shedding of the stag's antlers. He was one of the oldest animals, and possessed all the ancient knowledge of the earth itself.

In many an old tale, the mysterious white hart appears to the hero, challenging him to hunt it through the forest. The stag turns out to be his own soul, and the hunt a necessary lesson. The hunt is for the true self. He reminds you that the spiritual world overlays the material, interwoven with it as symbolised by the interweaving strands of the Celtic knot.

Choosing to follow the hart means action as opposed to inaction, change as opposed to maintaining the *status quo*, change and growth as opposed to stagnation and decline, choosing between self determination and living according to the expectations of others, between the spiritual and the material, and between the needs of the soul and the urgings of the world.

Swan

The swan was believed to be the king of water birds, and the only other bird the eagle thought it worthwhile to fight. Its sacredness is apparent in the taboo that is laid on killing it from Ireland to Siberia; to do so would result in great misfortune or even death.

In Celtic myth, the swan was associated with the dawn, the sun and water. It was the companion of gods and goddesses that combine the twin healing powers of sun and water, such as the goddess Brighid. Swans were often depicted with solar discs suspended from their necks, or linked together by gold or silver chains. The latter generally indicates a human being under an enchantment, living in the guise of a swan. Kings, princes, knights and maidens are the subjects of such transformations in Celtic tales.

One tale concerns Angus, the son of the Dagda, who fell in love with the swan maiden Cáer Ibormeith ('Yew Berry'), who appeared to him in a dream. He asked her parents for her hand in marriage, but they told him their daughter chose to live as a swan on alternate years, so they couldn't grant his request. At Samhain, she went to Lough Bel Dracon with one hundred and fifty other swan maidens, linked by silver chains. To win her, Aengus would have to go to the lough and pick her out from the other swans. Accordingly, the young god went to the lake, and called to her. In the end, he had to jump into the water and become a swan himself before she would go to him. Together they flew three times around the lough, singing sweetly, casting a spell that put everyone in the vicinity to sleep for three days and three nights. It is interesting to note that Caer's transformation was her own choice, and that it was Angus who had to transform himself to be with

her. Her name ('Yew Berry') may give us some clues as to her nature, since the yew is the death tree that stands in the graveyard, symbolising eternal life. They met at Samhain, the death time of the year.

The children of the sea god Lir were changed into swans by their jealous stepmother and had to spend nine hundred years in swan form, three hundred years at each of three places in Ireland. They could only become human when a prince from the north married a princess from the south and a church bell was rung in Ireland (an 'improvement' to the tale added by the Christian recorders). These things happened and St. Patrick's bell was rung. The children were restored, but were nine hundred years old and immediately died of old age.

Swans appear as guides to the dead, taking them to the Far Northern Otherworld, through the swan-veils. The Nordic Valkyries were such creatures, who could discard swan plumage to become human.

It was once believed that the mute swan sings only once, just before it dies, hence the phrase 'swan song', meaning a person's final work. Socrates and Plato both spoke of the belief that a swan only sings once, when it is dying. Its song was associated with prophecy (knowing its own death) and with Apollo, god of music, whose soul became a swan. Apollo's lye had a swan's neck, head, feet and feathers carved upon it. The singer Orpheus is also said to have become a swan after his death. Swans are very much associated with the bardic mysteries; swan skin and feathers were used to make the cloak of a Celtic shaman-poet. Celtic bards carried chains which

THE PATH OF THE SHAMAN

they shook for silence, and this may be the origin of the swan wearing a chain. In some stories, the song of a swan held magical properties that could make mortals sleep; it in this context that it became the bird of solitude and retreat.. The swan became the bird of poets, and Shakespeare is referred to as 'the swan of Avon'. Swan is the muse that inspires great poetry and music, one of her gifts is eloquence; an enchanting way with words that inspires others. She is the patron of bards, singers, musicians, writers and poets.

Swans are linked to thunder gods and folklore has it that swan's eggs will only hatch in a thunderstorm, requiring the lightning to strike the shell. It is said that if a swan stretches its head and neck over its wings in the day a thunderstorm is brewing. Swans pull the barque of the sun across the underworld Sea at night. Apollo's chariot was pulled by swans when he journeyed to the land of the Hyperboreans, the people who lived behind the North Wind, the country of his birth, identified with Britain.

The mist was poetically called 'the swan veil' and at certain times, passing through the swan veil could grant you entrance into the Otherworld. Part of Swan's magic is concerned with crossings boundaries.

In the Celtic tradition, Swan symbolises the eternal realm of spirit. She is the revealer of sacred things, a link to the world of the gods, a guide to the Otherworld. She may appear as a spiritual advisor or teacher, or may be the voice of your Higher Self, calling upon you to surrender to guidance by higher forces

Wolf

In Britain, wolves were once very numerous and people feared for their safety when travelling across the country. The wild forests of Scotland were said to be impassable because of wolves. The last wolf in Britain was killed by the deer hunter MacQueen in 1743.

Throughout the world, the wolf is regarded with awe and as the embodiment of all that is wild, associated with sorcery, ferocity and the night. In France, the twilight hour is described as being 'between the dog and the wolf'.[125] The wolf also symbolises death and the underworld. Hades, the ruler of the underworld in Greek myth, wore a wolf headdresss.

The wolf is a skilled hunter, and appears as the companion of several gods and goddesses of the hunt, such as the stag-horned god who is shown on the Gundestrup cauldron accompanied by a wolf. He was both the protector of the herds and the destroyer who culled them in due season. Hunting deities always have this duel role as protector and killer; he or she nurtures the herd, but kills when necessary to feed to the tribe.

THE PATH OF THE SHAMAN

Wolves have the reputation of being bloodthirsty killers. The Celts crossed their domestic dogs with wolves to produce a fierce fighting animal used in battle. Many warriors took 'wolf' as part of their names to denote ferocity, as did some Scottish clans like MacLennan ('Son of the Wolf') and MacMillan ('Son of the Wolf Servant'). The wolf was sacred to the Gaulish war god Esus (equated with Mars or Silvanus), and the Irish battle goddess the Morrigan, who assumed both wolf and raven forms. Wolves and ravens range the battlefields in search of carrion; during war it was said that whoever lost the battle the wolf always won, feeding on the bodies of the dead.

In actual fact, wolf packs are very loyal and care for their weakest members. When the hunters return from the kill, the first meat is offered to nursing mothers. Wolf mothers are supposed to be particularly kindly and nurturing, even adopting abandoned human babies. The Roman legend of Romulus and Remus is well known, but such stories also appear in Celtic myth. King Cormac of Ireland was suckled by a wolf. When he later became king, he retained his wolf companions, and was known as the 'Irish Solomon', the owner of a magic cup which shattered when three lies were told, and mended when three truths were spoken.

In February, the Romans held an early spring festival called the Lupercalia, dedicated to the she-wolf that suckled Romulus and Remus. The celebration bore a marked similarity to the Celtic February festival of Imbolc, which marked the early stirrings of spring, and sacred to the goddess Brighid who had a wolf companion. In Celtic lore the wolf ruled over the winter quarter from Samhain to Imbolc. February was called *Faoilleach* which means 'the wolf month' or 'the storm month'. January, in the Anglo-Saxon Chronicle, was called the *Wul-manoth* ('wolf month').

The days around the winter solstice, the time when the sun was at its weakest and its rebirth uncertain, were thought to be a time of chaos, when the forces of disorder, winter and blight threatened to overwhelm the world. They were particularly associated with ravening wolves, representative of the primeval wildness that came before order emerged. In Poland an excitable drunk was said to be like one 'who runs round at Christmas in a wolfskin'. [126]

Legends of werewolves were known in the ancient world. *Wer* simply means 'man' and there have also been stories of were-hares, were-foxes, were-cats and so on- all common shape changing forms of the witch or shaman, and it may be the legends are related to the shamanic journey.

The French historian I. Simon Goulart (1607) said that when Christmas day is past, a lame boy goes into the countryside and calls the Devil's slaves together in great numbers, and a great man comes holding a

THE PATH OF THE SHAMAN

whip made of iron chains and they are changed into wolves.[127] Reginald Scott (*Discoverie of Witchcraft* 1584) wrote that every year, at the end of December, a knave summons witches to a certain place and leads them though a pool of water, when they change into wolves. To change back, they have to go back through the water. [128] Presumably the water they travel though is that of the underworld river, mentioned in shamanic lore as the boundary between the worlds.

In seventeenth century Livonia certain men and women changed into werewolves on St Lucy's Eve (13th December), the Twelve Nights of Christmas and Midsummer Night. They would travel to the swamps of Malpils in Latvia, the entrance to the underworld where Devils and evil sorcerers took the fertility of barley, oats and rye which they stole from the upper world, and feasted on them in the lower world. The werewolves had iron whips and battled the evil sorcerers who fought with broomsticks hung with horsetails, fighting for the fertility of the grain harvest.

An elderly werewolf, questioned in 1692 in Jurgensburg, said that at the time of the seeds forming, sorcerers take away the blessings to hell. The werewolves would rescue it and bring it back again. They were called 'The Dogs of God.'[129] In the Baltic, the *Miezvilki* ('Barley Wolves') chased away Devils and brought abundance to the land. There was a procession led by the Barley Wolf Father and the Barley Wolf Mother, possibly representing the god and goddess of the cult.[130]

The early chronicler Giraldus Cambrensis reported that all Irishmen could change into wolves. Merlin changed Uther Pendragon into wolfform to visit Ygrainne the wife of Gorlois ('Wolf'). An old Irish tale tells of triplet sisters who became wolves and terrorised the countryside. Caoilte of the Fianna asked the fairy harper Cascarach to help him destroy them. He began to play some lovely music, and one by one, the three wolves sat at his feet. He advised them that they would better appreciate it they were in human form, so the three girls dropped their wolf skins to the floor. As they became human, Caoilte struck them with a spear in such a manner that it pierced all three hearts.

The Brotherhood of the Green Wolf held rites on Midsummer's Eve at Jumiege in Normandy. Every year a new leader, or Green Wolf, was chosen and dressed in a green robe and tall pointed hat. He led a procession from the village of Conihaut to a church at Chouquet where a mass was held. Everyone retraced their steps to the Green Wolf's house for a party, with dancing to the music of hand bells, and circle dancing a round a bonfire, miming the chase of the Green Wolf, pretending to throw him into the fire three times. A dignified feast followed, but at the stroke of midnight, lewd

155

songs were sung and fiddles played for the orgiastic revelries for the rest of the night.

Just as they are associated with the end of the year ay Yule, wolves are linked to the coming of the end of the world, when there will be a period of chaos, a 'wolf-age'. In Norse myth the Fenris wolf will overwhelm the established order at Ragnorok. Meanwhile, the wolves Skoll and Hati chase the sun and moon each day. They were born of the Etin-wife in the forest of Ironwood. She bred many sons in wolf shape, and from these ordinary wolves are descended. From this clan will come Moongarm who will fill himself with the lifeblood of all that die and he will swallow the heavenly bodies and scatter the skies with blood.

Ceridwen, the Welsh dark goddess of wisdom and inspiration, gave birth to a wolf cub called Rhiwgyverthwch when she was on her way to Anglesey in the guise of Henwen, the white sow. Ceridwen owned the magical cauldron in which all the wisdom of the world was brewed, with three drops of inspiration destined for humankind, an image that brings to mind the story of Cormac's enchanted cup.[131] A Druid rite to induce inspirational dreams included sleeping on a wolf skin. The Druid Bobaran once met the white wolf Emhain Abhlac. He threw three rowan berries into the air, three at the wolf, and three into his own mouth to receive the insight of the wolf.

Chapter 7
PLANT ALLIES

Herbs have been used since the dawn of time for healing ailments of the body, for magic, and for altering consciousness. Shamans understood that there was a way of maintaining the natural balance, a way of harvesting, of keeping the life force of the plants. Plants are linked to the living Earth from which they spring, and the plant itself is always the teacher. Witches and shamans both use plant powers, but to capture them without alienating or dissipating them is not simple a matter of walking three times around a tree and saying 'can I have a branch' and leaving a coin in return. Trees and herbs are not really 'used' magically. When properly approached they may share something of their life force, their spirit. Individual herbs and plants can be befriended as allies to enable the practitioner to travel to Otherworldly places, and to become in tune with different energies.

Sometimes a plant or tree will call to you, and you should listen and trust your instincts. Every plant has a meaning, a place within the great pattern. Accept any insight which is given to you, no matter what the circumstances. If the herb is approached with love and trust, its force will harmonise with the witch and share its secrets. If the plant is taken with the wrong motives, if it is mistreated or misused, it may cause discomfort, mislead or seek to gain control of the witch. If an enemy is made of the plant spirit, it can destroy:

"When we partake of a plant, we absorb its physical constituents, its substances. But we take into our bodies more than its material elements...in addition to the physical substances of the plant we also absorb its life forces, the particular qualities of strength and tenacity with which it confronted and mastered life...We can clearly see that a plant has a life of its won, a life very different from ours. If we take a large quantity of this alien into ourselves while we are well, it may act as a poison and overpower us with fatal consequences.'"[32]

It is a common misconception that a plant needs to have hallucinogenic properties to facilitate expansion of consciousness. Only a small number of power plants are psychedelic, and these plant spirits are the most difficult to deal with and easily overcome the weak will of anyone who uses them for recreational purposes. Every plant, from the common daisy to the mighty oak, has its own power and vibration, and by taking time to gain the trust of the plant spirit, these can be shared.

When working in conjunction with herbs and plant allies, the life force - or spirit - of the plant is more important than any 'active ingredient';

you must begin by getting to know the plants that grow in your local area, those vegetation spirits that live with you, along your local hedgerow, meadow, park, road or in your garden. Get a good field guide to help you identify them and a reputable modern herbal to tell you what they may be used for. You will need to refer to the botanical name (usually Latin or Greek) since these names are specific, while the same common name can refer to several very different plants.

Spend time with the plants, noting where they live, in sun or shade, on chalky soil or sandy soil and so on, their growth habits, when they flower, and when they set their seeds. Note the shape of the leaves, their texture and colour, their taste, if edible. In this way you will begin to learn from the plants themselves. Each plant is a living teacher and must be approached as an individual spirit, a vital life force which may become your ally if approached with love and respect. It is a knowledge that cannot be bought, and which cannot be learned from books, but only by doing. Allow yourself to trust your inner wisdom.

Each plant must be correctly approached and harvested in perfect condition. It must always be respected as a living being: its *life force* is the essence of its power.

Enteogens

The use of entheogenic (hallucinogenic) substances is central to a minority of shamanic traditions. The term entheogen was invented by Gordon Wasson, and means 'god containing' because these substances had the ability to allow people to unite the god-consciousness. The Aztecs of pre-Columbian Mexico revered psilocybin mushrooms so much that they named them *Teonanacatl*, meaning 'flesh of the gods' or 'divine flesh'. In Mexico and Guatemala, between 1000 and 500 BCE, people built temples to mushroom gods and carved mushroom stones. It is likely that at least some of the religions that speak of eating the flesh of the god mean the use of sacred plants.

Many early religions included the use of entheogenic plants as sacraments (i.e. Holy Communion with the gods), to evoke visions, or for divination and healing. Initiation to the Eleusinian Mysteries of ancient Greece probably involved the use of psilocybin mushrooms. Gilgamesh, the hero of an ancient Sumerian epic, went on a quest for a miraculous herb, which he eventually discovered only to have it taken from him by its guardian, the serpent. This may have influenced the Bible story which is told with a different slant- it is the serpent that actually offers the fruit of knowledge to Eve.[133] This 'forbidden fruit' may have been an

THE PATH OF THE SHAMAN

entheogen which opened the mind to the god-state. Eating the fruit of the tree of life (the World Tree) unites man with the gods- eating it is forbidden in the Bible.

The Peruvian *mestizo* shamans use *ayahuasca* as a sacrament. In the Amazon, the ayahuasceros regard the giant serpent as the "mother spirit" of all the other spirits of the forest, of the river and the air. [134] In legend, ayahuasca was created when the great grandmother Cosmos Yewa Velo (the great maloca of quartz was formed. The great ancestral shaman, made of smoke of tobacco, and during in his encounter with the ancestral shaman of quartz, made the sacred ayahuasca plant, which is the umbilical cord of the Cosmos.

Traditional shamanic rituals involving hallucinogenic plants are carefully structured experiences, in which a small group of people come together with a respectful, spiritual attitude to share a profound inner journey of healing and transformation, facilitated by these allies, usually accompanied by music, drumming and chanting. The mushroom ceremonies of the Mazatec Indians of Mexico involve the participants sitting or lying in a very dark room, with only a small candle. The healer sings almost uninterruptedly throughout the night, weaving into her chants the names of Christian saints, her spirit allies and the spirits of the earth, the elements, animals and plants, the sky, the waters and the fire.[135]

GUIDE TO PLANTS

Aconite *Aconite sp.*
Aconite was originally native to Europe, Asia and North America, thriving in windy mountainous regions and moist pastures. Aconite can be found growing wild in damp or shady places such as alder groves, and along stream courses, ditches or in highland meadows.

Aconite is a fatal poison, often causing death within a few minutes. In Anglo-Saxon it was called *thung*, which simply means a poisonous plant. The plant is also called 'wolfsbane' as it is said to have been used to poison spears and arrows employed in killing wolves.

The plant's reputation is a dark one, associated with death, black magic and the underworld. Hecate, the Greek witch goddess, is said to have created aconite from the deadly spittle scattered by Cerberus, the three-headed dog who was the guardian of the underworld, when Herakles dragged him out of Tartarus and fought with him on the hill Aconitus in Pontica. Aconite was said to grow at Heracli in Anatolia, which was one of the gateways to the underworld. It was poured as a libation to the ghosts of

THE PATH OF THE SHAMAN

the men who were sacrificed when the foundations of buildings were laid. It was used in funeral incenses, planted on graves and used for both suicide and euthanasia.

Aconite was known as a witches' plant and it was believed that it was used to poison the tips of elf bolts, the darts that witches and fairies threw at their victims. In ancient times the Thessalian witches used it in the manufacture of a flying ointment; used to anoint the skin it would cause hallucinations, visions and the sensation of flying. It appears as an ingredient in mediaeval flying ointment recipes. However, the dose of aconite needed to achieve hallucinations falls within the lethal range, and unless the practitioner was very skilled, death would probably be the result, and the trip one to the underworld one way.

NB: The deadly poison aconitine is present in all parts of the plant. The poison at first stimulates, causes a burning sensation on the tongue, vomiting, stomach pains and diarrhoea then paralyses the central and peripheral nervous system and finally death.

Alder *Alnus sp.*

The alder species consists of about thirty shrubs and small trees. They prefer moist soil and are found mainly on the banks of rivers, ponds and brooks, sometimes growing to well over ninety feet.

The common name of alder may be derived from the old German word *elawer* which means "reddish" as when the tree is cut the wood is at first white then appears to bleed crimson, like wounded flesh.

The British alder god Bran ("Raven") was the guardian of all Britain. After being fatally wounded in a battle, he instructed his companions to cut off his head and carry it to the White Mount in London and bury it there, facing France. He also made prophecies as to what would happen on the journey. The journey took eighty seven years, because of adventures that happened along the way, and all the time the head continued to speak. Eventually they came to the White Mount where the head was buried and continues to guard Britain against invasion; this is the present site of the Tower of London. The presence of ravens, Bran's totem birds, at the Tower confirms its association with the god. It is still said that as long as the ravens remain at the Tower then Britain is safe from invasion; if they should ever leave disaster will follow.

In laying himself across the river, so that his army might cross on his body, Bran became a bridge, referring to the use of alder pilings to make the footings for a bridge. The singing head of Bran refers to the topmost branch of the alder, called "the head", which was used to make magical flutes and whistles, through which the god was thought to speak- one of the old names for the alder is 'whistlewood'. The topmost branches of the alder move when the wind blows and the leaves rustle more musically than any other tree – the tree seems to sing. This makes the alder a bridge of another kind – the one between the worlds.

The alder is associated with another "singing head", that of Orpheus in Greek mythology. His story has many shamanic themes, including a journey to the underworld, death and dismemberment, prophecy and the use of music to enchant. His name is derived from *orphruoeis* which means 'on the river bank' i.e. the alder tree. Orpheus (the son of Apollo, the sun god, and the muse Calliope) could charm both men and beasts with his music.

His wife Eurydice trod on a venomous snake and died. Orpheus determined to seek her in the underworld and descended there to plead with Hades and Persephone, its rulers, for her release. The ghosts and even the tortured spirits of Tartarus stopped to listen to his beautiful, pleading music, and the two gods could not resist. They agreed that Eurydice should be returned to life on condition that Orpheus did not turn around to look at her until they were both out of the underworld. Orpheus journeyed upwards, but on reaching the sunlight and forgetting the injunction, turned around to make sure his wife was following. Seeing her in the shadows he reached out to embrace her, but alas, she was snatched away from him, back to the land of the dead.

The bereft Orpheus wandered the earth in misery and refused to give worship to Dionysus, the wild and joyful god of wine. Dionysus angrily sent his followers, the maddened Maenads, to tear Orpheus limb from limb. His head was laid to rest in a cave by the Muses, where it continued to prophesy day and night, until Apollo himself ordered it to be silent.

Angelica

Angelica (*Angelica sylvestris/ Angelica archangelica*) is universally known by its botanical name which is derived from the Greek *angelos* which means 'a messenger'.

Angelica has been known since ancient times and has at one time or another been credited with the ability to cure almost anything. It was frequently used as a remedy against all enchantments and evil potions, and was added to the bath water to remove curses or spells against an individual. The powdered root was sprinkled around the home to ward off evil. It is said to be a protection against all evil, and offer protection against evil spirits, apparitions, witches, Devils etc.

THE PATH OF THE SHAMAN

Angelica is closely associated with the Annunciation and with St. Michael who is said to have revealed the curative properties of angelica to a monk during the plague. Lore has it that angelica blooms on St. Michael's day, May 8th.

Angelica is a powerful purification herb, with its energy of the sun and the cleansing power of fire. As such it may be used to purify the person, sacred and personal space and in the fumigation on those rare occasions when exorcism may be necessary.

It is a plant of inspiration, the message imparted to the consciousness by higher powers. Shamanically, the leaves of angelica can be smoked to increase the ability to see into other realms. Angelica tea or incense may be used to communicate with the spirits of the Upperworld.

Apple *Malus sylvestris* (Crab Apple)/ *Pyrus malus* (Cultivated Apple)
The apple was a sacred plant in many parts of the world, associated with the World Tree and passage to the Otherworld. In European myth, the entrance to the Otherworld is often said to lie in the far west, the place of the setting sun.

In Baltic lore the sun goddess Saule rides across the sky in a chariot with copper wheels. At twilight she stops and washes her horses in the sea, then drives to her apple orchard in the west. The setting sun is a red apple that falls from the orchard. She rests there in an apple tree or iron post to which two horses (the means of journeying to the Otherworld) are tethered.

In Greek myth, the Hesperides were three maidens who lived in the western paradise where the golden Apples of Immortality grew. Aegle which means 'brightness'; Erythraea meaning 'the red one' and Hespera meaning 'evening light.'

Legendary isles of apples are common, and always lie in the west, the place of the dying sun, from which it proceeds to enter the underworld, or Land of Youth, travelling through the realms of death in preparation for its rebirth. The Sacred King or shaman was promised the same journey. In the story of King Arthur, after he is mortally wounded, he is taken on a magic barge to the Isle of Avalon, which means 'Isle of Apples', from the Welsh *afal* meaning 'apple'. Morgan (of the sea) is associated with Avalon as the goddess who guards the apple orchard of the Otherworld.

For the Celts, the afterlife was lived in a permanent summer, a land of the ever young, an apple orchard where the trees were always in fruit. The Elysian Fields of the ancient Greeks, the place of the afterlife,

THE PATH OF THE SHAMAN

also translates as 'apple orchards'. Elysium was ruled over by Cronus, its entrance close to the pool of memory, a happy land of perpetual day and the inhabitants may choose to be reborn on earth wherever they chose.

From its association with the underworld, the apple is seen as a passport to it, or symbol of it. The Greeks believed that carrying an apple bough that bore flowers, buds and fruit at the same time would enable them to enter the underworld. Bran, in Celtic myth, was summoned by the Goddess to enter the Land of Youth with a 'silver white blossomed branch from Emain, in which the bloom and branch were one'.

In the poem of *Thomas the Rhymer*, apple stands at the centre of the underworld as the tree of transformation. He does not pick the apple for himself, which would invoke the guardian, but for the queen of Elfland, a sacrifice which transforms himself and the queen. She tells him not to eat the fruit in its raw state as it is poison but transforms it to bread and wine.

The sacred apple tree of immortality was often protected by a serpent or dragon. In Greek myth the tree of the Hesperides, sheltered in the garden of paradise, was protected by the serpent Ladon. Hercules slew the serpent and stole the apples but they were later returned by Athene. In Judaic legend, the garden of Paradise had two trees, the Tree of Life and the Tree of Knowledge. Eve, the first woman was tempted by the serpent to eat the fruit of the Tree of Knowledge, and she in turn persuaded Adam to do the same. As they did they learned the nature of good and evil in the world.

The Celts accounted the rowan berry, red apple and red nut as food of the gods. There may have been a taboo against eating them, or perhaps they were reserved for the priesthood. The apple is the tree of transformation. It marks the gateway of transition from outward to inner consciousness. By eating the fruit, the gifts of the underworld are received, and understanding is purified through hardship. The underworld powers are brought through the body, attuned to the Cosmos and expressed in the world.

Ash *Fraxinus sp.*
Above all trees, the ash and the oak attract lightening. The ancients saw the lightening strike as the fertilising power of the sky god, darting from the heavens to be transmitted to the belly of Mother Earth through the agency of the tree, standing with its roots in the damp earth. The word 'ash'

THE PATH OF THE SHAMAN

derives from the Icelandic *aske* which means 'great fire blaze', while the botanical name *Fraxinus* means 'great fire-light'.

As the ash could channel lightening from the upper to the lower world it was viewed as a World Tree, symbolically linking all the realms of existence. The sacred pole of the Omaha is partly made of ash and partly of cottonwood, both sacred trees.

According to Norse mythology the chief god Odin created Yggdrasil, a massive ash tree which linked all the worlds of creation, stretching from the underworld, through Earth to Heaven. It had three roots in the primal source of being: one in Nifl-heim (the underworld or the cold north); one in Midgard (the Earth), home of mankind, and the third root in Asgard, the home of the gods, near the Urdar fountain. Yggdrasil's branches towered over all the other worlds and reached up into the heavens where its leaves were the clouds and its fruit the stars. The topmost bough was called Lerad which means 'the peace giver'. On it perched an eagle and between his eyes sat Vedfolnir, the falcon, looking down towards the earth , the underworld, and the heavens, reporting all that he saw to Odin.

The leaves of Yggdrasil never withered and were the food of Odin's goat, Heidrun, which supplied the mead the gods drank. They also sustained the four stags, Dain, Dvalin, Duneyr and Durathor, whose horns dripped honeydew upon the earth, which furnished the water for all the rivers of the world. The squirrel, Ratatosk,('branch borer') ran up and down the tree, gossiping about everything it saw and heard to both the dragon at the roots and to the eagle above.

At the Nifl-heim root the serpent or dragon Nidhug lived, continually gnawing at the root, aided by many worms, with the aim of killing the tree as its death would herald the end of the gods.

Legend tells us that Odin hung from the World Tree for nine days and nights to gain the secrets of the magical alphabet, the runes, which he was given in return for one of his eyes. The loss of the eye is significant from the viewpoint of the seer or shaman, who is often described as closing one eye to look into the inner world, while the open eye looks out on the everyday one. As might be expected, the ash figures heavily in the symbolism of the runic alphabet. In the Northumbrian system the thirty third rune *Gar* represents Yggdrasil itself, standing still at the centre, the beginning and the end, with all other runes falling under its influence. *Gar* means 'spear', specifically Odin's own ash spear Gungnir, a personal and moveable World Tree, just as the magician's ash staff or witch's ash-poled broomstick is a portable cosmic axis.

164

Perhaps the most significant rune connected with the ash is the horse rune *Ehwaz* or *Eh*. The horse is the sacred steed which carries the shaman on his journey throughout those realms connected by the axis mundi. The ash can be seen as the horse itself, with its buds and leaf scars resembling hooves. *Askr Yggr-drasill* can be translated as 'the ash tree that is the horse of Odin' (Yggr is one of Odin's titles) as Odin was the god of horses, runes and magic. The bark of Yggdrasil was said to exude a narcotic vapour which aided the shaman on his trance journeys. The dark ash leaf buds look very much like the underside of a horses hoof, from the fetlock to the frog - the centre of the hoof. These 'hooves' can be seen throughout winter and the twigs look like horses forelegs as they stretch to gallop or jump. Ash was used for the shafts of pony traps which not only supported the trap but controlled the power of the horse. At the World Tree, Yggdrasil, Odin's steed stands at the cross-roads linking the upper and lower worlds with middle earth.

The Greek ash god was the sea god Poseidon, whose sacred animal was also the horse. His father Cronos (the Crow God, Lord of Time and cognate with the Celtic alder god Bran) had castrated Uranus, and thrown the genitals into the sea. From the blood had sprung the ash spirits or *Meliei,* along with the three Furies or *Erinnyes,* death aspects of the goddess. Poseidon and his two brothers in turn deposed Cronos and assumed rulership of the realms as follows- Zeus the sky, Hades the underworld and Poseidon the sea. To the Greeks, the earth was the first element, the air that rises above it the second and the water that surrounds it the third element. Poseidon lived in an underwater palace where he kept white chariot horses: the white horses that are the white foam topped waves. He is said to have invented the bridle and horse racing. Both Odin and Poseidon were patrons of horses, shamanic and everyday travel, and both were patrons of seafaring.

In Celtic myth the ash connects the three circles of existence, *Abred, Gwynedd* and *Ceugant,* which can be interpreted as past, present and future or confusion, balance and creative force, there being only continual rebirth as passage is made from circle to circle until the Land of the Blessed is finally reached. In Ireland three ash trees comprised part of the five sacred trees of Ireland; The Tree of Tortu, The Tree of Dathi and The Branching Tree of Usnech. The felling of the five trees in AD 665 symbolised the triumph of Christianity over Paganism. The other trees were an oak and a yew.

The spiral arrangement of the buds of the ash is an ancient symbol of rebirth and the cycles of existence.

THE PATH OF THE SHAMAN

Aspen *Populus tremula*

In the *Odyssey*, the aspen is mentioned as one of the three trees of resurrection, along with the alder and the cypress. The valley of the Styx (in Greek myth the river which must be crossed to enter the underworld of the dead) was said to be full of white poplars, or aspen trees. Golden headdresses of aspen leaves were found in Mesopotamian burials of around 3,000 BCE.

The poplar is the sacred World Tree of the Lakota nation. For the sun dance ceremony a poplar is carefully cut and lowered into the centre of the dance circle. While being carried it must never touch the floor. Green branches, buffalo skulls and eagle feathers adorn the tree during the rite.

Bean *Leguminosae*

In many cultures the flowers of the bean, and the beans themselves, are associated with death; the spirits of the dead were thought to live in the blossoms. The Mystœ of Eleusis practised chastity abstaining from certain food and above all from beans before the great pagan sacrament. The Greek philosopher Pythagoras strongly believed that beans contained the souls of the departed. Legend has it that this caused his death when, pursued by enemies, he mistakenly ran into a bean field. Rather than trample on the souls of the dead he stood stock still, thus allowing his enemies to catch him. The Pythagoreans continued to abstain from beans on the grounds that their ancestors souls could be resident in them. If a man as opposed to a woman ate a bean he might be robbing an ancestor of his chance of reincarnation. Bean planting was at first a mystery confined to women. [136]

The taboo against eating beans was widespread. Today in Asia, bean flowers are scattered about the house to placate demons. There is an old English superstition that one white bean in a row of green plants signifies a death in the coming year. In Cornwall it was said that beans should only be planted on 3rd May or bad luck would follow. In the Midlands, the same belief is attributed to the 12th May.

In ancient Rome the head of the household would go out three days of the year, spitting beans from his mouth to rid the home of evil spirits. Beans were offered to the goddess Cardea on the first of June. Beans were distributed and eaten during funerals. To this day in Italy beans are distributed among the poor and bean dishes eaten on the anniversary of the death of famous people. In Britain beans were traditionally part of the funeral supper.

In the Middle Ages spitting beans into a witch's face was said to deprive her of her powers. They could also be spat at apparitions to make them vanish. Beans were used as a charm against evil sorcerers, they were made into rattles to scare away evil spirits and were believed to cure impotency if carried or eaten.

Belladonna *Atropa belladonna*
Belladonna is a perennial plant that is native to western, central and southern Europe, south-west Asia and North Africa. It is found all over the British Isles except for Scotland and Ireland. It grows on chalky soils, wastelands, in woods, thickets and on derelict building sites.

The generic name *atrop'* is derived from *Atropos*, one of the Greek Goddesses of Fate, daughters of Erebus and Night. Clotha span the thread of life at man's birth, her sister Lachesis determined its length, while the black veiled Atropos was the Goddess who wielded the shears to cut the thread of life, regardless of age, sex or position.

Belladonna or deadly nightshade is highly poisonous, causing death by the paralysis of the respiratory system. In small doses however, belladonna causes a feeling of euphoria and disorientation, followed by a deep sleep engendering vivid dreams, said to often be of an erotic nature. With a larger dose raving madness and death occur. This explains its use throughout history by shamans and witches. Some of its folk names such as 'dwaleberry' may derive from the Danish *dvaleboer* meaning 'trance berry'. This may be connected to the Scottish word *dul* and the French word *deuil* which both mean 'sorrow'. It was a principle ingredient of many of the flying ointments' used by witches.

The wine of the Maenads, worshippers of Dionysus in ancient Greece, may have included belladonna and datura to induce trance states and euphoria. In ancient Greece the plant was known as *circaeo* after the enchantress Circe, as the leaves were often employed in sleeping draughts. Circe caused the crew of Odysseus's ship to transform into animals.

Belladonna a herb of the underworld and connected with underworld deities. As such it may be used to consecrate tools used for underworld contacts, particularly those made of lead or onyx. It can be added to the Samhain incense, providing that it is used in the open air, to attract the spirits of the ancestors

NB: All parts of the plant contain atropine which is lethal in even small doses.

Betony *Betonica officinalis*
Betony is a hardy perennial that grows to a height to 2 ft. It is native throughout the British Isles and Europe, and is usually found growing in open woodlands and on heaths.

Throughout history betony has been grown in monastery gardens and around graveyards where it was thought to give protection from witchcraft and evil spirits. It was believed to protect the soul and body if worn on the person, and when placed beneath the pillow protected the sleeper from visions and bad dreams. Betony was often planted in the garden to protect the house from evil and was scattered near doors and windows to prevent evil from entering the home. If dried and sprinkled around the perimeter of the property it was believed to form a protective wall through which no evil could penetrate.

Carrying the herb is said to protect against drunkenness and act as a cure for the mysterious affliction known as 'elf sickness', or energy intrusion from malicious spirits.

Dried betony was often to be found hanging in country cottages for use in the treatment of winter illnesses. Betony was also smoked as a tobacco and powdered as a snuff to be used against headaches. The leaves were also taken as a tea.

The primary magical use of betony is for protection and the dispelling of negativity. Make an infusion and use it to clean the temple or house and make a protective seal by wiping betony around the edges of doors and windows. The bodily orifices can also be sealed with the plant when there is any danger. The incense can be used to cleanse contaminated magical tools and purify the atmosphere before and after ritual

Birch *Betula alba*

The common or silver birch is a graceful native tree found throughout the British Isles. The trees grow well on the poorest of soils, but they need plenty of light. They can often be found on pastures, fallow land and forest clearings.

One of the most important functions of the birch in lore is as a tree of fertility. In the Nordic tradition the birch (*Beorc, Byarka,* or *Berkana*) is a symbol of Mother Earth and represents the feminine powers of growth, healing and the natural world.

May poles were made of birch, associating the birch with the May Day sexual revels of sympathetic fertility magic. Sometimes, as in Wales, a living birch tree would be dressed and birch twigs used to light the Beltane fires of oak. The maypole formed part of Druidic ceremonies. It is a cosmic axis and a phallic symbol. Dancing round it celebrates the fertile energies in plants, animals and people in spring. It represents the phallic fertilising power of the God, thrust into the womb of the Earth Mother, and also functions as a cosmic axis, joining the worlds of Gods and men in the ritual cycle.

THE PATH OF THE SHAMAN

Shamans used a seven stepped birch pole to journey to the Otherworld. The birch is called *udeshi burkhan* or 'guardian of the door' and opens the door of heaven for the shaman. One Siberian shaman thought of World Tree as represented by birch. As he prepared for initiation, the master shaman took him to a birch tree possessed of a powerful life force. The neophyte rested his foot on the tree and examined the markings placed by the various shamans over the years. By carving his name into the tree, and calling to mind the names of the ancestors he shared their knowledge. [137] It association with shamanism may stem from the fact that the hallucinogenic fly agaric grows beneath it.

It was certainly associated with the Otherworld. In the traditional ballad of *The Wife of Usher's Well*, her three sons, when summoned back, wear hats of birch bark, showing they are no longer mortal.

In Russia the forest spirits are called Lieschi and were considered to be always present in clumps of trees, particularly the tops of birch trees. To invoke them young birches were cut down and placed in a circle with the points to the centre. Then one enters the circle and invokes the spirit which immediately appears. The magician should then stand on one of the tree stumps, face the east, look between their legs and say, Uncle Liechi, ascend thou, not as a grey wolf , not as an ardent fire, but as resembling myself. The leaves then tremble and the Liechi arises in human form and agrees to give the service for which he has been invoked providing the magician promises their soul.

Blackberry *Rubus fructicosus*

Blackberry is a common sprawling shrub native to Europe. It is widespread on waste ground, heaths, in woodlands and hedges.

The bramble was a sacred plant of the Celts. In Scotland the bramble, along with the rowan and the yew, constituted the sacred fire. In ogham the blackberry is an alternative for the vine, hence M – *muin*.

Blackberries are associated with death and the underworld. In Greek myth Baton, meaning 'blackberry', descended to Tartarus (the underworld) in the company of Amphiaraus.

On Old Michaelmas Day (11th October) it is said that the Devil enters blackberry thickets and spits on them, and hence they should not be picked after that date. A taboo on eating blackberries exists in Celtic countries. In Brittany and Cornwall the reason given is that the blackberry belongs to the fairy folk. In France some people still will not eat them as they are associated with the Devil. In one district, Blackberries were not eaten at all until quite recently, it being believed that "the trail of the Serpent" was upon them.

THE PATH OF THE SHAMAN

The Anglo-Saxons believed blackberry had the power to undo curses and the tricks of evil spirits:

"against any evil rune and for one full of elvish tricks...Take blackberries, pound and sift them, put them in a pouch, lay them under the altar and sing nine masses over them. Then put this dust into milk, drip Holy Water three times upon it and drink every three hours."

The Harvest Lord enters the underworld at Herfest, the realm of the fairy folk and the dead. The blackberry is a plant of the fairy folk, and the blackberries picked after the return of the dark time can be used to contact them. They can also be used for underworld journeys, in the form of wines or cordials. Meditate beneath a blackberry bush for these spirit contacts.

Blackberry Wine
4 lb. ripe blackberries
3 lb. sugar
1 gallon boiling water
Yeast and nutrient
Soak the blackberries in salted water to remove the tiny maggots that are sometimes found in the fruit. Wash thoroughly with clean cold water. Put them into a fermentation bin and pour over the boiling water. Stir thoroughly until all of the fruit are mashed. When lukewarm add the yeast and nutrient. Cover and leave for about a week, stirring daily. Strain the liquid into a demi-jon and add the sugar. Stir until completely dissolved. Fit an air lock and leave to ferment out. When fermentation is complete rack into a clean demi-jon and leave to clear. When clear bottle.

Blackthorn *Prunus spinosa*
The blackthorn is a widely distributed native tree of Britain, Europe and parts of Asia. It grows abundantly in hedgerows, thickets and on waste ground.

In Ogham the blackthorn is SS- *straif.* This translates as 'strife'. The words 'slay' and 'sloe' (the fruit of the blackthorn) are also closely linked. However, blackthorn in Ogham sayings is "the increaser of secrets" and "the rune of the great wheel", demonstrating its importance.

The blackthorn has an ominous image. The thorns of the blackthorn were used for pricking wax poppets for cursing. Witches were though to carry black rods of blackthorn which could cause miscarriages. When witches were burned, blackthorn sticks were thrown onto the fire. The sorcerer Major Weir was burned at the stake in 1670 with his blackthorn rod, which was described as the chief agent of his magic.

170

November 11th is recognised in Ireland as the day of the blackthorn spirits, the Lunantishees, Otherworldly beings who guard the sacred blackthorn from any human foolhardy enough to profane the sacred tree by cutting the wood after this date.

In some magical traditions the blackthorn is the tree of cursing or used to summon The Wild Hunt.

Sloe Gin
8 oz. ripe sloes
4 - 6 oz. sugar
14 fl oz. gin
Remove any stalks and ash the fruit. Prick the sloes at both ends to release their juice and put them into a screw top container which should be no more than half full. Add the sugar and top up with gin. Seal the container and shake vigorously. Repeat the shaking process for two to four weeks after which time the sloes will have turned the liquid a rich red colour. The liqueur should now be left to mature, although it can be drunk after a few weeks the flavour is much improved if left for twelve months. If required the liquid may be strained after three months and bottled before being left to finish maturing.

Sloe Wine
12 lb. fresh sloes
4 lb. sultanas
4 lb. honey
 4 pt. red grape concentrate
3 tsp. yeast nutrient
3 tsp. pectic enzyme
Yeast
Wash the sloes and stone them if possible. Crush the fruit and mix with the sultanas in a fermentation bin. Add the honey, nutrient and three gallons of boiling water. Cover and leave to go cool. Add the yeast and leave to ferment for three days. Strain and press lightly. Add the grape concentrate and top up to 4.5 gallons with cooled, boiled water. Leave for four days, stirring daily. Next strain into demi-jons, fit air locks and leave to ferment out. When fermentation has finished rack off into clean demi-jons and leave to clear. Bottle when clear. this wine will benefit from being stored for at least twelve months. It needs to be kept in the dark to preserve its colour.

THE PATH OF THE SHAMAN

Bluebell *Hyacinthoides non-scripta*

The bluebell has a small white round bulb which exudes thick mucus when crushed. The flowers appear in April and May.

The bluebell is intimately connected with the realm of spirits. The Succubus (Latin *cubare*= 'to lie', *sub*= 'beneath') is a female spirit who sexually assaults men in their sleep in order to conceive a demon child. A bluebell in the bedroom will keep her away. She is the female counterpart of an incubus and both are related to the various nightmare fairies.

In Greece, boys used to beat the statue of the horned god Pan with bluebells to solicit him to provide more meat and game.

The presence of bluebells in oak copses is a sure sign that those mischievous creatures called Oakmen are present and mortals should be wary. In Somerset it is believed that you should never go into the woods to pick bluebells, as it will anger the fairies. If you are a child you will never be seen again, as the fairies will take you away, but if you are an adult you will be pixy-led and will not be able to find your way out of the woods until someone rescues you. Oak Men are the most widespread tree fairies in England; sometimes they are merged with oak trees, like hamadryads, and sometimes they appear as forest dwarfs who offer tempting food to passing mortals, which will turn out to be poisonous fungi, disguised by fairy glamour (i.e. entheogens). They inhabit copses where saplings have grown from felled oaks. Oak men become extremely angry and dangerous if their tree is cut down. They also guard all the forest animals and punish those who harm them, such as foxhunters. The rain that gathers in their oak hollows has powerful magical healing qualities.

Witches were said to grow bluebells to attract fairies, and at one time their presence in a garden was a damning piece of evidence in a witch trial.

Bluebells may be planted at grave sites and incorporated into rituals of death and dying, and entering the underworld.

NB: Bluebells are poisonous and should not be ingested.

Borage *Borago officinalis*

Borage is a hardy annual plant that grows throughout most of North Africa, the Middle East, the Mediterranean and most of Europe. It grows to a height of between 1 - 2 ft and prefers an open, sunny position in a dry, well drained soil.

Borage is believed to be the famed 'nepenthe of Homer'. This was a herbal wine that supposedly brought complete forgetfulness.

172

THE PATH OF THE SHAMAN

Borage was one of the magical herbs of the Celts. The common name could be derived from the Celtic word '*borrach*' meaning 'person of strong courage or bravery'. Our Celtic ancestors would steep borage leaves in wine and the mixture would result in a very significant rise in the blood adrenaline level. To give courage to the Crusaders, borage was added to stirrup cups drunk at their departure.

The Welsh name for the plant *llawenlys* translates as 'herb of gladness' and bears testament to its use through the ages as a plant known for its ability to make men and women glad and merry. Borage is known to have been highly cultivated during medieval times and there is a saying 'a garden without borage is like a heart without courage'.

Borage can be used to an aid of psychic powers and to stimulate courage and strength. It is particularly useful when exploring the warrior path. Take the tea or wine, or use as an incense to explore the male aspects of your own personality. A strong infusion can be drunk to aid psychic awareness, and can be used in the ritual bath in preparation for inner journeying, vision quests and shamanic practices of an arduous nature.

Borage Tea
Pour 1 cup of boiling water onto 2 teaspoons of the dried herb and infuse for 10 - 15 minutes.

Borage Wine
2 pt. borage flowers and leaves
1 lb. raisins
2 lb. sugar
Juice and grated peel of one lemon
1 cup black tea
Yeast
Wash and chop the flowers and leaves. Put into 5 pints of water and b ring to the boil. Simmer for 5 minutes, remove from the heat and leave to infuse for 24 hours. Bring 1.5 pints of water to the boil and add the sugar, stirring until dissolved. Strain the infused mixture into a fermentation bin and add the sugar mixture. When cool add the raisins, tea, juice and grated peel of lemon and the yeast. Cover and leave for a week, stirring daily. Strain into a demi-jon and top up with cold boiled water. Fit an airlock and leave to ferment out. When fermentation is completed rack into a clean demi-jon and leave to clear. Some of the water may be substituted by 3 pints of pure apple juice.

THE PATH OF THE SHAMAN

Broom (Scotch)
Leaves and aged flowers of the broom have been smoked to produce euphoria. The freshly picked flowers should be sealed in a jar for two weeks until they go brown. It will ferment and smell foetid. It should then be dried. It can then be smoked to produce a mild altered state, though it is said that longer curing produced a mild hallucinogen. However, in some people it does cause headaches and nausea, and some may be allergic to it and suffer a reaction

NB: Oral ingestion or smoking of either the flower herbage of the broom may be toxic, especially in large amounts when eventual liver damage may result. It can cause nausea, vomiting, diarrhoea, dizziness, confusion, headache, gastrointestinal distress, weakness, palpitations, fatigue, sleepiness and dilation of the pupils. One of its constituents, Sparteine, has been associated with respiratory arrest, circulatory collapse, and death, although scotch broom itself has not.

Broom Beer
4 lb malt
2 lb sugar
3 oz fresh broom flowers
4 gallons water
Yeast
Add 2 gallons water to the flowers and simmer for 60 minutes. Strain. Add the malt and sugar and stir to dissolve. Add the rest of the water, and add the yeast. Ferment 1-2 weeks and bottle.

Catnip *Nepeta cataria*
Catnip is a hardy, herbaceous perennial that grows to a height of up to 3 ft. It is native to the whole of Europe and parts of Asia. It can be found growing in mountainous areas, near streams and river courses, along roadsides and in hedgerows.

The common name arises from the overwhelming attraction this plant holds for cats. Once the location of catnip has been found cats will happily chew the leaves, roll on the plant and curl up amongst its foliage. This reaction is thought to be caused because the smell of the plant is similar to the pheromones of the cat's opposite sex.

Catnip has been used throughout the centuries as a seasoning and as a medicinal herb. Brewed as a tea, catnip leaves are a sedative, or they can be smoked for a mildly hallucinogenic effect. It can be used for shape-shifting work, or to invoke or bond with a cat ally.

THE PATH OF THE SHAMAN

Chewing the root was believed to impart fierceness to even the most timid and make him quarrelsome. One hangman said he couldn't face his job until he'd eaten some.

Catnip Tea
2 tsp. herb
1 cup boiling water
Infuse for 15 minutes, strain and drink a cup three times a day.

Calamus, *Acorus calamus*
This ancient herb is mentioned in the Bible. It was used by the Mosos sorcerers of Yunnan, and in Chinese and Ayurvedic medicine. It is used extensively by Native Canadians. In small doses it is a stimulant, but in larger doses is hallucinogenic. It's main ingredient (TMA) is more psychoactive by weight than mescaline. Smoking it causes a relaxed, pleasant, mild psychotropic effect. A 2" piece of fresh root eaten raw will act as a stimulant, for hallucinogenic effects, a piece of 10" is needed. The root can also be boiled in water.

The active ingredient of calamus deteriorates within a two years leaving the herb useless.

NB: Large quantities have been found to produce tumours in rats, though the amount given was astronomical. The Cree chew it daily, and no such tumours have been reported in them.

Clary Sage *Salvia sclarea*
Clary is a form of sage. It is a perennial plant although it often acts as a biennial. It can grow up to a height of 2 ft. It is native to Syria and parts of southern Europe. It prefers a position in full sun and a light and chalky soil. The name 'clary' and the specific name '*sclarea*' are both thought to derive from the Latin word *clarus* which means 'to clear'.

Clary sage was used by the Germans in the making of beer and wine. In Britain clary was used as a substitute for hops and made a very intoxicating drink. Clary wine was famous for its narcotic properties.

Clary may be used to enhance visions within meditation. It has the power to protect the 'sight' and can be made into an infusion and applied directly to the eyes or to the third eye chakra. The wine may be used in rituals of divination. Clary may be used to enhance visions within meditation.

NB Do not use during pregnancy. Clary should not be taken over an extended period of time.

THE PATH OF THE SHAMAN

Clary Tea
1 oz dried herb
1 pt boiling water
Infuse for fifteen minutes and strain.

Clary Wine
1 gallon water
3.5 lb. sugar
8 oz chopped raisins
4 pt. clary blossoms
Yeast
Mix the sugar and water and warm gently until the sugar is completely dissolved. Remove from the heat and leave until luke warm. Put into a fermentation bin and add the blossoms (flowers only) and raisins. Add the yeast and leave for five days, stirring daily. Strain into a demi-jon, fit an air lock and leave to ferment out. When fermentation is completed rack into a clean demi-jon and leave to clear. When completely clear bottle and store for 12 months before drinking.

Coltsfoot *Tussilago farfara*
Coltsfoot is a hardy perennial plant that grows to a height of up to 1 ft. It is native to Europe, northern and western Asia and North Africa. It grows well on poor soil and is often found alongside streams, rivers in hedgerows and on the edges of woods.

The generic name *'tussilago'* is thought to be derived from the Latin *tussis agere* which literally means 'to take away cough'. This reflects one of the common uses of coltsfoot. It has been used for centuries as a herbal tobacco and the smoking of it was recommended by Pliny to ease asthma, bronchial complaints, excess mucus, catarrh and coughs.

The dried herb is known as 'British Tobacco' and has long been used in herbal smoking mixtures. It may be used as the base for shamanic smoking mixtures or added to incenses to promote tranquillity and induce visions.

NB: Tests on rats have shown that two alkaloids present in coltsfoot can cause liver cancer. The amounts used in the tests were very excessive and would not usually be taken by humans but it is not advisable to take large amounts of coltsfoot over extended periods of time.

THE PATH OF THE SHAMAN

Damiana *Turnera diffusa / Turnera aphrodisiaca*
Damiana is a small shrub. The leaves are ovate, pale green on the top and smooth on the underside with haired ribs. The flowers are yellow and aromatic and arise from the leaf axils.

Damiana can be used in incense to increase the levels of energy raised during a ritual. The tea can be used. The leaves may be dried and smoked to produce a mild marijuana-like effect for shamanic purposes.

NB Excessive long-term use may cause liver damage.

Datura *Datura stramonium*
Datura is a member of the *solanacea* family, which also includes potatoes and nightshade. It is native to south-western United States, Mexico, Central America, India and Asia. In Britain it occurs as an occasional weed on waste ground and rubbish dumps.

The name *datura* comes from the Arabic name for the drug *datora* or *tatorah*. Its gets its common name of 'thorn apple' from the spiny fruit capsules.

Datura has been used for medicinal and religious purposes since ancient times. Early Sanskrit writings refer to the drug as *dhurstura* and *unmata*. It is hallucinogenic and the priests of Apollo in ancient Greece used it to prophesy. It was also used by the ancients as an aphrodisiac.

Chinese herbalists would prepare an anaesthetic to carry out painless operations by gathering equal amounts of datura and cannabis sativa during the seventh and eighth moon. These would be dried in the shade and digested in wine.

In the medieval period it was supposedly introduced into Europe by gypsies who smoked it to experience hallucinations.

Because of its ability to give the sensation of flying and release sexual inhibitions, it was associated with witchcraft in the Middle Ages. Witches were said to inhale its vapours to cast spells. It was also a traditional ingredient of the 'flying ointment', along with water parsnip, aconite, belladonna and cinquefoil, all stewed in fat. The mixture would be mixed with soot and then smeared over the body. The hallucinations produced would be akin to flying. Some say that the ointment was smeared onto the handle of the broomstick and inserted into the vagina. The ecstatic witch would then be 'flying on her broomstick to the sabbat'.

Priests, medicine men and initiatory candidates of the Native American Indians in the south western states used the plant as a religious herb to produce visions. The Algonquin Indians would make a drink

177

THE PATH OF THE SHAMAN

containing datura, which was called *wysoccan* and given to boys about to be initiated into manhood. The candidate would enter a state of madness and visions for twenty days. On recovery he would have no memory of his former life as a child and enter into a state of manhood. Some tribes also used the herb as an anaesthetic for setting broken bones, and the Mariposa tribe used it as a female aphrodisiac.

In the *'Teachings of Don Juan'* Carlos Castenda describes firsthand experience of its use. Datura leaves were Don Juan's 'little smoke'.

NB: Datura is highly poisonous and should not be ingested. It produces symptoms similar to those of belladonna poisoning. Smoking datura damages the heart if it is used more than very infrequently.

Elder *Sambucus nigra*

Elder grows wild almost anywhere in Britain as its seeds are frequently dispersed by birds that eat the ripe berries. It is usually found as a large bush although it can grow into a small tree.

The generic name '*sambucus*' is derived from the Greek '*sambucu*', a musical instrument, as the Greeks and Romans made flutes from its hollow stems and a triangular stringed instrument from the hardwood. The Anglo Saxon for elder means hollow tree as used for whistles. A pan-pipe was made from the hollow stems. According to Pliny the shrillest notes came from those made from a tree which grew out of the sound of a cock-crow.

The elder is a tree associated with witches and the Crone aspect of the Goddess, and it is often treated with great caution and surrounded with warnings as a result. In Ireland witches used elder sticks for their broom staffs, not ash.

In Denmark the elder was sacred to Hulda, the Elder Mother or Elder Queen. She lived at its roots and was mother of the elves. The tree was hers and whoever wished to take a branch or cut the tree had to first ask her permission, otherwise grave misfortune would follow. She did not like floorboards or furniture to be made of elder, and if a child was placed in an elder cradle Hulda would come and pull him out by the legs. It was safe to take a branch from the elder on January 6th without permission if you spat on the ground three times. The elder branch could be used to draw a magic circle in a lonely place for the purpose of demanding magic fern seed, which would give one the strength of thirty men. Hulda would then see that a chalice was delivered by an unseen hand, containing the seed.

THE PATH OF THE SHAMAN

The Druids considered that any elder berries that remained in December were the last gift from the Earth Goddess, and they were ritually gathered and made into potent wine, only to be drunk by initiates to facilitate clairvoyance. The wine was also poured as a libation in sacred places and given to sacrificial victims at the solstices.

The elder is a tree associated with death and the underworld, in megalithic burial chambers the funerary flints are the shape of elder leaves. Even the scent of elder was thought to bring death and disease. It was planted on new graves by the Welsh and Manx Celts. If it blossomed, the dead soul was thought to be happy in the land of Tir-nan-og. To protect the dead from witchcraft green branches of elder were buried with them.

It is a tree of regeneration because of its ability to re-grow damaged branches easily and its ability to root and grow rapidly from any part. In the Tyrol elder branches, cut in the shape of a cross, were planted on graves. If it thrived and bloomed it meant that the departed soul was in paradise.

Elderberry Wine
5 lb. elderberries
1 gallon water
Juice and grate peel of 1 lemon
Yeast
Strip the berries from the stalks with a fork. Put into a fermentation bin,. pour over 6 pints of boiling water and mash down with the lemon juice and peel. Cover and leave for three days, stirring daily. strain into a demi-jon. Dissolve the sugar in 2 pints of water and add to the demi-jon. When cooled add the yeast. Fit an airlock and leave to ferment out. When fermentation has finished rack off into a clean demi-jon and leave to clear. bottle and keep for at least 12 months before drinking.

Fly Agaric *Amanita muscaria*
The white-spotted red fly agaric mushroom is psychotropic and has a long history of use among European mystics. The effects of the mushroom include auditory and visual hallucinations and spatial distortions. Subjects commonly report sensations of flying, or seeing little people or red-hatted mushrooms dancing. All of the Siberian tribes revere the birch, and the shaman builds his hut around a birch pole, cuts seven notches in it to travel to the realm of spirits (in other words, the shaman ingests the mushroom and flies up the World Tree or cosmic axis to the spirit realms, seeing the tutelary spirit of the agaric as a red-capped spirit). The fly agaric grows beneath birch trees, in mycorrhizal relationship to it.

179

The Father Christmas costume of white and red also suggests the mushroom. Siberian winter dwellings were excavated holes with a birch log roofs; the only entrance was through a smoke hole in the roof. Even the summer dwellings had smoke-hole exits for the spirit of the shaman to fly out of when he was in a trance. This might explain why Santa enters and exits through the chimney. Why does Santa bring gifts? The shaman is the middleman between humans and spirits and brings back knowledge from the spirit world. Ordinary individuals would write requests on pieces of paper and burn them so their messages would be carried to the spirits on the smoke.

A number of legends speak of one eyed, one legged creatures, and these may, in fact, be a code for psychotropic mushrooms. Like Cynon, the shamanic Lord of the Animals in the Celtic myth mentioned earlier, the fachan, a Highland fairy, has one eye, one hand, one leg, one ear, one arm and one toe all lined up down the centre of his body. He carries a spiked club with which he attacks any human who dares to approach his mountain realm. He hates all living creatures but especially birds, which he envies for their gift of flight. A number of writers have theorised that the fachan may be a folk memory of the Celtic shamans, who stood on one leg and closed one eye when casting spells. The usual explanation offered for this practice is so that one eye looks into the inner realms, and only standing on one leg

THE PATH OF THE SHAMAN

symbolises not being wholly in one realm or another. However, it may be that the stance is in imitation of the mushroom that gives the shaman his power, the one-legged, one-eyed fly agaric. The fact that the fachan inhabits a mountainous region is significant, as that is where the fly agaric grows. His hatred of birds, which he envies for their flight, may be a distorted folk memory of the gift of flight the mushroom bestows.

There was also an Irish race of one-legged, one-eyed beings described as the oldest inhabitants of the land, a race of wizards who intermarried with the Tuatha de Danaan. In Celtic lore all red food was taboo, including rowan berries and red nuts. These may be masks for the mushroom in Irish myth, as is the allusion to the fact the Celts were head hunters, believing that all wisdom and power resided in the head. Perhaps these heads were not only human ones but also the heads of vision-giving mushrooms.

It is likely that the Celts who settled Ireland brought with them knowledge of the use of fly agaric from their ancestors who migrated westward from an Indo-European heartland near the south-western edge of Siberia. Motifs of magical foods in Irish Celtic lore may be metaphoric references to *Amanita muscaria*, and it is certainly possible, though not provable, that the Druids used fly agaric, and the dried cap may even have been the magic egg so much written about. Fairy food, which is generally described as being red in colour, is prohibited for humans. Should they eat it, they can never return to the realm of men. This is comparable with the taboos placed on shamanic substances forbidding them to ordinary men and women. Among the Selkup fly agaric was believed to be fatal to non shamans (as indeed it can be for those who do not know how to prepare it). Among the Vogul consumption was limited to sacred occasions and it was abused on peril of death. The Indo-Europeans strictly limited the important ritual of *soma* to certain classes and the profane user risked death at the hands of the angry god. Amongst the Celts, red foods and mushrooms were taboo, designated as the food of the Otherworld or the dead. As the mushroom aids the shaman to visit other realms in spirit flight, see spirits and contact the spirit or god within, Robert Graves [138] argued that ambrosia, the food of the Greek gods, was in reality hallucinogenic mushrooms.

Wasson identified the Vedic soma with an hallucinogenic mushroom. It was called 'not-born, one-foot' suggesting the single stemmed mushroom which springs up overnight, unseeded, as though from nothing. Soma became a god in its own right. Of the more than a thousand holy

181

THE PATH OF THE SHAMAN

hymns in the Rig-Veda, one hundred and twenty are devoted exclusively to Soma. That the ritual is of Indo-European origin rather than being an indigenous Indian one is suggested to by the existence of the similar *haoma* fire ritual in ancient Persia.

An ancient Indian tradition recorded in the Rig-Veda asserts that *"Paranja, the god of thunder, was the father of Soma"* and mushrooms were commonly believed to spring from the strike of the thunder god. The Maya of highland Guatemala call *Amanita muscaria* the 'lightning mushroom' relating it to one of the gods, the 'Lord of Lightning'.

Fly agaric is also possibly the mushroom that Vikings took to enter the beserker state for battle. The Icelandic name for the fly agaric contains the word 'berserk' in it. [139]

Among many of the Siberian tribes that, in historic times, used the fly-agaric in their shamanic ceremonies, the name of the fly-agaric is also the word for 'inebriate'. Thus when a native sees a Russian drunk on alcohol he says that man is 'bemushroomed'.

NB: Fly agaric is poisonous and can cause vomiting, paralysis and death.

Galangal Root *Kaempferia galanga*
Galangal is a plant of the ginger family, used by natives of New Guinea and as a medicine and condiment in parts of Asia. Crowley mentioned the root in his incense formula for conversation with 'your Holy Guardian Angel'. A tablespoon of the root, chopped into small pieces, should be prepared by decoction in half a pint of boiling water, allowed to cool and drunk. The root may also be added to incense.

Grape Vine
All plants which had the ability to change consciousness were once considered sacred, including the grape. The vine grows in a spiral pattern, a very ancient symbol of immortality. Wine was thought to imbue the spirit with the divine inspiration of the god, freeing the imbiber from mundane thoughts and conventions, altering levels of consciousness and awakening the powers of the primal self within.

The story of the wine god is seen most clearly in the myth of Dionysus (Bacchus), the son of the god Zeus and Semele, a mortal woman. While Semele was pregnant, Zeus's jealous wife Hera visited her, disguised as an old woman, and advised her to ask her lover to reveal himself in his true form. Worried that she might be mating with a monster, Semele did as she was asked, making him forst swear by the river Styx (the underworld

182

THE PATH OF THE SHAMAN

river) that he would grant her request. Zeus was forced to comply, and appeared to her as thunder and lightening, which destroyed the unfortunate woman. Taking the six-month foetus from her womb, Hermes sewed it up into Zeus's thigh, where it matured for another three months and was duly delivered, both god and man, a horned child crowned with serpents, called the 'twice-born'.

At Hera's orders, the Titans seized Dionysus, and despite the fact that he transformed himself into a serpent, a lion and a bull, a goat and a stag, tore him into shreds. These they boiled in a cauldron and a pomegranate tree sprang from the soil where his blood had fallen. The pieces were rescued by his grandmother Rhea, who brought him to life again and so he became the thrice-born.

Zeus entrusted the boy to Persephone, the Queen of the underworld. She took him to King Athamas and his wife Ino who disguised him as a girl and placed him in the women's quarters. However, Hera was not fooled and drove the royal guardians mad, so that they killed their own son Learches, mistaking him for a stag.

Hermes transformed Dionysus into a kid goat and took him to the nymphs who lived on Mount Nysa. They tended him in a cave and fed him on honey, and here he invented wine.

Hera continued to pursue Dionysus and drove him insane. In this condition he wandered through many lands actively encouraging his cult, accompanied by the Maenads, wild women, flushed with wine, shoulders draped with a fawn skin, carrying ivy-twined staff tipped with pine cones called the *thyrsus*. In his company were also found the Satyrs, wild men with goat feet, carrying swords and serpents and fearsome bull-roarers. Always at his side was Silenus, his mentor and tutor who had a fondness for wine.

At Naxos, Dionysus met the beautiful Ariadne, who had been abandoned by the hero Theseus. Falling in love with her, they married. Her bridal crown was the Corona Borealis (also known as the Northern Crown or Caer Arianrhod around the Pole Star) and she bore him several children. From Naxos he sailed to Argos and caused the women to go insane until their king, the hero Perseus, acknowledged his divinity and built a temple in honour of Dionysus.

Dionysus was also one of the very few that was able to bring a dead person out of the underworld. Even though he had never seen Semele, he was concerned for her. Eventually he journeyed into the underworld to find her. He bribed Persephone with a gift of myrtle to release his mother, faced down Thanatos (Death) and brought Semele back to Mount Olympus. Still, just so other ghosts did not become jealous,

Dionysus changed his mother's name to Thyone ('Raging Queen') and that's how he introduced her to the other Olympians.

His festivals were the Dionysia, mainly celebrated by women who used alcohol to overcome inhibitions, to do and say things that social conventions would not normally allow them to do. Dionysus was a god that defied the social order, broke taboos and customs and gained knowledge through divine madness. As such he was the opposite of the god Apollo, logical, dignified, lord of the sun and daylight, while Dionysius was attracted to the night and dark places. They perhaps represent the two sides of human consciousness, both necessary in balance.

The story clearly has many shamanic elements- Dionysus is thrice born, like Taliesin. He is dismembered and boiled in a cauldron, reflecting shamanic dismemberment. His blood creates the World Tree. He experiences divine madness. He rescues his mother from the underworld. His wife is associated with the Northern Crown and the Pole Star, like Arianrhod. Mushrooms were believed to spring from the earth after lightening strikes, and Dionysus was engendered by the thunder god. The Maenads, followers of Dionysus, were said to rip apart the flesh of fawns and eaten them while the blood was still warm. One of the names of fly agaric was 'fawn'. Outsiders were forbidden on pain of death from attending the rites.[140]

Hellebore *Helleborus niger*
Hellebore is a perennial plant native to central and southern Europe. It was probably introduced into Britain by the Romans. It grows to a height of 1 ft and likes a moist, limey soil and a sheltered position. It can sometimes be found growing in woods and thickets and is also cultivated in many gardens.

The plant was formerly known by the name of *melampode* after Melampus, a physician of around 1,400 BCE. He used hellebore to treat nervous disorders and hysteria. According to the Greek tradition Melampus was originally a herdsman who first realised the properties of hellebore after observing the effects of the herb on his goats. He is said to have later used the milk of the goats who had eaten hellebore to cure mental derangement in the daughters of Proetus, King of Argus.

The ancient Greeks used great ceremony when collecting hellebore. A circle was drawn around the plant with a sword and then incantations and prayers to the gods were said while the black roots were being lifted.

THE PATH OF THE SHAMAN

Legend has it that witches picked this plant barefoot and dressed in white. The plant was never cut but plucked from the soil with the right hand, and was then transferred to the left.

Hellebore was scattered on the floor by sorcerers to make themselves invisible. It was one of the ingredients in the so called flying ointment. It was used to induce astral projection and in rituals of exorcism.

NB: Hellebore is highly poisonous and should not be used except under the guidance of an experienced practitioner.

Hemlock *Conium maculatum*

Hemlock is a biennial plant that grows to a height of up to 7 ft. It is native to Britain, Europe, Asia and North Africa. It can be found growing wild in damp places, along roadsides, on waste ground and in woodlands.

The generic name *conium* is thought to be derived from the Greek word *kona* which means 'to whirl about'. This is thought to describe the vertigo and eventual death caused when the plant is eaten.

The poisonous nature of hemlock has been recognised since ancient times. In ancient Greece it was a method of execution. In Rome and Greece it was taken, mixed with opium, as a method of suicide by life-weary philosophers. Socrates drank an infusion of hemlock rather renounce his philosophical beliefs. Plato wrote a graphic account of his death.

Hemlock has a dark reputation all over the world, the Russians called it 'the satanic herb' whilst the Germans thought it belonged to the infernal regions.

NB: The use of this plant is not recommended and it should never be taken internally. The difference between the narcotic and fatal dose is very small. Hemlock has a bitter taste and a mouse-like smell. If hemlock is taken it paralyses the motor functions of the body although the mind remains clear. If an overdose is taken the body becomes completely paralysed, the respiratory system is repressed and death occurs through suffocation.

Hemp *Cannabis sativa*

Cannabis is an annual herb thought to have originated in the area just north of the Himalayan Mountains. It is native to Central Asia and India and is widely cultivated in many parts of the world, including the Far East and Mexico. Occasionally, stray plants may be found on waste ground in Britain.

THE PATH OF THE SHAMAN

The hemp plant has been known for thousands of years, both for its mind altering abilities and for the useful fibre it provides. In ancient Greece, cannabis was burned by Pythoness at the Oracle of Delphi to induce trance.

Herodotus (c. 450 BCE) recorded that the Scythians used hemp as a power plant. They would roast the seeds and inhale the fumes. Pliny believed that the whole plant had wonderful medicinal properties, and regarded this as a better use for the plant than in the manufacture of rope. Some think that the nepenthe of Homer, the magic potion enabling unhappy mortals to forget their grief, was hemp.

Cannabis has been used for centuries as a sacred herb, allowing the magician to loosen the hold of the material world and gain access to the other realms.

However, any relationship with a power plant is precarious, and its spirit must be approached with respect. To use a power plant for a recreational purpose is an abuse of its energies and will lead to the subjugation of the magician's will by the plant spirit.

NB: The use and possession of cannabis is illegal in many countries, including Britain at the time of writing. It can have adverse effects on the short term memory and there is some recent evidence that it can cause psychosis in a tiny number of habitual users.

Henbane *Hyoscyamus niger*

Henbane is sometimes an annual but more usually a biennial plant that is native to Europe, western Asia and North Africa. It grows to a height of around 2 ft and is usually found on waste ground and along roadsides, especially on sandy soil.

It is associated with the underworld. In Hades the dead souls were crowned with wreaths of henbane.

During the Middle Ages henbane was associated with witchcraft. Witches supposedly used it to give their victims convulsions. It was one of the ingredients of flying ointment. Traditionally, henbane was mixed with the cup of wine which welcomes witches to the sabbat.

Henbane can be dried and added to incenses to increase the powers of clairvoyance and psychic perception. It is a herb of the underworld and as such can be used to contact the spirits of those who have gone before. It is a traditional Samhain herb.

A traditional spell for raising spirits involves that practitioner making an incense of henbane, fennel root, frankincense, coriander and cassia, going to a dark, haunted and enchanted forest. The incense should

THE PATH OF THE SHAMAN

be burned in a censer on a stump surrounded by black candles. The candles will suddenly be extinguished by the spirits that have formed there. To banish the spirits burn an incense of asafoetida and frankincense.

NB: Henbane is a highly poisonous plant which can be fatal if taken in large doses. It should not be used except under the guidance of an experienced person.

Hop *Humulus lupulus*
The hop is a hardy perennial deciduous climbing plant that can reach a height of up to 23 ft. It is native to Europe, Asia and North America. It likes a sunny and open position in deeply dug, fertile soil. It can be found growing wild along hedgerows and in thickets in Britain.

The specific name *lupulus* means 'wolf' and is thought to refer to the strangling habit this plant has as it climbs, similar to the way in which the wolf strangles its prey.

Hops have been used for many purposes over the centuries. They were recommended by the Roman writer Pliny as a garden plant and vegetable. By the 8th century hops were used throughout most of Europe in the brewing industry because of their clearing, flavouring and preserving qualities, although the British people resisted the introduction of hops for brewing. Initially Henry VIII banned them, but during the 16th century they became more widespread and by the late 17th century their bitter flavour and preserving qualities were being recognised.

An infusion of the fresh herb or dried plant makes a sedative and calming tea. Hop sleep pillows can be made by stuffing small cushions with dried hop flowers and leaves to induce restful sleep and dreams.

Beer or hop infusion helps to connect with the animal energy within, particularly wolf allies. The hop is associated with the wild wolf, which in Celtic mythology ruled over the winter months of the dead time. The wolf has connections with underworld deities, and stands beside Cernunnos on the Gundestrop cauldron.

Beer
2 pt. beer hops
1 lb. malt
1 lb. sugar
2 gallon water
yeast
Activate the yeast. Place the hops in a large pan, add sufficient water to cover and boil for 15 minutes. Strain the liquid into a brewing bin, add the

187

THE PATH OF THE SHAMAN

sugar and malt and stir until dissolved. Immediately add the rest of the water. When cool add the yeast and cover and leaves for five days. Bottle in screw top bottles and leave for at least a week before drinking.

Stout
2 oz dried hop flowers
4 oz black malt grains
1 lb. Demerara sugar
1 gallon water
1 lb. malt extract
Yeast
Activate the yeast. Put half the water in a pan and bring to the boil. Add the hops , malt grains and sugar and simmer for 30 minutes. Add the malt extract and stir until dissolved. Add the remaining water and the yeast. Cover and leave in a warm place for five days. Bottle in screw top bottles, adding half a teaspoon of brown sugar to each pint of liquid. Leave for at least four weeks before drinking.

Lotus
Lotus is the common name for many different kinds of plants. The Egyptian, East Indian and American lotuses are in the water lily family, *Nymphaeaceae.*

The Egyptian white lotus *Nymphaea lotus* is believed to be the original sacred lotus of ancient Egypt. The blue lotus, *N. caerulea,* and the *Nelumbium speciosum* or 'sacred bean' with red flowers, were also often pictured in ancient Egyptian art. The blue lotus has psychotropic properties.

In Egyptian myth, the first appearance of light gives the separation of earth and sky. The myth of Shu, or first dawn, when the sun arose out of the waters, was often symbolised as a lotus containing a divine child with its finger in its mouth. Life is spontaneous movement upwards, a flower rising from the waters and opening its petals to reveal the first light. The Egyptians sometimes symbolised the appearance of the great Life Spirit out of the waters as a lotus rising and opening its flower. The petals bent back to reveal the rising god of light and movement.

There is some evidence that the blue lotus was taken to induce altered states of consciousness by the ancient Egyptians.

The ancient Greeks wrote of a race of lotus eaters, *Lotophagi,* living in North Africa. It is said that their only food came from the lotus tree. Anyone who ate of this tree forgot their homes and families.

188

THE PATH OF THE SHAMAN

In the 1960s blue lotus was used in the Congo, when the Babembi warriors drank potions of *chanvre* (blue lotus), during the ritual of the *Dhawa* or witchcraft which sustained them in their rapid campaigns:

"The plant juice creates a wild exhilaration and immunity to fear and pain. As one battle eye-witness told me, "The onrush of men having eaten blue lotus was not affected by bullets striking them in the body. I saw one man still advance after four heavy calibre bullets had struck him, and he fell only a few feet from me." [141]

Mandrake *Mandragora officinarum*
Mandrake, which is member of the potato family, is a perennial plant that grows to a height of 1 ft. It is native to south-eastern Europe and is now cultivated in gardens throughout Europe.

People have had superstitious beliefs about the mandrake since early times. The plant contains scopolamine and hyoscyamine, two chemical compounds that may be used as medicines or poisons.

The generic name *mandragora* is derived from the Greek word *mandra* which means 'a stall' or 'a herd of cattle'. This is thought to be a reference to the fact that this plant is poisonous to cattle. Another possible derivation is from a corruption of the Greek *mandragorus* which is derived in turn from the Sanskrit words *mangros* and *agora*, meaning 'sleep substances'. The specific name *officinarum* relates to the fact that this plant was included on the list of officially recognised herbal medicines. The mandrake has a more comprehensive reputation as a magical plant than any other since primitive times.

It was mentioned in the Ebers papyrus, written around 1700 BC, and sections of mandrake roots have been found in the pyramids. The Egyptians honoured Ra as the first to administer mandrake as a soporific and they called it 'phallus of the field'. The Egyptians probably used the plant to prepare sedatives and pain-relieving drugs. Mandrakes were also described on Assyrian clay tablets of 800 BCE. The ancient peoples of the Near East and Europe used the root of the plant as a narcotic and anaesthetic.

During the time of Pliny, mandrake was given to people to chew before operations. This is because of its ability to deaden pain and induce sleep. As a wine of the condemned mandrake was given on a sponge to those about to be crucified or hung. It is said that Christ was given vinegar instead of mandrake wine as an added cruelty. The death-like sleep that was induced by mandrake led the Romans to begin their practice of spearing the bodies of crucifixion victims to ensure that they were really dead and not just under the sedation of mandrake.

In 1874 Sir Benjamin Ward Richardson wrote in *The British and Foreign Medico-chirurgical Revue* that he had prepared wine of mandragora according to Discorides and used it successfully as a surgical anaesthetic.

The roots were thought for many years to be an all-purpose good luck charm. In Germany they were called *alrauns* after the legendary Teutonic sorceress, the Alrauna Maiden, who used such plant charms. The Anglo-Saxons used mandrake roots to free a person from possession by a demon.

In Paris in 1638, Lauren Catelan wrote a treatise on mandrake saying that it grows from the semen discharged by men hung or broken on the wheel. In 1665 Jakob Thomasius wrote that mandragora grows from urine voided by innocent men hung for theft. It was believed that this plant grew under the gallows where murderers had died and if these plants were dug up, death would stalk the digger. Since gallows were situated at crossroads, in no-man's-land, mandrakes are plants of the Otherworld.

The mandrake can be employed as a plant familiar, giving contact with the Otherworld. The mandrake should be dug up, washed in wine and given a name which should be called out three times. The root should then be re-buried. This process should be carried out three times in all. The mandrake should then be always be addressed by its name.

NB: Using mandrake internally is not recommended.

Mugwort *Artemisia vulgaris*
Mugwort is an aromatic, perennial herb that grows to a height of between 2 - 4 ft. It is native to Europe and most of temperate regions of the northern hemisphere. It will grow in most soils and can be found growing along roadside, in hedgerows and on waste ground.

The English name 'mugwort' may derive from its use in brewing or from flavouring drinking cups, or mugs.

An 11th century herbal recommended that a root of mugwort, hung over the door, would act as a protective charm. Mugwort was believed to have magical properties which would ward off evil and disease.
"There is my moly of much fame
In magic often used;
Mugwort and nightshade for the same,
But not by me abused"
Michael Drayton
Anglo Saxons used mugwort for general protection. It was also used extensively by wizards, strengthened in the midsummer fires and made into

garlands. Wizards used it for counter magic. The *Lacnunga* or 'Lay of Nine Herbs' begins with:

"Have in mind, mugwort, what you made known,
What you laid down, at the great denouncing,
Una, your name is, oldest of herbs, of might against thirty and against three,
Of might against venom and onflying,
Of might against the vile She who fares through the land".

The 'vile She' may be the elves who act as agents of the Wyrd Sisters.

Mugwort is also a herb of clairvoyance and may be taken as a tea to aid divination. It may be used as incense. It can be placed by the bed or used in a dream pillow to aid prophetic dreams. Mugwort intensifies the dreaming process and helps in lucid dreaming. It can be smoked, preferably in combination with coltsfoot or mullein.

NB: Mugwort should not be taken during pregnancy. Internal use of mugwort has physiological effects on the stomach and female reproductive system though this will not transfer through smoking.

Oak *Quercus robur*

There are two types of native oak, the pendunculate and the sessile oak. The pendunculate oak is the most common and is distinguished by the fact that the acorns are set on long stalks. The oak is a lowland tree, needing moisture.

The oak is perhaps more honoured in lore than any other tree. The oak is the king of the forest, huge, living for centuries. In Britain there are reputed to be oaks which have been standing for a thousand years. All of these have, at some time in their history, been pollarded, a process which expands their life-span. Most of them have decayed and have hollow centres. Oak woods, together with other mixed trees, form the natural native cover over most of the better soil on the lowlands of the British Isles.

The roots of the oak are said to extend as far underground as its branches do above, making a perfect symbol for the World Tree, as well as a god whose powers royally extend to the heavens, middle earth and the underworld equally. It is a symbol of the law 'as above, so below'. It appears as a World Tree in the Welsh shamanic story of Lleu who was slain by his wife's lover and lived as an eagle in an oak tree until rescued by his uncle.

In ogham the oak is '*duir*' meaning 'door' in Gaelic (the word for door and oak come from the same root in many European languages), perhaps because a door made form oak offers protection and solidity and because oaks often marked boundaries; or perhaps because the oak is the door to knowledge and marks boundaries of a different kind. Pliny recognised the Greek *drus*, meaning 'oak' is related to the word 'Druid'. The second syllable may be related to the indo- European *wid* meaning 'know' and the derived meaning would be 'oak knowledge'.

In Slavic myth, the afterlife paradise was called Bouyan, meaning 'fruitful'. It was ruled by Zaryá, a sun maiden who represented the dawn and dusk. She sits under a dripping oak on the fiery stone Alatuir, which was made of amber. She sews with a red gold thread and was often asked to sew up wounds since there was a healing river flowing from beneath her seat; perhaps the river that marks the boundaries of this world and the next.

Gwyn ap Nudd, lord of Annwn (the underworld), rides out with the wild hunt, some say at Beltane, some say at midwinter. The old British legend is the distinctive whirring of the wild geese in their migration is the sound of the flight of damned souls flying to the frozen wastelands of the northern hell. Gwyn, which means 'the white one' is an underworld god, perhaps cognate with Bran. He was also an oak god. At his death he was buried in a boat shaped coffin made of oak in honour of his father, Llyr.

The oak was a tree of prophecy, a method by which gods could communicate with their followers. Zeus was worshipped in a grove of oaks at Dodona, one of the most ancient Greek sanctuaries. His sacred oak, Quercus, was an oracle tree which gave messages in the rustle of its leaves, or in the murmur of the sacred spring which rose from its roots. Ovid said *"The high oak trembled and branches moved without the wind"*. Lots could also be drawn from an urn which stood beneath it. The oracular powers of this oak were preserved in pieces taken from it, and a beam from the Dodona oak was incorporated in Jason's ship, the Argo, where it continued to give advice to the Argonauts. The Golden Fleece itself was nailed to an oak tree, while lindens stood nearby, the linden tree being the feminine partner of the oak according to some systems.

Like the ash, the tree of Poseidon, the oak, tree of His brother Zeus is said to attract lightning. Both Poseidon and Zeus were armed with thunderbolts. The oak seems to attract more lightning than any other tree, apart from the ash The Druids would carve a quartered circle on an oak as protection against lightning. In some places in Britain, this practice is still maintained by foresters. Several countries had thunder gods connected with the oak, such as the god Thor or Thunor. In Russia he was called Perun, the name meaning 'thunderbolt'. In Lithuania he was called Perkunas.

THE PATH OF THE SHAMAN

The oak's associated animal is the bull. In Britain many old oaks are known as 'bull oaks' including Herne's Oak in Windsor Forest. The bull is also connected with thunder gods, since its bellow sounds like thunder. The strength and virility of the bull is the animal kingdoms equivalent of the oak's. When the mistletoe, semen of the Forest Lord, was gathered from the sacred oak at midwinter, two white bulls were chosen for sacrifice. When the ancients sacrificed the powerful and fertile bull, its blood was believed to impart these qualities to the land.

Oak Bark Tea
Place one handful of oak bark in one pint of water. Simmer for 10 minutes, strain and drink.

Oak Leaf Wine
1 gallon oak leaves
1 gallon water
2 lb. sugar
3 oranges
Yeast
Pectinol
Boil the water and pour onto the leaves. Leave overnight. Strain and boil the liquid for 20 minutes. Pour into a fermentation bin and add the sugar and the juice and grated rind of the oranges. Leaves to cool and then add the yeast. Cover and leave to ferment for 5 days. Strain into a demi-jon, fit an airlock and leave to ferment out. When fermentation has completed, strain into a clean demi-jon and leave to clear. Add pectic enzyme to remove any haze. Leave for 24 hours and filter into bottles. This can be drunk immediately.

Passionflower *Passiflora incarnata*
Passionflower is used as a tea in herbal medicine for headaches and insomnia. The dried plant can be smoked to give a short lasting marijuana-like effect, especially when combined with skullcap and damiana.[142]

Psilocybin *Psilocybe semilanceata*
Psilocybin mushrooms are found in meadowland, golf courses, lawns, roadsides and recreation grounds from late summer to autumn.
Witches in Britain commonly used the psilocybin mushroom in certain ceremonies, such as initiation, either made into a tea or steeped in brandy to make a potent Sabbat brew for Samhain.

193

THE PATH OF THE SHAMAN

Dosage is a matter of experimentation. A light dreamy trance can be induced with as few as four mushrooms, while higher doses of fifty or more cause hallucinations.

NB: Possession and preparation of these mushrooms is now illegal in Britain.

Reed *Phragmites communis*
The reed belongs to a genus of tall grasses. The common reed is a perennial plant commonly found growing in damp places such as marshes, fenlands, water edges and in moist woodland

The peace pipe or *calumet* ('reed') was a ceremonial tobacco pipe that North American Indians smoked as a sign of peace and friendship, passing it from person to person. A reed formed the stem of the pipe.

The pipe is probably the oldest of musical instruments after the drum. Pipes are the ancestors of all other wind instruments. According to Greek mythology, the god Pan invented them. Pan fell in love with a water nymph called Syrinx and pursued her until she reached the river Ladon, where she cried out to her sister nymphs to enable her to cross it. Pan reached out to grasp her, but instead found his arms filled with reeds. Hearing the breeze as it passed through the reeds make a low musical sound, he plucked seven of them and made a pipe which he named Syrinx. The pipe had seven reeds in accordance with the harmony of heaven which was said to contain seven sounds.

Virgil wrote that Mænalus, a mountain in Arcadia sacred to Pan, clad with pine trees "...*always has a vocal grove and shaking pines; he ever hears, the loves of shepherds, and Pan, the first who suffered not the reeds to be neglected*". Hermes (a messenger and psychopomp god) cut reeds and made them into a shepherd's pipe and played a tune. Apollo was delighted and offered to swap his golden cattle-herding staff for them, which would make Hermes the god of all herdsmen and shepherds.

King Midas attended a musical contest between Apollo and the *korybante* Marsyas, which was judged by the river god Tmolus, who awarded the prize to Apollo. Marsyas was flayed alive. Midas dissented and Apollo punished him with ass's ears which Midas concealed under a Phrygian cap but his barber found it impossible to keep the secret and dug a hole in a riverbank and whispered into it "King Midas has ass's ears." Unfortunately a reed sprouted from the hole and whispered the secret to all who passed. When Midas learned his disgrace was public knowledge he condemned the barber to death, drank bull's blood (believed to be a deadly poison) and perished miserably.

THE PATH OF THE SHAMAN

The korybantes were the attendants of the orgiastic goddess Cybele. It was believed they could bind and release men from spells and both induce and heal madness. They wandered around the country in the manner of shamans, employing ecstatic dance, trance, and the playing of the flute and reed pipe.

The reed is hollow, filed mostly with air or spirit. The Gaelic word *gaothaiche* relates to the reed and means 'hollow' and refers to the mouth of the bagpipe. The pipes of the bagpipe were originally made from reeds and in Celtic legend were invented by the fairies.

Because of its thick root the Celts identified it with a submerged dryad. They also associated it with an entrance to the underworld, from which the sun is reborn. In myth the Sun Child is often set afloat in a coracle or moon basket.

Both Moses and Taliesin were taken from the reeds after being set afloat shortly after birth.

In a Zulu myth which tells of the origin of man, humans emerged from a bed of reeds (*Uthlanga*) which still exists, though not one knows where.

In the Egyptian *Book of The Dead*, there is a dialogue between the aspiring soul and the guardian of the hall of judgement, when the aspiring soul is asked his name and replies: "*Gleaming Sceptre of Papyrus is my name*," and the initiate goes on to describe a journey to the stars by way of a Cosmic Tree, through the lands of lamentation for Osiris (the underworld), and describes being given the key of the winds, a brazier and an amulet.

Rowan *Sorbus aucuparia*

The rowan is widespread as a native tree in Britain. It is usually seen as a solitary specimen, throughout woodlands or scattered in rocky and mountainous regions. Rowan draws its name from the old Norse word *runa* meaning 'a charm'.

In Ireland, Druids lit fires of rowan wood to summon the spirits of the dead to assist warriors in battle. Some think the rowan berry may have been the magical serpent's egg mentioned by the Druids.

The rowan is associated with protection, particularly from witchcraft and lightning. Bewitched horses can only be controlled with a rowan whip: "If your whipstock's made of rowan you can ride through any town". The berries are marked at the base with the sign of the pentagram, the universal sign of protection. Lambs were given rowan collars to protect them from witchcraft. Rowan witchposts, carved with billets and St Andrew's crosses standing between the chimney and door would prevent

THE PATH OF THE SHAMAN

witches entering, and were common in cottages in Eskdale, Yorkshire. Boiling jam was stirred with a hazel or rowan stick to prevent the fairies from stealing it

The other property of rowan is divination. The Welsh once brewed a visionary drink from the rowan, although the recipe for this is now lost. The Druids spread flayed bulls hide over wattles of rowan to ride into the other realms to gain knowledge. The Irish Druids used rowan fires to invoke spirits to aid armies in battle. As it played a central role in Druid ceremonies it was named '*fid na druad*' or 'the Druid's tree'. Another name for rowan is 'witchwand' for divining rods for metal are made form rowan.

Rowan frequently occurred around stone circles. The three fiery arrows of the goddess Brighid were said to be made of rowan and may relate to the triple arrow sign of *awen*, meaning inspiration.

Magical rowan berries appear in Celtic legend. In the legend of Fraoth rowan berries were guarded by a dragon and were said to give sustenance equal to nine meals. It was also the food of the gods, probably associated with a taboo on red foods, red being the colour of death and rebirth in Bronze Age Britain. Perhaps, as in Greece, red foods were reserved for feasts of the dead.

Special properties are associated with a rowan growing out of the top of another tree. It is believed to be doubly effective against witchcraft, and since it does not grow on the ground, witches have no power over it. In this it has parallels with mistletoe. The growths which form on a rowan tree were considered to contain all knowledge, thus the wattles were valued and the tree considered oracular.

A mystic rowan tree was believed to grow in one of the Orkney isles in which the fate of the island was bound up. If even one leaf of this tree was carried away from the island, the whole group would pass under the dominion of a foreign lord.

In Wales, the rowan tree was so sacred there was not a churchyard without one and on a certain day everyone wore a cross made from its wood. Rowan was planted in the churchyard as a warning to evil spirits and coffins on the way to the churchyard were frequently rested under it.

Rowan's associations are with witchcraft, protection, divination, the underworld and the dead. The berries and leaves can be dried and burned as incense to invoke spirits, familiars, spirit guides and elementals, to ask for their help when seeking visions, particularly at Samhain. The berries can also be used in an incense to banish undesirable entities and thoughtforms. A rowan cross, made of two twigs of rowan, tied with red

196

THE PATH OF THE SHAMAN

thread, may be hung in the home for protection. A rowan wand is used for casting a protective circle. The wine or tea may be taken to induce prophetic dreams and the incense burned whilst seeking visions.

Rowan Wine
2 lb. rowan berries
2 oranges
3 lb. sugar
2 tsp. dried yeast
1/2 gallon boiling water
Remove the stalks from the berries, wash and place in a fermentation bin. Pour the boiling water over them and leave for three days, stirring daily. Put 1.5 pints of water in a saucepan and bring to the boil. Add the sugar to make a syrup then add to the fermentation bin along with the juice and grated rind of the oranges. Stir thoroughly and then strain into a demi-jon. Top up with cooled, boiled water, add the yeast and leave to ferment out. When fermentation is complete rack off into a clear demi-jon and leave to clear. Bottle when clear.

NB: Eating the raw berries can cause stomach upsets.

Sage *Salvia officinalis*
Sage is a hardy, aromatic, evergreen shrub that grows to a height of between 1 - 2 ft. The common sage is a native of the Mediterranean. It likes a position in full sun and a light, dry and well drained soil.

The generic name *salvia* and the common name 'sage' both come from the Latin *salvia* meaning 'I save'. The specific name *officinalis* recognises sage as a medicinal plant.

Sage was a sacred herb to the Romans who believed that the use of it benefited most illnesses. They believed it had the ability to both save and create life. It was collected ritually by a priest dressed in a white tunic, barefoot and purified. The sage would be cut by a tool that contained no iron after sacrifices of bread and wine were offered. It was dedicated to their chief god Jupiter.

The French writer Saint-Simon, of the court of Louis XIV, took an infusion of sage every night and attributed his long life to it. Sage tea was once drunk in the same way as ordinary tea or coffee is today. It was also used by fasting churchmen.

Sage is a sacred herb amongst the Native American peoples, who have used it for purification, healing and cleansing.

THE PATH OF THE SHAMAN

In the Bible sage is mentioned as one of the herbs that Solomon used to purify his temple.

Sage is a herb of purification and its smoke may be directed to cleanse the aura, the working area and magical tools. An infusion of the leaves may also be used for the same purpose. Sage tea may be taken whilst fasting to purify the body and spirit. Dried sage leaves may be smoked to connect with the plant's energies.

Sage Tea
2 tsp. herb
1/2 pt. boiling water
Pour the boiling water over the herb and infuse for 15 minutes. Strain and drink.

Sage Purification Incense
1 part sage leaves
2 parts frankincense
1/2 part rosemary leaves
Combine the ingredients and burn on charcoal.

NB: Sage is slightly toxic and should not be used in large doses over an extended period of time.

Skullcap /Scullcap *Scutellaria lateriflora / Scutellaria galericulata*
Skullcap is a hardy perennial member of the mint family that grows to a height of between 1 - 3 ft. It is native to eastern North America and as far west as New Mexico. It grows readily in Britain.

Skullcap is a sedative and if the leaves are smoked it has similar effects to marijuana. It may be employed in relaxation and meditation incenses. The tea may be taken for trance work.

NB: When taken in large doses skullcap can cause giddiness, stupor and twitching. Do not take in combination with prescribed tranquillisers.

Skullcap Tea
1 oz skullcap
1 pt. boiling water
Pour the boiling water over the herb and infuse for 20 minutes. strain and take one cup for medicinal purposes and up to four for trance work.

THE PATH OF THE SHAMAN

Valerian *Valeriana officinalis*
Valerian is a hardy, herbaceous perennial which grows to a height of between 2 - 5 ft. It is native to Europe and northern Asia. It likes a rich, moist soil in full sun or light shade.

Valerian is calming and stress relieving and can be taken in moderation during difficult times.

Witches have long employed valerian for bonding with their cats, and for attracting cat familiars. The Wildfolk were often thought to take cat disguises and valerian is used to attract some types of fairy allies. Cats' divine status in ancient Egypt was corrupted in the usual manner of Christian take over into association with evil and the Devil. Many innocent animals in Medieval times suffered cruel torture and death, often along with their owners, as a result. Certainly the cat is an enigmatic creature, nocturnal, reputedly psychic with the power to see spirits and ghosts. Cats, like pigs, are associated with underworld and moon goddesses.

As a burrowing animal, the rat is also an underworld guide, and rat allies can be encouraged with valerian root.

The dried roots of the herb are used as a sedative and for nervous complaints, and give a mild, floating feeling. Steep a tablespoon of roots in half a pint of warm (not boiling or the essential oils will evaporate) water for one hour in a covered pan. Add peppermint and honey to taste.

NB: Taken over an extended period of time valerian can cause headaches and stupor.

Vervain *Verbena officinalis*
Vervain is a hardy herbaceous perennial that grows to a height of between 2 - 3 ft. It is native to Britain, Europe, North Africa and West Asia. It likes a fertile soil and a position in full sun or light shade and can often be found growing along roadsides, in pastures or on waste ground.

Vervain was one of the three most sacred herbs of the Druids, who used it in their 'lustral water' for the ritual cleansing of the altar, and to sweep the sacred space. The Druids gathered vervain only at the rising of the Dog Star Sirius, when neither the sun or the moon cast a light. It was dug up with the left hand and a libation of honey was used to propitiate the earth. The Druids also used vervain for divination and as a charm against ill luck and curses.

Verbena was the Roman name for altar plants in genera, calling it *herba sacra*. It was placed on the altar during ceremonies and was used for spiritual purification. In the Bible Solomon used vervain, amongst other herbs, to cleanse his temple.

It was also considered to be a plant of protection, and for this reason Roman soldiers carried vervain during battle. The Anglo-Saxons included vervain in their *Holy Salve* as they considered it to be a powerful protector against the demons of disease. In Medieval Europe it was also believed to guard the carrier against the plague and to protect the eyesight. Persian magicians greeted the newly risen sun naked and holding aloft bunches of vervain. It was employed by the Pawnee Indians to enhance their dreams. In the Middle Ages vervain was considered to be a plant much used by witches, though only for beneficial purposes such as love spells. Indeed it was thought to be so kindly disposed towards humankind that it would only grow within a mile of human habitation.

The poem *The Chair of Taliesin* describes the initiation of a bard with a magical drink containing vervain. This was the Cauldron of Cerridwen, which bestowed the powers of eloquence, inspiration, prophecy and song, of which vervain was one of the main constituents. Cerridwen is a shape shifter and has aspects as a Cat Goddess, a Moon Goddess, the Harvest Mother and as a Crone or white sow. She is the underworld initiator of the Native British Tradition.

The story of Gwion is a metaphor about the initiation of a bard. First of all he stokes the cauldron of knowledge, then, when he least expects it, he gains a new consciousness of All. The knowledge then makes him afraid and he tries to run away from it. The Goddess challenges him by assuming a frightening form to test his worthiness. He goes through different personifications of animal totems, assimilating the knowledge of different realities, while the confrontation of the Goddess forces him on, refining his being. Eventually he has to be reassumed into the womb of the Goddess in order to be reborn as a true initiate. The womb of the underworld goddess contains both the seeds of new growth and the souls of the dead. In the incubation chamber the would-be initiate must encounter both of these aspects.

Vervain is a powerful plant ally and should be treated with great respect. To befriend the spirit within it the tea can safely be taken, or an incense of it burned. Gather it consciously, at the dark moon, and give thanks to the Earth Womb that produced it. It is traditional to harvest enough for the coming year, and any left from the previous year should be cast on the Midsummer bonfire.

Sweeping the sacred space with bunches of vervain will cleanse and purify it as well as raising its vibrations. The temple and magical tools can also be washed with lustral water. Vervain leaves can be used in the ritual bath to detoxify the physical body and refine the aura prior to ritual.

THE PATH OF THE SHAMAN

Taking the tea before the ritual will heighten the consciousness and intensify clairvoyant powers. The assocaited animal of vervain is the hawk; the plant spirit may allow you to journey on the wings of the far seeing bird and receive the messages and omens only its clear eyes detect. Use vervain oil to anoint the third eye chakra and to consecrate tools used for divination. If you need to examine your life from a greater perspective, seek vervain as your partner.

Wild Lettuce *Lactuca virosa*
Traditionally, the leaves and roots of wild lettuce was dried and smoked to create a mild, dreamy state by the Native Americans. The Hopi believed these dreams contain more information about reality than the waking state.

NB Wild lettuce should not be ingested by anyone with stomach ulcers or other digestive disorders, as it will hinder the digestive process. It can also affect the sex drive. [143]

Wild Lettuce Beer
1 gallon water
12 oz molasses
10 oz sugar
3 oz wild lettuce
Yeast
Combine the treacle, sugar and water. Bring to the boil. Pour into the brewing bin and add the wild lettuce. Cool to 20 degrees C and add the yeast. Allow to ferment out and strain into bottles.

Willow *Salix* species.
Willows usually grow near water. Sometimes they are planted in damp regions so that their roots take up water and dry the soil. The roots interlace to form a tough network that holds the soil together and prevents soil erosion. Willows also are planted to provide shade and to protect fields from winds.

The word 'witch' is derived from a root word for willow which also yields 'wicker'. The witches besom is made of an ash stake with birch twigs and an osier or willow binding.

In classical mythology the willow was sacred to Hecate, Circe, Hera and Persephone, all death and underworld goddesses, worshipped by witches. It is sacred to all deities of the underworld and may be used as a funeral herb.

An old Celtic custom associated with the willow was the practice of tying cloths to the trees near wells and sacred fountains.

201

The willow is a tree of inspiration and initiation for bards and poets. In the *Song of the Forests* an injunction is made *"Burn not the willow, a tree sacred to poets"*. Orpheus is depicted as touching the bough of a willow in a grove of Persephone for eloquence when passing through the underworld. The Celts also associated it with bards.

The sorcerers of the Abipones of Argentina were believed to have unparalleled powers over the forces of nature and the spirits of the dead. Those who aspired to become a shaman sat upon an aged willow overhanging a lake and abstained from food for several days until they began to have visions.

Willow tea and incense can be used when working on the feminine side of your nature, the Goddess and the gentle rhythms of the moon and Nature's cycles, on the feminine gift of fertility.

It is sacred to the pan-Celtic goddess Brighid, the daughter of the Great god Dagda. She is a Triple Fire Goddess and her name come s from '*breo-saigit*' which means 'fiery arrow'. Hers are the three fire arrows of inspiration, healing and the hearth or forge. She is the muse of poets, who lived under her patronage and who carried a golden branch hung with small bells in her honour. She is the goddess of holy wells, where offerings were left to solicit healing. She was also a goddess of the hearth fire and forge, patroness of the magician/ shaman smith who transformed, by his alchemy, elements of the underworld into beautiful or useful objects.

Yarrow *Achillea millefolium*
Yarrow is native to the whole of Europe, including Britain. It is a hardy herbaceous perennial and grows to a height of around 3 ft. It prefers a sunny position but will tolerate light shade. It likes a rich, moist soil.

Stems were used by the Druids to divine seasonal weather in Europe, while in China the stems are used for the fifty *I Ching* sticks to foretell the future. The Chinese considered yarrow to be a sacred plant.

Yarrow is sacred to the Horned God, the Lord of the Animals. Yarrow tea may be used for connection with the God. Yarrow tea and incense can be used to promote divination and clairvoyance. The dried leaves can be used in smoking mixtures to aid clairvoyance and contact with the masculine principle.

Yarrow Infusion
1 oz herb
1 pt boiling water
Pour the boiling water over the herb. Infuse 15 minutes, strain and drink.

THE PATH OF THE SHAMAN

NB: Yarrow should not be used by pregnant women. It should not be used over a long period of time as it can cause skin irritation.

Yew *Taxus baccata*
Although the yew is a large tree it is not necessarily a tall tree, reaching a height of between 15 - 20 ft. It has a short but massive bole which is covered in thin red bark that flakes off in patches. Large specimens can have a girth of over 50 ft, although a girth of around 25 ft is more common. A girth of this proportion represents many centuries growth because the annual growth rings are very thin. The produces hard but elastic wood that is extremely durable. The yew is reputed to be one of the longest lived trees. Its capacity for longevity is provided by its peculiar form of growth. Its branches grow down to the ground to form new stems which grow to become the trunks of separate but linked growth. In time the central trunk becomes old and the inside decays but a new tree grows within the spongy mass of the old and eventually cannot be recognised from the original.

In all European countries the yew is associated with death and the underworld. Many ancient cemeteries are full of yew trees. In Ireland the yew was described as the coffin of the vine as wine barrels were made of yew staves.

The yew was one of the five magical trees of Ireland described as 'the renown of Banbha' (the Crone or Death aspect of the Goddess), 'the spell of knowledge' and 'the king's wheel'. Every ancient Irish king wore a yew brooch in the shape of a wheel to remind him of the turning of the life's wheel and the inevitability of death. It was then passed to his successor.

In Greece and Rome the yew was sacred to Hecate, the Crone Goddess of the underworld and patron of witches. In Rome black bulls were sacrificed to Hecate, wreathed in yew, so that the ghosts would lap up their blood and it would keep them happy.

The yew however, is also a tree of regeneration arising from death. As the central trunk becomes old and the insides decay but a new tree grows within the spongy dying mass of the old. In Brittany it is said that a churchyard yew will send a root to the mouth of each corpse. This root is a symbol of the spirit reborn in much the same way as the tree is reborn.

In ogham the yew is *Idho*, one of the Cauldron of Five Trees. A mistake in the translation of a 5th century manuscript meant that the name of a sacred island off the western coast of Scotland was changed from Ioha to Iona. The traditional connections with Iona are linked to rebirth and reincarnation. The ancient bardic groves were taken over by St. Columba, who had fled from Ireland to seek fresh lands in which to spread the word. The clouds that pass over Iona and fall as rain on the mainland are said to be a reminder of the strength of the soul and its continuing ability to be reborn.

In Norse mythology, the yew was the sacred tree of Uller, god of winter, from which he made his bows and arrows. He lived at Ydalir, a vale of yews. He ruled Asgard while Odin was absent for the winter months. Odin would return and drive him away and be greeted with rejoicing as he bestowed gifts on mankind. Uller took refuge in the far north, or some say, the underworld. He was also a god of death and rode in the Wild Hunt. His place was taken by St Hubert, the hunter, patron of the first month of the year, beginning November 22nd in Sagittarius, the bowman.

Yews are either male or female. The oldest know artefact in the world is a yew spear that is 250,000 BCE found in Clacton in Somerset. A yew longbow was found with the Iceman mummy 3500 BCE found on Italian/Austrian border in 1999. In Britain there are yew trees as old a Stonehenge. They were sometimes planted on burial mounds. A mound in Taplow churchyard in Bucks contained a Saxon warrior with gold buckles, arms, and drinking horn. The yew seems to have been planted at time of burial. Churchyard yews often predate the churches. According to the Irish *Book of Lismore*:

Three life times of the stag for the Blackbird;
Three life times of the Blackbird for the Eagle;
Three life times of the Eagle for the Salmon;
Three life times of the Salmon for the Yew.

Yew needles may be used in an underworld incense.

NB: The yew is deadly poisonous and should not be used internally.

RECIPES

Flying Ointment
One part each of:
Dittany of Crete
Cinquefoil
Parsley
Mandrake root
Calamus
Valerian Root
Catnip

Mugwort
Damiana
6 parts Petroleum Jelly
Few drops fennel oil
Few drops clary sage oil
Heat the petroleum jelly in a double boiler. Add the herbs and heat until the fat has extracted the scent, which will take about thirty minutes. Strain through cheesecloth into glass jars, and add a few drops of fennel and clary sage oil to each.

Shaman Smokes

Some plants have leaves which can be dried and smoked. Tobacco, for example, has a long history as a sacred plant. However, if you use a plant recreationally, if you are addicted to it, you can never use it as a sacred herb. Other herbs that can be smoked include coltsfoot, peppermint, wild lettuce, passionflowers, broom flowers and damiana.

Dreambringer Smoke

1/8 part cinnamon
3 parts damiana
1 part crushed juniper berries
3 parts passion flower
3 parts wild lettuce
4 parts coltsfoot
2 parts catnip

Meditation Smoke

1/8 part cinnamon
3 parts damiana
1 part juniper berries, crushed
1 part rose petals
3 parts coltsfoot
3 parts catnip

Clairvoyance Tea

1 oz peppermint
¼ oz dried orange peel
¼ oz rose petals
½ oz lemon grass
½ cinnamon stick, crushed

THE PATH OF THE SHAMAN

6 cloves, crushed
1 oz mugwort
¼ oz wild lettuce
Combine the ingredients and keep in an airtight container in a dark place. To use, steep ½ oz – 1 oz in half a pint of boiling water for 20 minutes, strain and drink.

Shaman's Tea
½ oz sage
½ oz mugwort
1 oz catnip
½ oz skullcap
1 oz passionflower
¼ oz ginger powder
Combine the ingredients and keep in an airtight container in a dark place. To use, steep ½ oz – 1 oz in half a pint of boiling water for 20 minutes, strain and drink.

Trance Incense
1 part broom flowers
½ part broom seeds
2 parts crushed juniper berries
½ part foxglove seeds
1 part crushed sloes
1 part ragwort flowers
1 part mistletoe
1 part valerian root
1 part wild lettuce
Combine and burn on charcoal blocks.

Chapter 8
SHAMANIC PRACTICE

In tribal cultures, the witch or shaman is the bridge between the world on men and the world of the gods. He or she enters the spirit realm to return with healing, messages from the gods and ancestors, or visions that benefit the community.

PERSONAL POWER

What is Personal Power? Perhaps it is easier to say what happens when you have lost your Personal Power. You feel as though control of your life lies in other hands- the authorities, doctors, your parents, your spouse, your friends, your enemies, fate. You feel weak and unable to control what happens to you. You might feel worn out, tired and ill. In shamanic societies it is said that when this happens it is because a person has lost their soul, their spirit allies, life force or their Personal Power. Personal Power is cohesion of mind, body and spirit, whole and centred, balanced and harmonious. Once it is attained you feel in control, whole and centred.

Personal Power is something that needs constant maintenance. It is easy to give away, to lose. We often give away our Personal Power when we judge ourselves by other people's standards, only see ourselves as reflected in other people's eyes, allow others to dictate what we should think, wear, do. You give away your Personal Power when you see yourself as a failure because you haven't achieved what someone else thinks you should have achieved not what you yourself want to achieve. When you think that your health is not your responsibility but a doctor's, a therapist's. When you blame other people for the deficiencies in your life and never yourself. This is to give away your power, to place it in the hands of other people.

You can take back the power. You can make your Personal Power whole and strong. You can regain control of your life. This power lies within you, and no one else can do it for you. As candidates approached initiation into the ancient Eleusinian mysteries they would see, carved above the door of the chamber, the words '*Know Thyself*'. It is the root of all Personal Power and happiness. It's only when we fail to be in touch with ourselves that we lose our paths in life, together with our happiness with a resulting ill effect on our health and lives.

Today, many people are coming to realise what the ancients took for granted- that the mind, body and spirit are connected. Doctors recognise that a patient's mental attitude can have a dramatic effect on recovery and

THE PATH OF THE SHAMAN

serious illness survival rates. Most complimentary therapists would go a step further and say that all illness is a manifestation of imbalance or *dis*-ease within the whole being- mind, body, emotions and the soul or life force; a problem in one area will eventually affect the others. No problem exists in isolation, it may have several causes and a variety of effects. Any treatment needs to address the whole being- not just the body, not just the mind and certainly not just the spirit.

Reclaiming your Personal Power enables you to re-shape your life into a happier, more harmonious, more fulfilling existence. Reclaiming your Personal Power means taking on the responsibility for your own life, well being, growth and happiness.

Giving away your Personal Power leaves you weak and vulnerable. To blame another for your unhappiness is to hand over power to them. To stay in an abusive relationship or a situation that is damaging constitutes a relinquishing of personal power. To make someone else responsible for your happiness and well being is to give away your Personal Power.

Fear is a natural function of the mind. It warns the body when it is in danger and triggers the release of adrenaline. This gives the body the energy to either fight or take flight. Without this fear response the human race would not have survived, our ancestors would all have been gobbled up by sabre tooth tigers or trampled by hairy mammoths. It is still a vital part of the body's survival mechanism. We all have our fears and most of them are quite natural. It is normal to be a apprehensive if you are standing on the edge of a cliff, bungie jumping off a bridge, riding your motorbike at 100 miles an hour down the M1 or facing surgery- the body is merely expressing some concern for its safety. Most people would experience a little stage fright if called upon to address a meeting or speak to a large audience- there is a moment when you feel like chickening out and running away.

Problems occur when the fear response is triggered when you are not in any immediate physical danger. People have phobias about all kinds of things from spiders and frogs to spectacles and barrels of apples. Often these are the product of a frightening childhood experience or may be passed down from parent to child- if your mother screamed every time she saw a spider you would grow up thinking a spider was a terrifying thing. Sufferers know that their fear response is inappropriate: spectacles and frogs cannot harm them and we have no poisonous spiders in Britain, but the response is there all the same.

We become afraid when we are in a situation we cannot control. The body responds by giving us the immediate means to deal with it- physically fight it or run away. However, in many cases, this is not much use and may actually be damaging. When you walk into an exam room you can't fight the examiner or run away; either reaction would damage your career prospects. If you have been told you have a serious illness it doesn't help to punch the doctor and you can't run away from your aberrant body.

I was recently talking to an old friend who has suffered from panic attacks for nearly thirty years. He has tried various medications, but none of them seem to help very much. He has recently realised that his panic attacks started when his parents split up while he was still a child. He was a small boy who wanted his parents to stay together but was powerless to bring this about. He was in a frightening situation he couldn't control and his fear response brought about panic attacks. This is understandable, but his body and mind have now got used to responding to situations he cannot control by bringing on panic attacks. He gets them in pubs, crowded streets and shops. They grow much worse when there is an underlying uncertainty like moving to a new town, becoming unemployed or starting a new job. When he feels not quite in control he gets panic attacks.

This kind of fear can be seen as a loss of Personal Power. When we lose control over our lives, and ourselves we suffer a loss of Personal Power. The answer is to take steps to reclaim the power. Margaret had cancer:

MARGARET: *"When you get a serious illness, the first response is one of enormous fear. You don't know what is going to happen to you, you don't know how ill you may become, you don't know whether you are going to die. You are afraid of dying. Your body does not seem to be in your control, and the effects the illness is going to have on your life don't seem to be in your control. You are overwhelmed by fear. This is quite natural I suppose. But the effects of continual fear can be worse than any illness: nightmares, retreating inward to dark spaces, trying to run away from yourself, depression, panic attacks, the physical effects on the body of stress. You torture yourself quite literally. The strange thing about fear is that it cannot be sustained indefinitely. Sooner or later, you realise that it is worse than the illness and you get fed up with it. I started to take an interest in my treatments, I wanted to know what was really going on. I researched my illness, I found out all I could about it, then I came to you. You made me start eating properly and the treatments made me feel more relaxed. You talked to me about how I felt which was the most important thing. I felt like I was doing something to help my body to heal itself. The treatments you gave me made me feel like I was doing something positive myself, I wasn't just a slab of meat in the hands of men in white coats. Then I started the meditation and visualisation techniques you gave me, and bit by bit the nightmares stopped. I felt like I was getting to know myself for the first time in my life. I could still have some control over what happened to me. I realised I was not so afraid anymore. I was still me."*

SHAMANIC HEALING

One of the most important functions of the shaman is as a healer, whether the disease is physical, psychological or spiritual in nature. To effect healing, he will make a journey (or several journeys) to the Otherworld to determine the cause of the problem, and what forms of healing are necessary. He will make contact with the spirit allies that are necessary for the healing process, and perform a ritual to bring about the healing. As with all other forms of healing, including modern medicine, this may not bring about a complete cure, but instead give the patient the tools to better cope with the problem.

From the shamanic point of view, people who are prone to illness, accidents and bad luck have lost their personal power, and it is the job of the shaman to re-establish a link with that power, and reconnect the personal with the flow of the universe, restoring the lost parts of their souls. The shaman does not see the body as a solid object that carries you through life.

It is a network of energy and information in dynamic exchange with the rest of the Cosmos, existing in a constant stage of transformation. With every breath, every mouthful of food, every noise you hear and sight you see, your body changes. In the last few seconds, it has exchanged four hundred billion trillion atoms with your environment.[144] Every year 98% of the atoms have been exchanged. In three years every single atom is different. So when we get a new liver every few months, why does a diseased liver renew itself with diseased cells? It does it because the body consciousness programmes it to. We expect it to happen, and so it does. It has been shown over and over again, that people who expect to recover do so, and that people who have poor expectations deteriorate much faster and have a poorer prognosis. A sick person surrounded with stress, anger and negativity is having the sickness continually fed and exacerbated and will deteriorate fast. A sick person surrounded by calm, love and positivity can experience miracles.

In Japan there was a polluted lake called Lake Biwa, covered with invading foul-smelling algae. On July 25th 1999 three hundred and fifty people gathered, led by Dr Shioya to recite the Great Declaration: "*the infinite power of the universe takes shape and takes shape, the world became truly great and powerful*". A month later most of the algae had gone.[145]

Also in Japan, Masaru Emoto has been conducting experiments with the effect of intent on water crystals (these experiments have been duplicated and repeated thousands of times). On one jar of water, he pasted the words 'thank you', and beautiful crystals formed. On another jar he pasted the 'you fool' and the structure of the water was so affected that crystals refused to form. If thoughts can do that to water, what can they do to us? Holistic healers state that illness begins in the psyche, and that illness follows on from trauma, emotional upset, stress, rage and so on. When we project these emotions onto our body, illnesses follow. Trauma, stress and negative emotions trigger the disease process, and a portion of the soul may be lost or fixated on a particular point in time, a time of trauma of emotional change, and is lost to the present 'whole' because of its fixation on the past, leading to illness or depression.

Soul Retrieval

The shaman may undertake a journey to recover the lost portion of a person's soul, retrieve the life-essence and restore it to the person, and refocus the patient on the present. To do this, he may lie down beside the patient; enter an altered state of consciousness and journey to the underworld. When he has found the lost portion of the soul, he will bend to the patient's chest, and blow it back into the patient's body with his lips and breath.

I recently undertook a series of journeys to determine the source of my physical problems. In the first I was in the vortex of the Grail, it was overflowing with energy but I couldn't connect to it. I was a swan, flying up towards the Pole Star. In the next, I again became the swan, and flew upwards towards the Pole Star. A shaman clad in deerskin and antlers waited for me. In his hand he held a pink sphere, and it contained my youth and its idealistic and romantic fantasies. He did not return it to me, but stored it in a wooden chest.

In my third journey, I was overtaken with fear and panic as soon as I began, and this was the terror of illness. I realised that it stemmed back by to my childhood when my adoptive mother told me I had cancer (I didn't, there was nothing wrong with me). I spent the years of my child-hood being terribly afraid, and this fear shaped me; I have always been afraid for my health. The shaman appeared once more, accompanied by a toad. This fear took the shape of a black crystal which was in my heart, and the shaman sucked it out.

In the next journey, I became a crystal body, filled with golden light. I called some of my allies to me, stag, toad and fox, to seek the origin of the chronic pain in my shoulder. Frustration and trauma relating to certain events in my past were stored there, accreting in the form of something that looked like black coal. Toad came and sucked the poison from my shoulder, and

THE PATH OF THE SHAMAN

dived immediately into a nearby pond. At the bottom of the pond was a golden ball, the side of myself that had been abandoned at the time of trauma. I sank into the pool, became toad myself, and retrieved it. I expected the shaman to put it in his wooden box, but he didn't, instead I absorbed it back inside myself.

The next day, and there is no such thing as coincidence in this interwoven Cosmos, a friend came to visit. She is a counsellor, and got me talking about my ME triggers. I know that these include simply over-reaching my energy reserves, which I do constantly because I hate sitting still, but also conflict and boredom. She made me realise that a big part of me longs for the deep and continually sustained spiritual connection I experienced during the time of my shamanic crisis - and sometimes even looked back with nostalgia upon it - something which is inconsistent with also having to deal with everyday life. This was why I had not been able to let go of my illness completely. I had realised there had to be a balance between the two sides of myself, physical and spiritual, but I hadn't realised before why I wasn't achieving it.

To make a soul retrieving journey for another, you may need the help of a drummer. You and the patient should fast during the day, and for the operation, find a quiet dimly lit place where you will not be disturbed. Honour the four directions. Make a statement of intent. Begin the drumming and the dance to summon your animal or other spirit allies, with the help of your power song, if you have one.

When you have entered a light trance, the state of dreaming with the eyes open, lie down beside the patient. Find the entrance to the underworld, and begin to journey downwards. State that you are looking for the patient's lost soul, or his lost power animal. As you journey, this animal soul may then appear to you several times. When you are sure it is the right one, take it in your arms and return to the middle world. Place the animal on the chest of the patient, and blow hard to force it into the chest of the patient.

Afterwards, relate the experience to the patient, and help him to dance his animal.

Intrusions

My experience with the Great Shaman and the toad touches on another shamanic healing technique, that of extraction. Extraction involves removing a spiritual intrusion. This does not mean that an evil spirit has taken possession of the body, but is a kind of spiritual infection that affects on the functioning of the body, mind and spirit.

THE PATH OF THE SHAMAN

Among the Untsuri Shuar and Jívaro people of eastern Ecuador, the intrusions are called 'magical darts', and sometimes these were deliberately inserted into enemies. This has direct parallels with the elf bolts of British lore, called in Gaelic *saighead sith* (elf-arrows). They were said to have been manufactured by fairies and evil witches for use in causing harm, shooting them at humans or livestock. Deaths were attributed to them and it was thought they could induce paralysis: the word 'stroke' for paralysis is derived from 'elf-stroke'.[146] In 1662 the Scottish witch Isobel Gowdie confessed to her dealings with fairies and testified:

> *"As for Elf-arrow-heidis, the Divell shapes them with his awin hand, and syne deliveris thame to Elf-boyes, who whyttis and dightis them with a sharp thing lyk a paking neidle."*

If a cow were suspected of being elf shot, then it would be necessary to send for a wise woman or cunning man who would examine the cow for hairless patches or lumps under the skin. The wise woman would then proceed to remove the intrusion. An eminent 'fairy doctor' (a wise woman who specialised in curing spirit-inflicted ills) made the cure of fairy darts her speciality and was sent for all round Ireland. She had no power unless she was asked to cure, and she took no reward until the dart was extracted and the cure effected. The treatment included a salve, the ingredients of which she kept secret.

In Britain, the cunning folk engaged in many practices from using herbs to the laying on of hands, charms, invocations, prayers and magic. However, the cunning woman who practiced such magic laid herself open to prosecution for witchcraft. While any woman practicing fortune telling, midwifery or herbalism could be executed as a witch, male doctors, astrologers and alchemists were left unscathed- powerful women were something to be feared and put down.

The shaman will locate the position of the intrusion, while in an altered state of consciousness, and remove it by plucking it out with his hand, sucking it out, or scooping it out with a crystal. The intrusion is then put, or spat, into something neutral, like water or earth, so that it can dissipate. In order to remove the intrusion, the shaman is sometimes obliged to take it into himself, and suffers pain and discomfort in consequence. If the shaman is not powerful enough, he may not be able to get rid of the intrusion from his own body afterwards.

THE PATH OF THE SHAMAN

Psychopomp Work

Shamans do another type of healing by acting as psychopomps. A psychopomp is a spirit or individual or divine entity which accompanies the soul of the recently deceased to a place in the Otherworld. This might involve dealing with cases of haunting and possession, when the shaman conducts the soul beyond the middle realm where it has got stuck for whatever reason to the realm beyond. In the case of a possessed person, the shaman must them return to them their own, complete soul.

In the case of a person lying in a coma, a shaman would say that the soul has left the body, and he must journey to the Otherworld and find it, and determine whether it wishes to return to the body, and if it does, conduct it back there. If it does not, the shaman will escort it to the realm where it can be reunited with loved ones.

DIVINATION

The dictionary defines divination as the various methods by which events are interpreted or explained as predictions by seers. Divination is probably as old as man himself. For the shaman, since all of the Cosmos is connected, any aspect or realm of the Cosmos is available to him, including all its knowledge, the past and future as well as the present, and even the language of animals and plants. In an altered state of consciousness, the shaman can determine what herbs might help a patient, for example.

Many methods of divination have been employed through the ages, including cards, tea leaves, palmistry, dominoes, dice, the I Ching, the reading of oracles, the interpretation of dreams and the runes. In modern times many new methods of divination have been invented, some based on old lore, some not. There are two types of diviners, one will go into a trance to make contact with the voices of the inner world, the other will observe events, whether that be the flight of certain birds or the fall of the runes, which are then interpreted according to particular rules. The Cosmos and its various concepts are presented as a series of symbols that are read according to their individual meanings and by their relationship to each other.

A shaman's work might also involve divination to get an answer to a specific question. The answers are known by the spirits and he might enter a state of altered consciousness in order to question his allies. He might even use divinatory tools, such as bones, runes and so on, with the aid of his spirits.

WEATHER WORKING

One of the traditional roles of the shaman is as a weather worker. For the shaman, everything has spirit, including the spirits of the wind, rain and so on. In the 1800s, Alexander Carmichael wrote of the Scottish Highlanders:

".... the old people had runes which they sang to the spirits dwelling in the sea and in the mountains, in the wind and in the whirlwind, in the lightning and in the thunder, in the sun and in the moon and m the stars of heaven".[147]

For the Koyukon peoples, the shamans were not seen so much as owners of power for themselves, but instead as ones who knew how to influence the spiritual forces of nature for good or no good, according to their purpose. Everything in nature, including the weather, has spirit. Some peoples use intimidation and threat to achieve their desired result. The Guajiro of South America shoot arrows into clouds to pierce them and force the release of rain. However, weather magic is only used on serious situations like drought, not simply because you don't want it to rain on your barbecue. When the weather is affected in one place, this will have a knock on effect in others, possibly with serious consequences for others.

STORYTELLING

The Celtic bards preserved the knowledge of the Otherworld and the magic of how to deal with it. Through their skill, they were able to take their audience into their story, telling it to the silent audience in the darkness, altering the reality around them. The stories were more than entertainment; they imparted traditional lore, and helped the listeners to journey into the Otherworld along with the heroes and fairy maidens.

In the North, skalds fulfilled a similar role. Much of the poetry contained kennings, a way of expressing a thing in terms of another, and to understand them, a great knowledge of mythology was necessary.

Through the tales of the Otherworld, we gain knowledge of the Otherworld, since they often come from the shaman's direct experience of it, the spirits, and the words the gods speak through him. They help us remember the Otherworld knowledge we all contain within.

In many ancient societies, the story could be the path to initiation. In Greece, the mysteries of Eleusis were presented as a drama, [148] with candidates taking the parts of the gods, something that is still done in ritual today.

THE PATH OF THE SHAMAN

Quartz

In prehistoric times, it is possible that extracting stone from the earth was considered to be contact with the spirit or ancestral world. In ancient Europe stones bearing white quartz crystal were chosen for stone circles, and used extensively in burials chambers like New Grange in Ireland. Quartz was carried to sacred sites, making rock art as part of the pilgrimage, sometimes pushing quartz into the rock cracks which were portals into the spirit realm. The dead have been found with quartz crystals beside them or in their hands. Even the early Christian church took over the custom and scattered quartz on graves. Quartz seems to have been regarded as a gateway to other dimensions.

Quartz was very important throughout the native shamanic cultures of the world from America to Borneo. The medicine men of Australia carry quartz and call it 'solidified sacred water' which was sprinkled on neophytes, where it was symbolically absorbed and grew into wings over the course of two days. Amazonian shamans consider that spirits can materialize and become visible in quartz crystals. Some *sheripiari* even feed tobacco juice to their stones daily. In Malaysia, the people of the Semang Tribe believed that Celestial Beings presented quartz crystals to their shamans. Spirits lived inside these crystals, which were called "stones of light". The Chinese called quartz crystals "living stones" as they believed that they were alive. Japanese shamans believed that quartz crystals were the solidified breath of sacred dragons.

Shamans were often thought to have quartz inside their bodies. The Wiradjeri believe a supernatural being called Baiame sings a piece of quartz into their foreheads so they will be able to see inside people, and fly. For them, quartz comes from the depths of the earth to mediate the light of the sun, bridging the tiers of the Cosmos.

In south America the Desana shaman wears a polished cylinder of white or yellowish quartz and carries smaller pieces in his purse- hexagonal crystals are a model of the universe for them (hexagonal patterns are often experienced in hallucinations). Crystals symbolise sacred space wherein all essential transformations are thought to take place. The refraction of light is an image if dynamic change. The Desana dead are buried in a canoe cut in half and folded over, thus creating an hexagonal space.

When rubbed together, quartz crystals generate a bright flashing light, like lightening. They also produce an electrical voltage. Raised form the earth, quartz drew power form the sun.[149] Quartz is associated with lightening and semen, especially the semen of the sun. A Desana shaman can throw lightening at a person in the form of a crystal. It was thought that

216

THE PATH OF THE SHAMAN

if small pieces penetrate the body they are poisonous and a shaman causes illness by sending small splinters into a person, and cures them by sucking them out. The shaman of the Sea Dyaks or Iban of East Malaysia (Sarawak) has a box containing a collection of magical objects, the most important being quartz crystals, "the stones of light".

Native American shamans pounded quartz crystals to release the divine light that was trapped inside to attract the souls of deceased ancestors. They also placed quartz crystals over their eyes to stimulate clairvoyant abilities. The shamans of some tribes even inserted a tiny quartz crystal between two of their ribs on the left-hand side of their bodies. When a shaman died, the crystal was removed and inserted between two ribs of a new shaman, granting him all the knowledge gained by his predecessor.

In ecstatic trance, crystals are used as a bridge to the realms of Spirit, empowering the initiate to communicate with beings in other worlds.

SHAMANIC EXERCISES

Shutting Off the World

It is a fact that while children are often aware of fairy folk, most people lose contact as they get older. The cares and stresses of the everyday world intrude; we get caught up in other things. The Otherworld may be trying to communicate with you, but cannot get through the babble of *'what shall I make for dinner? What shall I wear tonight; I must get my suit from the dry cleaners,'* and so on. We must be able to slow down and listen to the rhythms of Elphame.

Sometimes the Otherworld forces us to do this. One of the ways it uses is to make us too ill to have any interaction with the outside world. In illness we stop trying to achieve and simply learn to exist, to *be*. In the ensuing quiet, the world of spirits opens.

You will never contact the spirits while your mind is cluttered with the business of everyday life. To work with spirits you have to learn to shut out the prattle of the human world, and the inner chatter of your mind. When you find the still, silent place within, the Otherworld can begin to communicate with you. Don't rush, don't try to force it, stop trying to accomplish it, and simply learn to *be*.

Meditation helps in this aim; it develops mental clarity, and imagination is the greatest tool we posses when working with spiritual disciplines. You may use meditation and pathworking as the first step in recovering lost levels of consciousness, to clear the mind and even establish contact with the Otherworld.

Stopping the Internal Dialogue

Have you noticed that you are constantly talking to yourself inside your mind? This constant dialogue of the logical left brain with the ego prevents other levels of consciousness becoming apparent, and reinforces the existing state of perceptions of the world. You must learn to stop this 'internal dialogue' still the mind, empty it in order to become aware of greater levels of consciousness and to develop clairvoyant and other psychic facilities.

Light a candle and gaze at the flame. Try to empty your mind of all thoughts and let it be empty and still. This is very difficult. If you find thoughts creeping in, gently push them away, and re-centre your concentration on the candle flame. Try to do this exercise for five minutes a day. You could try doing it by concentrating on any object, it doesn't have to be a candle flame, and so, for example, you could do it on the bus to work, or sitting in the park at lunchtime. When you have progressed, do the exercise with your eyes open or closed, not looking at any object in particular.

Trance through Chant

Start by humming, and then as the spirit moves you, begin to utter syllables. It doesn't matter if they are nonsense words. Begin to sing or chant them. Allow the voice to speak without conscious motivation.

Trance through Dance

Use drumming or music for this exercise, or simply go out to some secluded place and use the sounds of nature. Start to move slowly with your eyes closed. Find a speed and rhythm as your body dictates. Feel patterns of movement. Allow your body to fulfil its desire for movement. Forget about what you look like- leave your ego behind. Go deep inside and experience the movement in your core.

Trance through Circular Breathing

Breathe in through your nose and out through your mouth without stopping between breaths to create a cycle of breath.

Finding Your Power Song

Many shamans believe that it is important to acquire a power song, with which the guardian spirit or ally can be summoned. To find you song, you will need to spend a lengthy period fasting and meditating in solitude, preferably in some wild place. As you enter an altered state, concentrate on your intent of finding your power song. Listen with your inner ears for the melody and words. Many shamans find these songs on their journeys ir during their initiation period. You will be able to use the song in future to help you enter trance and summon your allies.

Pathworking

Pathworking, or guided meditation, is a tool used by mystics to foster spiritual development, to open the psychic senses, and to visit all the realms of the Otherworld. After a time, the pathworker begins to realise that the landscapes and persons met do not all belong to his or her internal world, but constitute messages and lessons from the Otherworld. In time, he or she will also learn to recognise spiritual lessons manifesting in the physical realm, since the realms co-exist in the same space.

The pathworkings given below consist of three parts. The first stage is the relaxation stage, and to avoid onerous repetition, the instruction given for this is 'relax'. This means the whole of the relaxation exercise in this chapter should be gone through. Then is the pathworking proper. The third stage is the awakening stage, given at the end of each pathworking as 'return yourself to waking consciousness', but meaning that the awakening exercise given in this chapter should be gone through each time.

Preparing To Meditate

At first you may find pathworking difficult. You will itch and want to fidget, or find that you can't concentrate. Many people have problems with visualisation at first. The trick is to make sure your body is completely relaxed and allow yourself to drift into it: don't try too hard; this is counter-productive. Once you have experienced the pleasant feeling of deep relaxation you will find it easier to achieve it a second time. The next time will be even easier. I have taught pathworking meditation for over twenty years and I have never found anyone who was incapable of using the method.

The relaxation technique below is the one I always use, counting people down into relaxation and walking them down five imaginary steps into the pathworking. There are many other methods, and some teachers will ask their students to imagine themselves going down an escalator, climbing up steps and so on. It doesn't really matter as long as the meditators can relate to the imagery, but I find it that helps if the same method is used every time. The words and images act as an instant mental trigger. As soon as I begin talking, my students know what is coming. After many sessions with someone, all I have to say is 'lie down and relax', and they are already in a meditative state.

A good pathworking is not too detailed. It will take the meditator into a place or situation, and then leave them plenty of time to look around and experience what they need to. Any pathworking that charts each step and image is merely showing you what the author imagines, not what is true for you: you might as well just read a short story- this is not meditation!

After a pathworking, write down as much of it as you can remember, in as much detail as possible. You will find that some of it fades like a dream. As you progress and continue to record your experiences, you may discover that the small details that seemed insignificant were, with hindsight, very important.

Relaxation Before Pathworking
Remember, during a pathworking a narrator helps you to enter a state of relaxation, and then relates an imaginary scene. After the experience is over, the narrator helps you to bring yourself back to waking consciousness. You are not under someone else's control, just deeply relaxed, and you can stop and return to ordinary waking consciousness whenever you like. If you wish, you can record the narration yourself on tape, and use it.

Find a comfortable, warm space where you can be undisturbed. Take the phone off the hook. You might like to lie down on the floor with a cushion under your head, on your bed, or sit upright on a comfortable chair. Lie or sit comfortably, arms and legs uncrossed, and allow all your muscles to relax.

Concentrate on your breathing; with each breath, you become more and more relaxed. With each outward breath you let go of tensions, you let go of the events of the day; you let go of problems.

Centre your attention on your toes, be fully aware of them, and let them relax.

Move your attention to the soles of your feet, be fully aware of them, and let them relax, feel the tension drain away.

Move slowly in the same way through the tops of your feet, your ankles, your shins and calves, your knees, your thighs, your bottom, your stomach, your spine (feel each vertebrae separate and relax), your chest (be aware that your breathing has become slow and rhythmical), your shoulders, your arms and elbows, your hands and fingers, your neck, your scalp, your face, feel the muscles of your forehead relax, the muscles around your eyes, your nose, mouth, cheeks, jaw.

THE PATH OF THE SHAMAN

Concentrate again on your breathing; with each breath you become more and more relaxed. With each breath, you go deeper and deeper into a warm, pleasant state of relaxation.

Now imagine that you are at the top of a flight of five steps, leading downwards. As you go down each step in turn you will go deeper and deeper into relaxation. Go down one step at a time, noticing what the steps are made of, how they feel. Five...four...three...two...one...(now continue with the pathworking chosen).

Returning From the Pathworking

When you are ready to return, walk back the way you came until you reach the flight of five steps.

As you ascend each step, you become more and more awake, more conscious of your body and the room in which you are sitting or lying, until at the fifth step you are completely awake. One... two. three.... four.... five....Slowly open your eyes and stretch.

You may be surprised at how long you spent in your meditational state. What seemed like ten minutes may have turned out to be an hour in real time. In meditation, time and space become irrelevant. As soon as you can, write down what you experienced during your meditation, including as many details as possible.

The Hollow Oak Pathworking

Relax.

It is Midsummer Eve. The sky is clear and studded with stars. You find yourself in a primeval forest, alive with the power of magic.

You begin to follow an ancient pathway, which leads you to a clearing.

In the centre stands a massive oak tree. It is the king of the forest, colossal, centuries old. The branches spread like a leafy canopy above, while you know that its roots extend as wide below ground.

221

THE PATH OF THE SHAMAN

The oak is a magical cosmic axis, linking all the realms of existence, from the human world where you stand, to the upper world of the gods and spirits, and the underworld of the fairies.

The oak is hollow, and you squeeze yourself inside a natural doorway into the warm trunk.
The oak stands at the boundary of the year, between the time of the waxing sun and the time of the waning sun. You can feel the year turning, and the gates between the worlds opening.

You burrow down inside the hollow oak, and a passageway deep into the earth opens up before you. The way is lit by lanterns.

Gradually, as you walk downwards, you begin to make out the sound of music, a beautiful, haunting tune, played on harp and pipes. As you travel further, it gets louder, and you are aware of lights ahead.

You emerge from the passageway into a bright hall, full of dazzling fairy folk. They are beautiful, slender, tall, with shining pale skin and white robes. They are laughing and feasting at tables heavily laden with food and wine.

They become aware of your presence, and greet you with delight.

You feel yourself being led through the hall towards a pair of golden thrones. On them, sit the Fairy King and Queen. You bow before them courteously.

The Fairy Queen takes an apple from the low silver table at her side and offers it to you.

As you reach for it, she warns you sternly "Know that if you eat of this Otherworldly fruit, you will be changed forever. You will be part human and part fairy, and your path will be difficult and often painful. When you are away from the Otherworld you will long for it, but when you return to us the sweetness of this realm is almost unbearable."

You may eat, or decline politely. The choice is yours alone.

You can spend some time among the fairies now, and speak to them as you wish; they may answer your questions, if they like you.

When it seems time for you to leave, say your goodbyes, and remember that you can take nothing away from Fairyland.

THE PATH OF THE SHAMAN

You return to the underground passage, and travel up it into the hollow oak.

You realise that the sun has risen, and you feel the warmth on your skin.

Return yourself to waking consciousness.

Discovering Your Animal Ally Pathworking

Imagine that you are walking in a beautiful forest. The sun glances through the branches forming dappled light on the forest floor. It is peaceful and silent but for the rustle of the leaves and the occasional bird song. You are following a faint but clear path through the trees.

Pause

Eventually you come to a clearing. Seated beneath the tree you recognize Cernunnos, the stag horned god who is Lord of the Animals. He is surrounded by animals large and small, all gathered peacefully around him. Though cats rub shoulders with mice, and lions with deer they are all calm and content under his influence. You gaze in wonder at the beasts.

Pause.

Cernunnos beckons you forward and as you move towards him the animals scatter and retreat into the trees. Soon they are all out of sight.

Pause

You may be disappointed, but Cernunnos smiles. He alone is Lord of the Animals with the power to still them all. He knows that you have come to discover your own totem animal and nods. He will help you.

Pause.

He lifts up his arms and utters a piercing whistle. The forest falls silent.

Pause.

Then from the trees an animal emerges. It is your totem. You may be surprised, it may not be the animal you were expecting, but you must accept it.

Pause.

223

THE PATH OF THE SHAMAN

The animal moves towards you and you touch it, make friends with it.

Pause.

When you are ready, you thank Cernunnos, and accompanied by your animal make your way back down the forest path.

Pause.

Let the scene fade around you, and return yourself to waking consciousness.

Dancing Your Animal

You will need someone to drum for you, or use a drumming CD with a fairly steady and rapid beat. Begin to move to the rhythm of the drum, moving around the space. Allow your conscious thoughts to drift away, and be one with the music. Be aware of any sense of an animal on the edge of your consciousness, and begin to move in accordance with that animal, be it bird, bear, reptile or fish. You might wish to move your wings, stamp your feet, cry out and make the noises of the animal. Close your eyes if you wish to, and be aware of the animal's natural environment. When you feel that the connection is made, and the animal has possessed you, stop dancing, and welcome the animal with words of honour.

Dreaming With the Eyes Open

When you first arrive at a place, greet it as you would a living being. Stand or sit quietly for a while. Try to relax your body as you would for a pathworking. Still your mind by closing your eyes and concentrating on the sounds around you, perhaps you can hear the birds and the wind, or the rolling of the sea on the shore. Be aware of your mind probing around the area, seeking for its ambience, its energies and its places of interaction with the Otherworld.

Then open your eyes. While maintaining this heightened consciousness, you can walk though the place and explore it with new levels of awareness.

The Witch Walk

The Witch Walk is a pilgrimage that relies on the Otherworld to give you direction. To begin, dedicate the journey to the higher powers, and ask that you will be guided. Put yourself in the light trance state called *dreaming with the eyes open*. Now ask the spirits to direct your footsteps (or driving), turning right or

224

left as they dictate. Sometimes, you will feel the direction as a magnetic pull, at others as a heat on your face. Sometimes the Otherworld will send messengers in the form of birds, animals or butterflies to lead the way. Treat everything that happens to you on a Witch Walk as significant, whether this is a person or animal that you meet, a place or plant you discover and so on.

The Medicine Wheel
Take eight small pebbles (not crystals) and lay them out in a large circle. Place a single pebble in the centre of the circle and five more around that.

Elemental Medicine Wheel
This medicine wheel works with the power of the elements as they are understood and used in British magic. The pebble at the north of the circle represents earth, the one at the south fire, the one on the east, air, the one on the west, water. Decide which element you most need to work on, and sit by that pebble.

For example, if you need to work on water, sit by the water stone, and imagine all the aspects of water- the waves of the sea, a river, and the gentle rain. Be aware of the ebb and free flowing of water. Feel the element flowing freely within you. Feel your emotions flowing freely within you. if you have severe emotional blocks, you may be find the water of your tears flowing from you.

When you feel you have absorbed all the element of water you need for the present, imagine all the negative things you wish to be rid of as a black sludge within your body. Feel the sludge drain away down your body and out through your feet. It flows towards the centre of the circle and drains away beneath the central stone, like water draining down a plughole.

When you have finished, thank the elements and clear away the pebbles.

Herbal Medicine Wheel
This is adapted from the herbal medicine wheel suggested by Susun Weed, an American Wise Woman at www.susunweed.com. It utilises the principle of the medicine wheel to work with plant allies.

The east is the place of dawn, newness and freshness. Its taste is sweet and bland. Mother's milk is sweet and bland. It is the place of the plants that give us nourishment, such as the cereal crops.

The south is the realm of fire, passion, sweat and blood. Its taste is salty or hot. It includes the plants that provoke passion and heat, such as ginger, cinnamon and so on.

THE PATH OF THE SHAMAN

The west is the place of water, death and the entrance to the Otherworld. Its taste is bitter, and it is the place of plants that alter consciousness, such as mushrooms, but also powerful and bitter medicinal pants. Susun Weed points out that the closer to the west a plant lies, the more critical the dose, as too much may be the difference between life and death.

The north is the direction of earth, of deepness and clarity. The taste is aromatic, and includes such aromatic and volatile oil containing plants as mint, marjoram and so on. The north is the place of wisdom.

ENDNOTES

[1] In some places, the role of shaman is hereditary, but only if the spirits have chosen the successor, and he has undergone the crisis.

[2] David Lewis Williams & David Pearce, *The Neolithic Mind*, Thames and Hudson Ltd, London, 2005

[3] Joseph Campbell, *The Way of Animal Powers*, Harper and Row, New York, 1988

[4] Joseph Campbell, *Primitive Mythology*, Penguin Arkana, New York, 1976

[5] *ibid*

[6] John Matthews, *Taliesin, Shamanism and the Bardic Mysteries in Britain and Ireland*, Thorsons, Scranton, 1991

[7] *ibid*

[8] *ibid*

[9] Taliesin's Song of his Origins, *Taliesin, Shamanism and the Bardic Mysteries in Britain and Ireland*, p 281

[10] http://www.vikinganswerlady.com/seidhr.shtml

[11] *ibid*

[12] *ibid*

[13] M. Eliade, *Shamanism: Archaic Techniques of Ecstasy*, Bollingen Series, New York, 1964

[14] C. Rae, *The Bluffer's Guide to the Occult*, Ravette Publishing, 1988

[15] M. Eliade, *Shamanism: Archaic Techniques of Ecstasy*, Bollingen Series, New York, 1964

[16] Nigel Jackson, *The Compleat Vampyre*, Capall Bann, Chieveley, 1995

[17] Quoted in Brian Bates, *The Real Middle Earth*, Pan Books, London, 2003

[18] Mircea Eliade, *Shamanism: Archaic Techniques of Ecstasy*, Bollingen Series, New York, 1964

[19] ibid

[20] A. W. Howitt, *The Native Tribes of South-East Australia,* London, 1904

[21] B. Spencer and J. Gillen, *The Northern Tribes of Central Australia*, London, 1904

[22] *The Ethnography of Franz Boas 1858-1942*, University of Chicago Press, 1969

[23] M. Eliade, *Shamanism: Archaic Techniques of Ecstasy*, Bollingen Series, New York, 1964,
based on and quoted from Knud Rasmussen. Intellectual Culture of the Iglulik Eskimos (Copenhagen, 1930) pp.112-13

[24] Abstracted from David Lewis Williams & David Pearce, *The Neolithic Mind*, Thames and Hudson Ltd, London, 2005

THE PATH OF THE SHAMAN

[25] Daniel Goleman, *Emotional Intelligence*, Bloomsbury, London, 1996
[26] Nigel Pennick *The Eldritch World* Lear Books, Earl Shilton, 2006
[27] *ibid*
[28] *ibid*
[29] *ibid*
[30] Nigel Jackson, *The Compleat Vampyre*, Capall Bann, Chieveley, 1995
[31] *What the Bleep Do We Know*, www.thebleep.co.uk
[32] Nigel Jackson, *The Compleat Vampyre*, Capall Bann, Chieveley, 1995
[33] David Lewis Williams & David Pearce, *The Neolithic Mind*, Thames and Hudson Ltd, London, 2005
[34] Ronald Hutton, *Shamans: Siberian Spirituality and the Western Imagination*, Hambledon and London, London, 2001
[35] David Lewis Williams & David Pearce, *The Neolithic Mind*, Thames and Hudson Ltd, London, 2005
[36] Mike Dixon-Kennedy, *European Myth and Legend*, Blanford, London, 1997
[37] Nigel Pennick, *pers comm.*
[38] Nigel Pennick, *The Ancient Science of Geometry*, Thames and Hudson, 1979
[39] John Michell, *At the Centre of the World*, Thames and Hudson, London, 1994
[40] *ibid*
[41] *ibid*
[42] *ibid*
[43] Bob Trubshaw, *The Quest for the Omphalos*, Heart of Albion Press, Wymeswold, 1991
[44] *ibid*
[45] http://www.indigogroup.co.uk/edge/ Goddess of the Black Stone Alby Stone
[46] *ibid*
[47] *ibid*
[48] *ibid*
[49] Bob Trubshaw, *The Quest for the Omphalos*, Heart of Albion Press, Wymeswold, 1991
[50] John G. Neihardt *Black Elk Speaks*, Pocket Books, 1982
[51] John Michell, *At the Centre of the World*, Thames and Hudson, London, 1994
[52] *ibid*
[53] Mike Dixon-Kennedy, *European Myth and Legend*, Blanford, London, 1997
[54] David Lewis Williams & David Pearce, *The Neolithic Mind*, Thames and Hudson Ltd, London, 2005
[55] *ibid*

THE PATH OF THE SHAMAN

[56] John Michell, *At the Centre of the World*, Thames and Hudson, London, 1994

[57] http://www.indigogroup.co.uk/edge/ *The Cosmic Mill* Alby Stone

[58] Gracheva; G. K. *Etnokulturnye kontakty narodov Sibiri*. 1984, p 91

[59] http://www.indigogroup.co.uk/edge/ *'In Heaven as on Earth' Royal Roads and the Milky Way* Penny Drayton

[60] http://www.indigogroup.co.uk/edge/ *The Cosmic Mill* Alby Stone

[61] David Lewis Williams & David Pearce, *The Neolithic Mind*, Thames and Hudson Ltd, London, 2005

[62] John Michell, *At the Centre of the World*, Thames and Hudson, London, 1994

[63] David Lewis Williams & David Pearce, *The Neolithic Mind*, Thames and Hudson Ltd, London, 2005

[64] Douglas Hill, 'Pueblo Indians', *Man, Myth and Magic*, n/d

[65] David Lewis Williams & David Pearce, *The Neolithic Mind*, Thames and Hudson Ltd, London, 2005

[66] http://www.themystica.com/mystica/articles/c/chanting.html

[67] Vilmos Diószegi, *Tuva Shamanism*, Acta Ethnographica, 1962

[68] David Lewis Williams & David Pearce, *The Neolithic Mind*, Thames and Hudson Ltd, London, 2005

[69] Nigel Jackson, *The Compleat Vampyre*, Capall Bann, Chieveley, 1995

[70] David Lewis Williams & David Pearce, *The Neolithic Mind*, Thames and Hudson Ltd, London, 2005

[71] *ibid*

[72] Nigel Pennick pers comm

[73] David Lewis Williams & David Pearce, *The Neolithic Mind*, Thames and Hudson Ltd, London, 2005

[74] Nigel Pennick, *Spirits of the Landscape*, Silver Wheel Magazine, Beltane 2005

[75] Quoted in Brian Bates, *The Real Middle Earth*, Pan Books, London, 2003

[76] Emma Wilby, *Cunning Folk and Familiar Spirits*, Sussex Academic Press, 2005

[77] *ibid*

[78] *ibid*

[7979] Reginald Scott, *The Discoverie of Witchcraft*, Leiden, 1637

[80] Quoted in Emma Wilby, *Cunning Folk and Familiar Spirits*, Sussex Academic Press, 2005

[81] *ibid*

[82] Institute of Ethnology and Folk-lore Research 2004, www.ief.hr

[83] Emma Wilby, *Cunning Folk and Familiar Spirits*, Sussex Academic Press, 2005

THE PATH OF THE SHAMAN

[84] John Webster, *The Displaying of Supposed Witchcraft*, London 1677

[85] Reginald Scot, The Discoverie of Witchcraft, Leiden, 1637

[86] Emma Wilby, *Cunning Folk and Familiar Spirits*, Sussex Academic Press, 2005

[87] *ibid*

[88] *The Witch's Familiar and the Fairy in Early Modern England and Scotland, Folklore*, Oct, 2000 by Emma Wilby

[89] Emma Wilby, *Cunning Folk and Familiar Spirits*, Sussex Academic Press, 2005

[90] David Lewis Williams & David Pearce, *The Neolithic Mind*, Thames and Hudson Ltd, London, 2005

[91] W.C.Hazlitt, *The Romance of King Orfeo*, London, 1875

[92] Quoted in Emma Wilby, *Cunning Folk and Familiar Spirits*, Sussex Academic Press, 2005

[93] W. Bottrell, *Traditions and Hearthside Stories of the West of Cornwall*, Penzance, 1870

[94] Nigel Pennick, *Spirits of the Landscape*, Silver Wheel Magazine, Beltane 2005

[95] M. Eliade, *Shamanism*, PP. 72-3,

[96] W.B.Yeats, *Folk and Fairy Tales of the Irish Peasantry, 1888*

[97] David Lewis Williams & David Pearce, *The Neolithic Mind*, Thames and Hudson Ltd, London, 2005

[98] A. W. Howitt, *The Native Tribes of South-East Australia*, London, 1904

[99] Nigel Jackson, *The Compleat Vampyre*, Capall Bann, Chieveley, 1995

[100] *ibid*

[101] M. Eliade, PP. 72-3, quoting Leo Stemberg, 'Divine Election in Primitive Religion' (1924),

[102] Triinu Ojamaa *The Shaman As The Zoomorphic Human*

[103] *ibid*

[104] http://www.vikinganswerlady.com/seidhr.shtml

[105] *ibid*

[106] Nigel Jackson, *The Compleat Vampyre*, Capall Bann, Chieveley, 1995

[107] *ibid*

[108] *ibid*

[109] Joan Halifax, *Shamanic Voices*, Penguin Arkana, New York, 1979

[110] Kaledon Naddair, *Keltic Folk and Faerie Tales*, Century Paperbacks, London, 1987

[111] Joseph Campbell, *The Way of Animal Powers*, Harper and Row, New York, 1988

[112] Marion Davies, *Sacred Celtic Animals*, Capall Bann, Chieveley, 1998

THE PATH OF THE SHAMAN

[113] Madeleine Johnson, http://www.yewgrove.demon.co.uk/starsong/arcturus.htm, 1997

[114] Miranda Green, *Animals in Celtic Life and Myth*, Routledge, London, 1992

[115] *ibid*

[116] D. Ó HÓgáin, *The Sacred Isle*, The Collins Press, Cork, 1999

[117] Marion Pearce, *Sacred Celtic Animals*, Capall Bann, Chieveley, 1998

[118] Robert Graves, *The White Goddess*, Faber and Faber, London, 1961

[119] *ibid*

[120] Miranda Green, *Animals in Celtic Life and Myth*, Routledge, London, 1992

[121] *ibid*

[122] *ibid*

[123] Lewis Spence, *The Minor Traditions of British Mythology*, London 1948

[124] Marion Davies, *Sacred Celtic Animals*, Chieveley, 1998

[125] Nigel Jackson, *The Compleat Vampyre*, Capall Bann, Chieveley, 1995

[126] *ibid*

[127] *ibid*

[128] *ibid*

[129] *ibid*

[130] *ibid*

[131] Marion Davies, *Sacred Celtic Animals*, Capall Bann, Chieveley, 1998

[132] Gustav Schenk, *The Book of Poisons*, Rinehart and Co, New York, 1955

[133] *Soma and the Fly-Agaric*, (Ethno-Mycological Studies No. 2), by Wasson, R. Gordon, Cambridge, 1972

[134] *The Reunification of the Sacred and Natural* by Ralph Metzner, PhD

[135] *ibid*

[136] Robert Graves, *The Greek Myths*, Faber and Faber, London, 1979

[137] Brian Bates, *The Real Middle Earth*, Pan Books, London, 2003

[138] Graves, Robert, *The White Goddess*, Faber and Faber, London, 1961

[139] Georg Heinrich von Langsdorf, *Divine Mushroom of Immortality*, Canadian Whole Earth Almanac, Vol 3 (No 1) 1972,

[140] John M. Allegro, *The Sacred Mushroom and the Cross*, Bantam, London, 1971

[141] Ian Colvin, *The Daily Telegraph*, August 1965

[142] Richard Alan Miller, *The Magical and Ritual Use of Herbs*, Destiny Books, Rochester, 1983

[143] *ibid*

[144] Deepak Chopra, *Grow Younger, Live Longer*, Rider, London, 2001

[145] Masaru Emoto, *The True Power of Water*, Beyond Words Publishing, Oregon, 2005

THE PATH OF THE SHAMAN

[146] Crofton Croker, *Fairy Legends and Traditions of the South of Ireland*, John Murray, London, 1827
[147] Carmichael, Alexander *Carmina Gadelica: Hymns and Incantations*, Landisfarne Press. New York, 1992.
[148] Caitlin Matthews, *The Celtic Book of the Dead*, Grange Books, Rochester, 2001
[149] David Lewis Williams & David Pearce, *The Neolithic Mind*, Thames and Hudson Ltd, London, 2005

Illustrations
Crane by Paul Mason [from the Celtic Animal Oracle by Anna Franklin & Paul Mason, Vega]
Raven by Paul Mason [ibid]
Wolf by Paul Mason [ibid]
Swan by Paul Mason [ibid]
Snake by Paul Mason [ibid]
Fachan by Paul Mason [The Fairy Ring Oracle by Anna Franklin and Paul Mason, Llewellyn]